THE BUSINESS ANALYST'S HANDBOOK

Howard Podeswa

Course Technology PTR
A part of Cengage Learning

COURSE TECHNOLOGY
CENGAGE Learning·

Australia, Brazil, Japan, Korea, Mexico, Singapore, Spain, United Kingdom, United States

COURSE TECHNOLOGY
CENGAGE Learning·

The Business Analyst's Handbook
Howard Podeswa

Publisher and General Manager, Course Technology PTR:
Stacy L. Hiquet

Associate Director of Marketing:
Sarah Panella

Manager of Editorial Services:
Heather Talbot

Marketing Manager:
Mark Hughes

Acquisitions Editor:
Mitzi Koontz

Project Editor and Copy Editor:
Kim Benbow

Technical Reviewers:
Rick Guyatt, Chris Reynolds, and Ken Clyne

PTR Editorial Services Coordinator:
Jen Blaney

Interior Layout Tech:
William Hartman

Cover Designer:
Mike Tanamachi

Indexer:
Sharon Shock

Proofreader:
Kate Shoup

Course Technology
25 Thomson Place
Boston, MA 02210
USA

Cengage Learning is a leading provider of customized learning solutions with office locations around the globe, including Singapore, the United Kingdom, Australia, Mexico, Brazil, and Japan. Locate your local office at: **international.cengage.com/region**.

Cengage Learning products are represented in Canada by Nelson Education, Ltd.

For your lifelong learning solutions, visit **courseptr.com**.

Visit our corporate Web site at **cengage.com**

For product information and technology assistance, contact us at
Cengage Learning Customer & Sales Support, 1-800-354-9706

For permission to use material from this text or product, submit all requests online at **cengage.com/permissions**
Further permissions questions can be e-mailed to
permissionrequest@cengage.com

Library of Congress Control Number: 2008902400

ISBN-13: 978-1-59863-565-2

ISBN-10: 1-59863-565-4

Printed in Canada
6 7 8 9 15 14 13 12

This book is dedicated to Joy Walker, my partner in both life and business. It has been my greatest fortune to find someone who enriches every area of my life—and who does it with such style, beauty, and grace. Joy had a particularly important role with respect to this book, as it was she who saw the need for it and encouraged me to write it. For that, and much more, I am most grateful.

Acknowledgments

A special thank you goes to:

- My editor, Mitzi Koontz. I can't imagine a better, more effective, tougher (when she needs to be), and, at the same time, more supportive editor. Any author is lucky to have her in his or her corner.

- Kim Benbow, copy editor, for doing a great job on one of her more "challenging" assignments—and, in particular, for putting up with my penchant for multiple and last-minute revisions. In the midst of it all, she kept an eye on the ball, indulging me when it served the book and keeping me in line when it didn't—and did it all with warmth and humour.

- Rick Guyatt for his invaluable insight into ITIL and its implementation in the public sector.

- Chris Reynolds for the benefit of his rich experience in BA best practices within the private sector.

- Ken Clyne of Number Six for the deep perspective he provided on many issues and, in particular, those related to the agile approach, the UML, RUP, and iterative development.

- Keith Sarre, a fellow reviewer of the *BABOK®*, for his valuable input regarding the *BABOK®* and best BA practices.

- John Welch for drawing my attention to the existing gap between ITIL and the BA role. John is the visionary who, early on, saw the importance of making the ITIL-BA link and who worked tirelessly to ensure it was addressed.

- Beth Brook (OPSI) for her help in expediting the applications to license the ITIL material in this book.

- Mike Bonamassa of Number Six.

- My kids, Yasha Podeswa and Samantha Stillar.

- My parents, Yidel and Ruth Podeswa, for giving me the confidence to do anything I put my mind to.

In Memory

And finally, a note in memory of Brian Lyons, a founder of Number Six. I met Brian years ago in Toronto, while we were both working with a telecommunications client. Brian was one of the most brilliant and unconventional people I had ever met in this business. We had kept in touch since then and, when my previous book was about to come out, he consented to act as technical editor. As this book was nearing completion, I was looking forward to another round, when I learned that he had died in a tragic motorcycle accident. He has been an inspiration to me and many others.

ABOUT THE AUTHOR

Howard Podeswa is the co-founder of Noble Inc., a business analysis training and consulting company. He has 29 years of experience in many aspects of the software industry, beginning as a developer for Atomic Energy of Canada Ltd. and continuing as systems analyst, business analyst, consultant, and author of courseware and books for business analysts, including *UML for the IT Business Analyst*. Directly, and through his company, he has provided training and consulting services to a diverse client base covering a broad range of industry sectors, including health care, defense, energy, government, and banking and financial institutions. Podeswa has developed BA training programs for numerous colleges, universities, and corporate education centres. He has been a subject matter expert in Business Analysis for NITAS—a BA apprenticeship program for CompTIA—and a contributing reviewer for the IIBA's *Business Analysis Body of Knowledge* (*BABOK®*). For more information on the Noble Business Analysis curriculum, please visit www.nobleinc.ca or e-mail info@nobleinc.ca.

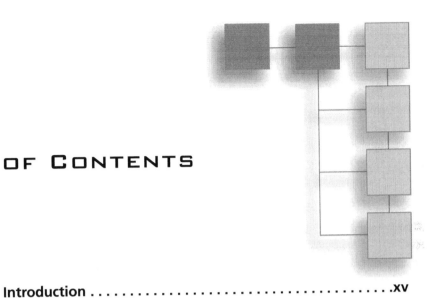

TABLE OF CONTENTS

INTRODUCTION

In my previous life in chemical engineering, I used to carry around *Perry's Chemical Engineers' Handbook*—a working reference book containing every table and tool the professional might need to refer to in carrying out his or her role. When I began working as a business analyst, I looked for a similar handbook for my new profession; not finding anything as comprehensive, I began to compile my own handbook. We began dispensing this handbook to Noble Inc. clients a number of years ago as the "Noble Cheat Sheets," and it soon became a much sought-after "value-added" item. By presenting this book to the general BA public, my hope is that the book will fill the need for a comprehensive working reference for the business analysis profession—a "Perry's" for the working BA.

Standards and This Book

One of the objectives of this book is to incorporate best practices and standards into the BA role. While a number of standards and guidelines, such as Business Process Modeling Notation (BPMN), have been incorporated, particular emphasis has been placed on the *Business Analysis Body of Knowledge* (*BABOK®*), the Information Technology Infrastructure Library (ITIL), and the Unified Modeling Language (UML).

The *BABOK®* is a publication of the International Institute for Business Analysis (IIBA™), outlining the knowledge areas required for the practice of business analysis. In this handbook, you'll find an overview of the *BABOK®* as well as definitions and examples for many of the techniques recommended in the *BABOK®*, such as functional decomposition, state models, process models, use cases, structured walkthroughs, non-functional requirements, and data models.

ITIL is an international publicly available framework of best practices owned by the Office of Government Commerce (OGC), with broad acceptance in Europe and Canada and growing acceptance in the U.S. An explicit mapping of ITIL guidelines to the BA role within the software development process has been long overdue. ITIL V3 (the latest version of ITIL), with its introduction of the Service Life Cycle, is a significant move forward. This handbook aims to complement that work by embedding ITIL best practices right into the BA role. For example, ITIL artifacts and steps are included in the Noble Path (an end-to-end process for performing the BA role), ITIL considerations are incorporated into templates and meeting guides, and a section mapping ITIL to the BA role has been included.

The UML is a standard notation for the specification, visualization, and modeling of the structure and behaviour of business and software systems. The UML is owned by the Object Management Group (OMG), a not-for-profit computer industry specifications consortium. This handbook focuses on those aspects of the UML of value to the BA, while excluding those aspects used only in a technical context.

Terminology

This book uses some terms which, though widely used within the BA and broader IT community, are not always used consistently. Therefore, some clarification is in order.

As used in this book, the term *requirement* refers to a capability that a solution must provide (such as the capability to conduct online transactions) or a condition that it must meet (such as compliance with a set of regulations). A requirement is differentiated from a *specification* in that a requirement describes what is required, whereas a specification defines how it will be satisfied.

A related term is *business requirements*. In some usages, it applies only to business objectives, such as increasing market share and reducing costs, and excludes other requirements, such as user requirements. In other usages, it refers to any requirements that stem from the business side—including both higher-level business requirements (such as increasing market share) and more detailed requirements (such as user requirements) that also stem from business stakeholders. This latter usage is the one used in the book.

Other contentious terms are functional and non-functional requirements. In this handbook, *functional* requirements denote externally visible behavior that a system must be able to perform and include features and use cases written from the customer, user, and system perspective. The term *non-functional* requirements means anything other than functional requirements. (This is in accordance with requirements classification schemes, such as FURPS+; however, there are other references, such as ITIL, that have a more restrictive definition of non-functional requirements.)

There is some confusion, as well, about whether the ITIL terms Service Level Management (SLM), Service Level Requirements (SLR), and Service Level Agreements (SLA) refer to non-functional requirements only or also include functional requirements. Some have proposed the acronyms SM, SA, and SR be used to make the inclusion of functional requirements clear, but the term Service Management (SM) already has an ITIL definition (one that is too broad for our purpose) and the others are not ITIL terms. In this book, I have used S(L)M, S(L)R, and S(L)A when I intend to include functional requirements (the parentheses suggesting that the reader not take the word "Level" too restrictively) and the acronyms SLM, SLR, and SLA (without parentheses) to specifically refer to non-functional requirements as well as across-the-board system capabilities.

Other terms used in this book that overlap with ITIL are *business service* and *IT service*. In this book, a business service represents a capability or need that the business area provides to those who interact with it; the service itself may be realized with or without IT. ITIL V3 provides two alternative definitions of a business service. The usage in this book is consistent with the second definition, which declares that business services "often"—but not always—"depend on. . .IT services." Following is the full text of the ITIL V3 definition of a business service:

> An IT Service that directly supports a Business Process, as opposed to an Infrastructure Service which is used internally by the IT Service Provider and is not usually visible to the Business. The term Business Service is also used to mean a Service that is delivered to Business Customers by Business Units, for example, delivery of financial services to Customers of a bank, or goods to the Customers of a retail store. Successful delivery of Business Services often depends on one or more IT Services.

An IT service, as defined in this book, is a service that the IT organization must provide to its customers. This is in accordance with the ITIL V3 definition:

> A Service provided to one or more Customers by an IT Service Provider. An IT Service is based on the use of Information Technology and supports the Customer's Business Processes. An IT Service is made up from a combination of people, Processes, and technology and should be defined in a Service Level Agreement.

The term *tool* is sometimes used in other contexts to refer to software used in the development process; an example of such a tool is IBM Rational Rose. In this book, however, it refers to any job aid or technique that facilitates the practice of business analysis. Examples of BA tools are Pareto Analysis and class diagrams. Tools are described in Chapter 4 of this book.

In this book, the term *systems analyst* refers to a role distinct from the business analyst; the business analyst analyzes the business, whereas the systems analyst designs the software solution. (Please be advised, however, that in some other usages, the systems analyst is responsible for the analysis and modeling not only of software, but business structure and processes as well.)

The term *user task* is used in its English-usage sense of "a usually assigned piece of work often to be finished within a certain time." It corresponds to a system use case—a unit of work performed by an actor with the assistance of the IT system that yields a valuable result for the initiating actor. (This is not to be confused with a technical usage of the term task that connotes a small-scale programming action.)

A number of terms refer to the documentation and visualization of the requirements. A *template* is a standardized form used for textual documentation. A *description* is something that tells you what something is like; it is the actual documentation and may be in the form of text and/or diagrams. For example, a system use-case description usually consists of text whose format may be based on a system use-case template; if the workflow is complex, the description should also contain an activity diagram. (Please note that what is referred to in this book as a use-case description, is referred to in RUP as a use-case specification.) A *brief* is a short textual description. For example, a use-case brief is a one-paragraph summary of a use case. A model is a representation of something, often expressed in diagrams (for example, flowcharts, use-case diagrams, and class diagrams).

Finally, a note on the use of hyphens. In general, this handbook uses a hyphen between two nouns when, together, they qualify a third noun, as is the case, for example, with use-case diagram and all other occurrences of the use-case qualifier. An exception has been made with respect to ITIL terms that are widely written without a hyphen, such as Service Level Agreement (and all other occurrences of Service Level as a qualifier).

How to Use This Book

The Business Analyst's Handbook is a reference book. You do not need to read it from cover to cover; rather, keep it by your side as you work and refer to the relevant section as required.

Chapter 1, "Overview of BA Activities Throughout the Life Cycle," contains an overview of the BA role over the course of a project. Use this chapter to ensure that you have considered all business analysis steps when planning and executing your role on the project. The chapter also contains instructions to the reader on where further details about the steps, artifacts, and tools that appear in this chapter can be found in the other chapters of the book.

Chapter 2, "Meeting Guide," contains guidelines for planning and executing business analysis meetings. Use this chapter if you need to prepare for a meeting; it provides useful lists of input documents to be distributed to participants, as well as agendas and specific questions to ask stakeholders for each type of meeting.

Chapter 3, "Standards and Guidelines Used in This Book," describes the standards and guidance used in this book: the *BABOK®*, the UML, and ITIL. Refer to this chapter if your project is using any of these best practices; it explains how they map to the BA role.

Chapter 4, "BA Toolkit," describes BA tools (techniques), listed alphabetically. This is the key chapter of the book and the one you will likely refer to most. For example, if you need to create or review an Entity Relationship diagram, look it up in this chapter; you will find an example of the diagram and a glossary of symbols.

Chapter 5, "Tips and Checklists," contains miscellaneous tips, rules of thumb, and checklists useful for performing the BA role, such as tips for managing requirements risks.

Chapter 6, "Templates," contains templates used to create business analysis documentation. If your organization does not currently have templates for the documents described in this chapter, use the provided templates as is or as a starting point to build your own. If you already have templates, you can check their completeness by comparing them with the templates in this book (keeping in mind that while all sections in the provided templates should be considered, they will not necessarily be completed).

The book also contains appendices of acronyms and business analysis terms. Refer to the appendices whenever you encounter a term or acronym you are not familiar with or whose relevance to business analysis is unclear. Appendix A, "Glossary of BA Terms," provides official definitions, where applicable, as well as an explanation of what each term means from the perspective of the BA.

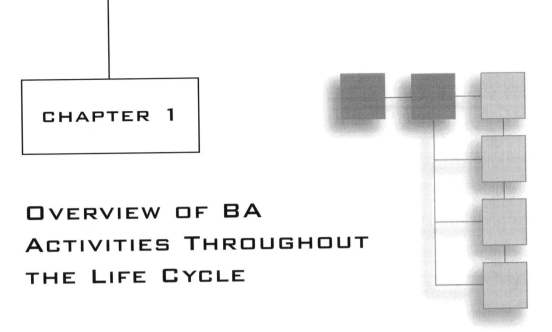

CHAPTER 1

OVERVIEW OF BA ACTIVITIES THROUGHOUT THE LIFE CYCLE

The purpose of this chapter is to provide an overview of the entire life cycle of a project with a focus on the involvement of the business analyst (BA). The chapter includes a step-by-step guide for the BA over the course of an IT project and the Spectrum Diagram, which places the software development life cycle in the context of the end-to-end initiative—including phases that lead up to and follow the IT project.

The BA guide, referred to as the Noble Path, is a based on a job aid that my company, Noble Inc., has been using internally and distributing to our clients. The Noble Path is not a methodology, but rather a summary of all of the steps, questions, etc., that a BA needs to consider regardless of methodology; it pulls together BA tools and techniques, described elsewhere in this handbook, indicating when each is used and the questions that the BA needs to ask in order to produce each deliverable. The Path presumes that an iterative, incremental process is being used on the project—an approach in accordance with industry best practices, standards, and methodologies, such as the IT Infrastructure Library (ITIL), IBM Rational Unified Process (RUP), Microsoft Solutions Framework (MSF), and agile processes. In iterative, incremental processes, the software is developed in a number of passes, with each pass resulting in executable code. (See "Adapting the Noble Path" later in this chapter for guidelines on customizing the Noble Path for different types of projects and processes.)

Figure 1.1 shows an overview of the phases of the Noble Path. Each phase represents a span of time within the Software Development Life Cycle (SDLC), marked at each end by milestones. The phase names (Initiation, Discovery, etc.) highlight the main theme of behaviour for each phase; however, in the iterative process presumed by the Path, all types of activities—such as analysis, design, coding, and testing—may occur in any phase[1] and are

---

[1]This is not true, however, for waterfall processes, where each activity must be completed before the next may begin.

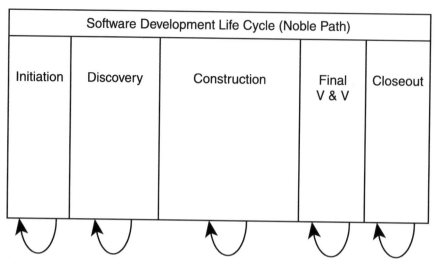

Figure 1.1 Noble Path overview

not dedicated to specific phases. The loops below each phase indicate that each phase is accomplished through one or more iterations (the number of iterations varying based on the approach being used and the nature of the project).

Phase names have been chosen to be as generic as possible. In practice, the names used for each phase, as well as the number of phases and the way activities are apportioned to phases, can be expected to differ from those used in the Noble Path, as there is no universally accepted standard for IT project management (and, in any case, one approach is unlikely to fit all projects). Consequently, you may need to adapt the Path by mapping Path phase names, artifact names, and so on, to those used on your project. The phase names used in the Path are as follows:

- **Initiation:** Make the business case for the project. Work also begins on the user experience and on architectural proof of concepts.

- **Discovery:** Conduct investigation leading to an understanding of the solution's desired behaviour.[2] Requirements analysis peaks during this phase but never disappears entirely. During this phase, architectural proof of concepts are also constructed.

- **Construction:** Complete the analysis and design, code, integrate, and test the software. (On iterative projects, these activities are performed for each iteration within the phase.) Design and coding appear in all phases, but peak during this phase.

---

[2]This definition for "discovery" is derived from *Object Solutions: Managing the Object-Oriented Project* by Grady Booch (Pearson Education, 1995), as quoted by Brian Lyons in the Number Six Software PowerPoint presentation "Three Key Features." In Booch's usage, the term refers to an activity that may occur in any phase but peaks early; in the Noble Path, it is used to name the phase during which most of this activity occurs.

- **Final V & V**: Perform final testing before the product or service is transitioned into production. (While final testing occurs in this phase, testing activities may occur throughout the SDLC, for example, before design or as a replacement for it.)
- **Closeout**: Manage and coordinate deployment into production and close the IT project.

Adapting the Noble Path

The analysis steps and documentation listed in the Noble Path are meant to be used as a checklist of items for the BA to consider as the project progresses; the intention is not to prescribe all of these items for every project. A number of parameters will vary depending on the nature of the project and the methodology used to manage it. These include the following:

- The number of life cycle phases and their names.
- The number of iterations in each phase.
- The duration (time box) of each iteration.
- The distribution of activities over the project life cycle.
- The amount and type of documentation produced.
- The amount of rework expected. (Iterative processes, in contrast to waterfall processes, are based on the expectation of rework.)

The relative emphasis placed on each step in the Path (and the other parameters listed in the previous paragraph) varies according to the type of life cycle approach being used. Life cycles may be described as definitive or empirical. Definitive life cycles are well-defined processes. To adapt the Noble Path to definitive life cycles, map Path steps and artifacts to those used in the life cycle. Use the Noble Path as a complement to the methodology, adding in those Path steps not detailed in your current process, if they are appropriate for the project.

Empirical approaches are less defined and adapt quickly to circumstances; they are characterized by minimal analysis and documentation. Factors favouring empirical approaches include volatile requirements, experimental technology, and small teams and projects for which the customer requires results quickly. When adapting the Path to empirical life cycles, use Path steps and artifacts as a checklist but implement only those items that are essential for the project. (An example of an essential step is the creation of architectural models.)

When adapting the Path for an agile approach, use the following guidelines[3]:

- Short iterations (for example, two-week sprints).
- Many iterations.
- Minimal requirements analysis and documentation, except as necessary to minimize risk and address architectural concerns.
- Frequent replanning.
- Constant collaboration.
- Continuous testing.
- No baselining of requirements for the purposes of change management.[4]
- The requirements may be changed at any time by the product owner as long as they are not being implemented.

As described earlier, the Path presumes an iterative, incremental process. To adapt the Path for a waterfall process, apply the following constraints:

- The number of iterations in each phase is one.
- All requirements analysis must be complete before design and coding begin.

Project size and complexity also have an impact on the BA role and, consequently, on the implementation of the Noble Path. As project size increases, so does the need for documentation to facilitate communication within the group. As complexity rises, more time must be spent on understanding the problem domain and establishing a solid architecture.

How to Use the Tables

Each of the Tables 1.1 through 1.5 describes a phase of the life cycle, focusing on the BA role. Each row in the tables represents one BA activity, described in the first column. (For example, the activity in the third row in Table 1.1 is "Analyze impact on business services and processes.") The row provides an overview of the activity; more detailed descriptions for many of these activities can be found throughout this handbook, such as in the "Meeting Guide" chapter, which provides participant lists and additional questions for the interview.

The BA does not need to execute the activities sequentially from the top to bottom row; in fact, many activities may be carried out in parallel. The second column (Predecessors, Timing) provides guidance regarding when each activity may begin. Use this information

---

[3]A number of these items are listed in the article "What Is Agile Software Development?" by Jim Highsmith in *Crosstalk, the Journal of Defense Software Engineering*, October 2002 issue. See http://www.stsc.hill.af.mil/Crosstalk/2002/10/highsmith.html.

[4]There is no point in freezing requirements because there is no investment in a requirement until it is scheduled for an iteration.

initially to plan the timing of activities. (Keep in mind that on iterative projects, many activities will occur repeatedly in the phase—once per iteration.) When you are about to execute the activity, use the column again to verify whether you are truly ready to proceed.

The third column (Input Documents) lists artifacts that are required for the activity. Use the information in this column to prepare documentation packages for participants to review prior to meetings. Many of these inputs are described in more detail elsewhere in this handbook, either in the BA Toolkit or the Templates chapter. Artifacts marked "UML (extended)" in this and the next column are either part of the UML standard or a valid extension of it.[5] (An example of a valid extension to the UML is the Worker modeling element.) RUP readers please note that the use-case *descriptions* that appear in these columns are referred to in RUP as use-case *specifications*.[6] Where the term *model* appears in these columns, it refers to any abstractions and representations of a system or aspect of a system and includes diagrams, modeling elements, and related textual documentation. For example, the system use-case model includes system use-case diagrams, modeling elements, such as system use cases and actors, and system use-case textual descriptions.

The fourth column (Deliverables) describes artifacts produced as a result of the activity. Use the information in this column when building meeting agendas so that the agenda may be directed toward the creation of the specified deliverables. Use the column, also, when creating your Work Plan of BA activities over the course of the project; the column helps identify when each deliverable will be produced or updated. Some of the deliverables are referred to as "interim." This is meant to convey that the document is updated at that point; it is a draft but has not been finalized. On a non-agile project, documents described as "baselined" are saved at that point in the process so that changes may be evaluated against them later. They may be frozen at the same time (depending on the project and methodology), in order to indicate that subsequent changes must be subjected to a change-management process. On agile projects, however, the requirements (if they exist) often are not baselined; furthermore, they may be changed at any time without undergoing a change-management process as long as they are not being implemented. The column also notes where some of the deliverables are indicated as finalized or signed off. Here, as elsewhere, expect particulars to vary by methodology and by project.

The fifth column (Interview Planning, Questions) summarizes key questions used by the BA during interviews with stakeholders. Where appropriate, the reader is directed to the

---

[5]Role Maps are listed under the UML heading, since they represent a limited form of a UML use-case diagram (i.e., one only depicting actors and their relationships to each other).

[6]I have deviated from the RUP term in order to avoid confusion over the design implication of the term *specification* as it is used in this book.

Meeting Guide chapter. In that chapter, the reader will find more detailed guidance, a more comprehensive list of BA questions, and a detailed mapping of specific questions to specific deliverables.

Initiation Phase

> ITIL Service Life Cycle Phase: Service Strategy[7]

The objectives of the Initiation phase are to develop the business case for the project, establish project and product scope, and to explore solutions, including the preliminary architecture. (The prototyping effort during Initiation should be risk-driven and limited to gaining confidence that a solution is possible.) The BA assists the project manager by identifying stakeholders, business services and processes, and IT services impacted by the project (see Table 1.1). By the end of this phase, key functionality is identified—such as key user tasks and IT services. When a non-agile process is used, these requirements are baselined and subsequent changes to scope are managed in a controlled manner using a change-management process.

Discovery Phase

> ITIL Service Life Cycle Phase: Service Design

The main objective of the Discovery phase is to understand the solution's desired behaviour and baseline the architecture (see Table 1.2). This and the previous phase are the key phases for the BA. Requirements analysis peaks during this phase. (In iterative processes, analysis continues throughout the life cycle; in waterfall processes, it is completed in this phase.) Some user tasks are selected for development during this phase in order to demonstrate architectural proof of concepts. The Discovery phase corresponds to one aspect of the ITIL Service Life Cycle phase, Service Design, which deals with the development of the requirements. (The Construction phase that follows corresponds to the other aspect of Service Design—the development of technical design specifications.)

---

[7]The activities in the Initiation phase correspond to planning and the first steps of analysis as described in the itSMF® publication, *Service Agreements – A Management Guide* (itSMF-NL, Benyon and Johnston, 2006).

Table 1.1 Initiation Phase

Objective	Predecessors, Timing	Input Documents	Deliverables	Interview Planning, Questions
Kick-off meeting; identify opportunities and challenges	At start of project, to identify main issues, costs, and possible benefits; redo as necessary	Change request *ITIL:* Initial RFC (Request For Change[8])	■ Pareto chart ■ Cause-and-effect graph ■ Interim cost-benefit analysis (ROI,[9] payback period[10]) *ITIL:* Interim BIA (Business Impact Analysis)	*Refer to the "Identify Opportunities and Challenges" section in the Meeting Guide for a more comprehensive list of questions. Key questions include:* ■ What are the major problems you are experiencing? ■ How often do they occur? ■ What opportunities are we missing? ■ What are the costs and benefits of a change? ■ What are the risks?
Identify stakeholders and interests	A request for a change has been made, triggering the project	Initial business case *ITIL:* ■ High-level RFC(s)	***Vision Document:*** ■ Problem Statement ■ Problem Position Statement ■ Stakeholders and Interests Table ■ Objectives ■ Features	*Refer to the "Identify Stakeholders and Interests" section in the Meeting Guide for a more comprehensive list of questions. Key questions include:* ■ Who will be affected by the success or failure of the solution? ■ Who are the users? ■ Who is the customer? ■ Who will sign off on the solution? ■ What is each stakeholder's interest (an addressed need or opportunity) in the solution?

(continued)

Objective	Predecessors, Timing	Input Documents	Deliverables	Interview Planning, Questions
Analyze impact on business services and processes	Stakeholders and interests have been identified	Stakeholders and Interests Table **UML (extended)**[11]: ▪ As-Is business use-case model **ITIL:** ▪ CMS (Configuration Management System) ▪ Business Services Catalogue ▪ Technical Services Catalogue[12] ▪ Existing S(L)As[13] (Service Level Agreements)	▪ Interim BIA ▪ Impact of proposed changes on business services (BRD) **UML (extended):** ▪ To-Be business use-case diagrams, business use cases, actors and business use-case descriptions *Note:* A business use-case description (referred to in RUP as a business use-case specification) defines the interaction across the business boundary and is usually expressed using a text narrative. (See the Business Use-Case Description Template in the Templates chapter.) The text may be augmented with an activity diagram with one partition for the business and one for each actor.[14]	*Refer to the "Analyze Impact on Business Services and Processes" section in the Meeting Guide for a more comprehensive list of questions. Key questions include:* ▪ What existing business services and end-to-end processes will be affected by this project? ▪ What is the gap between what is required and what currently exists? ▪ What new business services or processes will be introduced by this project? ▪ For each identified service or process, what is the expected impact of the change on the business area and on other services and components?

Table 1.1 Initiation Phase (continued)

Objective	Predecessors, Timing	Input Documents	Deliverables	Interview Planning, Questions
			Alternatives to UML: ■ Interim business perspective DFDs (Data Flow Diagrams) **ITIL:** ■ Interim business S(L)Rs (Service Level Requirements) ■ Updates to Business Service Portfolio	
Business Impact Analysis: Analyze risk	Analyze risk at the start of each iteration; reassess regularly	■ Vision Document[15] ■ Interim BIA (Business Impact Analysis) ■ Impact of proposed changes on business services (BRD)	■ Interim Risk Analysis (see BRD template in the Templates chapter) **ITIL:** ■ Interim BIA ■ Interim Risk Analysis	*Meet with business and technical stakeholders. Refer to the "Analyze Risk" section in the Meeting Guide for a more comprehensive list of questions. Key questions include:* ■ Are there any threats that could have a negative impact on the outcome of this project? ■ Are there any desirable events (opportunities) that would have a positive impact? *For each identified risk:* ■ What is the likelihood it will occur? ■ What is the impact on the business if it occurs? ■ What is the best strategy for dealing with this risk?

Table 1.1 Initiation Phase (continued)

Objective	Predecessors, Timing	Input Documents	Deliverables	Interview Planning, Questions
Requirements Management: Setup and planning	Initial cost benefit, BIA reviewed; approval to proceed	▪ Vision Document *ITIL:* ▪ BIA	▪ Requirements Work Plan ▪ Requirements attributes table templates ▪ Requirements traceability matrix templates *ITIL:* ▪ CMS (Configuration Management System) framework,[16] updates to Service Portfolio	*Meet with the project manager and team leads. Refer to the "Requirements Management— Setup and Planning" section in the Meeting Guide for a more comprehensive list of questions. Key questions include:* ▪ What questions must the requirements-management process be able to answer? ▪ What level of requirements tracking is appropriate? ▪ What facts need to be documented about each requirement?
▪ Requirements Management: Update requirement attributes and traceability matrices with information about features and business services	▪ Requirements traceability matrix has been set up ▪ Requirements attribute table has been set up	▪ Vision Document ▪ Overview of business services[17] *UML (extended):* ▪ Business use-case diagrams ▪ Business use cases ▪ Actors ▪ Business use-case descriptions ▪ Business use-case documents *ITIL:* ▪ BIA ▪ RFCs, Business Service Portfolio[18]	Updates to requirements attributes table and traceability matrix *ITIL:* ▪ Updates for Service Portfolio, S(L)Rs, CMS	*Meet with stakeholders and team members to review and update requirements attributes and the relationships between new or changed requirements and other artifacts and Configuration Items. For each feature or service, use the requirements tables as a guide to questions and to document responses. Questions for all requirements include:* ▪ Who is the author? ▪ Who is responsible for it? ▪ How will we verify that it is supported in the final product? ▪ How likely is it to change over time?

Table 1.1 Initiation Phase (continued)

Objective	Predecessors, Timing	Input Documents	Deliverables	Interview Planning, Questions
Define To-Be internal workflow for end-to-end business processes	Business services impacted by the change have been identified	■ Impact of proposed changes on business services (see BRD template) *UML (extended):* ■ Business use-case diagrams ■ Business use cases ■ Actors ■ Business use-case descriptions *ITIL:* ■ Business Service Portfolio ■ BIA	■ Business process cross-functional workflow *UML (extended):* ■ Business use-case realizations (A business use-case realization is a description that includes internal workflow and is usually expressed visually using activity diagrams.) *Alternatives to UML:* ■ Text, BPD *ITIL:* ■ Interim S(L)Rs	*Refer to the "Define Internal Workflow for End-to-End Business Processes" section in the Meeting Guide for a more comprehensive list of questions. Key questions for each process include:* ■ What is the current (As-Is) workflow (if applicable)? ■ What is the desired (To-Be) workflow? ■ Which participant carries out each activity in the workflow?

Table 1.1 Initiation Phase (continued)

Objective	Predecessors, Timing	Input Documents	Deliverables	Interview Planning, Questions
Describe users	Impact on business-process workflow has been analyzed	■ Stakeholders and Interests Table ■ Business process model: participants (actors), workflow ■ User profile *UML (extended):* ■ To-Be business use-case model ■ Role Map[19] (if there is an existing one) *Alternatives to UML:* ■ DFD (Data Flow Diagram) ■ Updated BPD (Business Process Diagram) *ITIL:* ■ CMS[20]	User profile[21] *UML:* ■ Role Map *ITIL:* ■ Updates to user CIs (Configuration Items) by CMS[22]	*Refer to the "Describe Users" section in the Meeting Guide for a more comprehensive list of questions. Key questions include:* ■ Which of the business process participants (business actors and workers) will be direct users of the system? ■ Who will receive messages or reports from the system? ■ Which external computer systems will the system communicate with? ■ Is there any overlap between the roles of the various user groups?

Table 1.1 Initiation Phase (continued)

Objective	Predecessors, Timing	Input Documents	Deliverables	Interview Planning, Questions
Identify user tasks	■ Impact on business process workflow has been analyzed	■ Business process model: Cross-functional workflow ■ Existing IT services model *UML (extended):* ■ To-Be business use-case model ■ As-Is system use-case model *ITIL:* ■ RFCs (Requests for Change) ■ Business S(L)Rs ■ Technical Service Catalogue	Functional requirements: User tasks *UML:* ■ System use-case diagrams ■ System use cases ■ Actors ■ System use-case briefs (short textual descriptions) *Alternatives to the UML:* ■ DFDs *ITIL:* ■ Interim IT S(L)Rs ■ RFCs[23]	*Review workflow of each end-to-end business process (business use-case). Refer to the "Identify User Tasks" section in the Meeting Guide for a more comprehensive list of questions. Key questions include:* ■ Which tasks involve the IT system? ■ What is the best way to group the automated steps into tasks that can be accomplished by one user in one session? ■ What menu options would you like to see? ■ What electronic transactions must the system be able to process?
Requirements Management: Monitor requirements	■ Requirements attributes table (or equivalent) has been set up ■ Performed whenever requirements are identified or changed	New or changed requirements *UML:* ■ System use-case diagrams[24] ■ System use cases ■ Actors ■ System use-case briefs *ITIL:* ■ RFCs, interim IT S(L)Rs, CMS	■ Requirements attributes table ■ Requirements traceability matrix *ITIL:* ■ Updates for Service Portfolio, S(L)Rs, CMS	*Meet with stakeholders and team members to review and update requirements attributes and the relationships between new or changed requirements and other artifacts and Configuration Items. For each user task (system use case), use the requirements table as a guide to questions and to document responses. For example:* ■ Who will be responsible for ensuring that the requirements for this user task (system use case) are delivered as requested? ■ What methods will be used to verify that the solution meets the requirements (tests, walkthroughs, UAT [User Acceptance Testing])? ■ What business services or processes (business use cases) does this user task support? ■ What business goals does it support?

Table 1.1 Initiation Phase (continued)

Objective	Predecessors, Timing	Input Documents	Deliverables	Interview Planning, Questions
Static Modeling: Define business concepts, objects, and rules	■ Perform in parallel with dynamic modeling of IT services. As business nouns are introduced, elicit and document definitions and rules.	Business process model *UML (extended):* ■ Business use-case model: Business use cases, business actors and workers, business use-case diagrams, business use-case descriptions, business use-case realizations ■ System use-case model: System use cases, actors, Role Map, system use-case diagrams, system use-case briefs ■ Activity diagrams *Alternatives to UML:* ■ DFDs ■ BPDs ■ Flowcharts	■ Business rules ■ Data dictionary *UML:* ■ Entity classes ■ Business-perspective class diagrams *Alternatives to the UML:* ■ Business-perspective ERDs (Entity Relationship Diagrams)	*Refer to the "Define Business Concepts, Objects, and Rules" section in the Meeting Guide for a more comprehensive list of questions. Key questions include:* ■ What are the primary people, transactions, products, and services that the business needs to track with the aid of the software system? *For each entity (class) included in the model, ask stakeholders:* ■ Briefly explain the term ■ Provide a typical example ■ What type of information (attributes) does the business track about it? ■ Does the business need to link it to any other business objects and, if so, how many of each type?

Table 1.1 Initiation Phase (continued)

Objective	Predecessors, Timing	Input Documents	Deliverables	Interview Planning, Questions
Define non-functional business service level requirements	▪ May occur at any time	▪ Vision Document, features, existing requirements **UML (extended):** ▪ Business use-case model **ITIL:** ▪ Business Service Portfolio ▪ Interim S(L)Rs	▪ Interim non-functional requirements **ITIL:** ▪ Interim business SLRs ▪ Interim updates to Service Pipeline	*Refer to the "Define Non-Functional SLRs" section in the Meeting Guide for a more comprehensive list of questions. Key questions include:* ▪ What volume of transactions/customers must be accommodated? ▪ How available must the business services be? 24/7? ▪ What are the security requirements? ▪ Are there any accessibility guidelines that apply?
Investigate solutions/early design	▪ Impact on business services and processes has been analyzed ▪ Impacted IT services have been identified	▪ Vision Document ▪ Features ▪ Mid-level functional requirements ▪ Architectural documents: Enterprise architecture, business architecture, product line architecture, information system architecture **UML (extended):** ▪ Business use-case model ▪ System use-case model **ITIL:** ▪ S(L)Rs	▪ UI prototypes ▪ Proof of concept prototypes ▪ Design plan Prototypes created during this stage are likely to be disposed of later in the project. Architectural work is largely paper-based, including sketches of communications, basic large-scale interactions, and division of labour across systems. Design activities during this phase focus on developing a design plan. (The design plan describes the design approach and identifies design artifacts that may be leveraged.[25])	If a COTS or Service Provider solution is contemplated, meet with stakeholders and vendor or provider. If an internal or customized solution is planned, work with the technical team on high-priority or high-risk use cases at this time; review resulting design specifications and so on to ensure requirements are supported. Refer to the checklist "Selecting Solution Providers" in the Tips and Checklists chapter for suggested selection criteria.

Table 1.1 Initiation Phase (continued)

Objective	Predecessors, Timing	Input Documents	Deliverables	Interview Planning, Questions
QA: Plan tests (support role)	▪ Impacted IT Services have been identified	**UML** ▪ System use-case model **ITIL:** ▪ S(L)Rs ▪ Service Pipeline	Support the QA team in the development of: ▪ Master test plan ▪ High-value test cases	
Review and sign off on requirements	**Walkthroughs:** ▪ At regular intervals, as artifacts become available **Sign-off:** ▪ Requirements may be signed off iteratively, as they are developed OR ▪ One big sign-off is performed at the end of the phase	**Any changed requirements artifacts:** ▪ Vision Document ▪ Risk analysis ▪ Features ▪ Business services/ processes ▪ User requirements (tasks identified) ▪ Requirements attributes tables and traceability matrices ▪ Non-functional requirements **UML (extended):** ▪ Business use-case model and documents ▪ System use-case model and documents ▪ Role Map ▪ Class diagrams **Alternatives to UML:** ▪ Interim functional decomposition, DFD, BPD, ERD	**Walkthroughs:** ▪ Verified requirements documents **Sign-off:** On waterfall projects, the following items are baselined and finalized; on iterative projects, requirements are subject to change at any time as long as they are not being implemented. ▪ Vision Document ▪ Risk analysis ▪ Feature ▪ Business services/ processes ▪ User requirements (tasks identified) ▪ Requirements attributes tables and traceability matrices ▪ Non-functional requirement ▪ Requirements Work Plan	*Meet with business stakeholders, developers, QA, and the project manager to review requirements. For a compete list of questions see the "Review Meeting" section in the Meeting Guide. Key questions include:* ▪ Are the requirements complete, correct, realistic, testable, and within scope? ▪ Has all the necessary documentation been created or updated? Class diagrams? Traceability tables? Requirements attributes tables?

Table 1.1 Initiation Phase (continued)

Objective	Predecessors, Timing	Input Documents	Deliverables	Interview Planning, Questions
Review and sign off on requirements		**ITIL:** ■ RFC (initial request for change) ■ Interim Service (Level) Requirements	***UML (extended):*** ■ Business use-case model ■ System use-case model ■ Role map ■ Key business class diagrams ***Alternatives to UML:*** Functional decomposition BPD, DFD, ERD ***ITIL:*** BIA, S(L)Rs, RFCs, CMS updates	

[8]In ITIL, RFCs may originate from a number of sources, such as the IT and Marketing departments. In either case, the analysis should begin with the business impact. An example of a marketing-initiated RFC is a request to add or modify a business service. The implication of (and reason for) placing this type of request as an RFC is to place it under Change Management so that it can be properly monitored and controlled. Eventually, an RFC of this type will lead to lower-level RFCs that initiate changes to IT configuration items, such as programs, databases, and hardware units.

[9]ROI stands for Return on Investment. Other metrics, such as IRR (Internal Rate of Return) may also be used.

[10]Payback period is the measure of the time it will take to pay off the initial investment.

[11]Artifacts marked "Extended UML" are either part of the UML standard or a valid extension of it.

[12]The Business Service Catalogue consists of active and approved services and the "relations with departments and processes that depend on the service" (Foundations of ITIL Service Management, based on ITIL V3, p. 194) and contains policies, service level arrangements, and so on. The ITIL process governing this step is Service Catalogue Management.

[13]Use existing SLAs in performing a gap analysis. Also please note that, as described earlier, the parentheses in S(L)A and S(L)R are used to indicate that the term refers to any type of service level requirement or agreement (both functional and non-functional).

[14]Augmentation of text with an activity diagram is recommended for complex use cases where the flows connect to each other in complex ways.

Table 1.1 Initiation Phase (continued)

[15]This document will evolve over time. The input Vision Document used at this point is an early iteration of the artifact.

[16]The CMS (Configuration Management System) tracks CIs (Configuration Items) and their relationships to each other. Configuration standards, including requirements configuration, are often defined for a department or business and all projects are expected to comply with it. The senior BA should meet with the PM and leads to review and plan the types and levels of requirements to be tracked, what requirements attributes will be included in the CMS, and how these will be traced to other CIs.

[17]See the section "Impact of Proposed Changes on Business Services and Processes" of the BRD in the Templates chapter.

[18]The Business Service Portfolio consists of the Business Service Pipeline (services in development), Business Service Catalogue (current services), and Retired Services. New business services identified by the BA should be documented in the pipeline.

[19]*Role Map* is not a UML term; it is a limited form of a use-case diagram popularized by Larry Constantine, containing only actors and their relationships to each other. See the "Role Map" section of the BA Toolkit chapter for more on Role Maps.

[20]The CMS can provide information about users and their links to other CIs if the CMDB is set up accordingly (see footnote 16).

[21]See the "Actors" section of the BRD in the Templates chapter.

[22]Customers, users, suppliers, and other stakeholders may be treated as CIs (Configuration Items). Doing so allows their relationship to IT services (and system use cases) to be tracked by the CMS (Configuration Management Systems) so that the stakeholders impacted by a change can be easily identified.

[23]RFCs generated at this point include requests for changes to IT services (and their related CIs).

[24]Although the term *system use case* is not part of the UML, system use-case diagrams are classified as such in this handbook because they conform to standard UML use-case diagrams.

[25]These guidelines are sourced from an e-mail from Chris Reynolds.

Table 1.2 Discovery Phase

Objective	Predecessors, Timing	Input Documents	Deliverables	Interview Questions
Business Impact Analysis: Analyze risk	Analyze risk at the start of each iteration; reassess regularly	Vision Document	Interim Risk Analysis (see BRD template in the Templates chapter) *ITIL:* ■ Interim BIA	*Meet with business and technical stakeholders. Refer to the "Analyze Risk" section in the Meeting Guide for a more comprehensive list of questions. Key questions include:* ■ Are there any threats that could have a negative impact on the outcome of this project? ■ Are there any desirable events (opportunities) that would have a positive impact? *For each identified risk:* ■ What is the likelihood it will occur? ■ What is the impact on the business if it occurs? ■ What is the best strategy for dealing with this risk?

(continued)

Objective	Predecessors, Timing	Input Documents	Deliverables	Interview Questions
Plan IT service analysis and implementation	▪ Impact on business services and processes has been analyzed ▪ IT services have been identified	▪ Functional requirements (features, user tasks) ▪ Non-functional requirements ▪ Requirements Work Plan *UML:* ▪ System use-case model and documentation ▪ Role Map *ITIL:* ▪ S(L)Rs ▪ Schedule of Changes ▪ Service Portfolio	Updated Project Plan, Requirements Work Plan *ITIL:* Interim updates to SOC (Schedule of Changes)	*Meet with the project manager to advise on the mapping of requirements to project phases and iterations* ▪ During which phase and iteration will each functional requirement and non-functional requirement be elaborated? When will it be implemented? ▪ Are there any elements that we should implement in order to mitigate risk? For example, should we build proof of concepts of new technology components? *If your project follows the use-case approach, direct the above questions toward system use cases and their flow:* ▪ What system use cases and flows (basic, alternate, exception) will be described during this phase? What will wait until the Construction phase? ▪ During which phase and iteration will each system use case and flow be elaborated? When will it be implemented? ▪ Are there any system use cases that we should implement in order to mitigate risk? For example, should we build proof of concepts for system use cases that use new technology components?

Table 1.2 Discovery Phase (continued)

Objective	Predecessors, Timing	Input Documents	Deliverables	Interview Questions
Gather detailed user requirements	■ User tasks (within functional requirements), IT services have been identified *UML:* ■ System use cases have been identified	■ Project Plan ■ Business process models, high-level user requirements *UML (extended):* ■ Business use-case realizations ■ System use cases ■ Actors ■ Role Map ■ System use-case diagrams ■ System use-case briefs[26] (A use-case brief is a short paragraph describing the use case.) *Alternatives to UML:* ■ BPDs ■ DFDs *ITIL:* ■ RFCs ■ S(L)Rs	Interim user requirements *UML:* ■ System use-case descriptions *Note:* A system use-case description (referred to in RUP as a use-case specification) defines the interaction between actors and the business and is usually expressed using a text narrative. (See the System Use-Case Description Template in the Templates chapter.) The text may be augmented with an activity diagram with one partition for the system and one for each actor.[27] *ITIL:* ■ Interim S(L)Rs	*Meet with stakeholders to discuss user requirements. Refer to the "Gather Detailed User Requirements" section in the Meeting Guide for a more comprehensive list of questions. Key questions for each user task (system use case) include:* ■ What event triggers the interaction? ■ What is the net effect of a successful interaction? ■ Describe a typical, successful interaction. ■ Is there any other way each step in the interaction could play out? ■ At what points during the interaction might the user or system cancel the transaction?

Table 1.2 Discovery Phase (continued)

Objective	Predecessors, Timing	Input Documents	Deliverables	Interview Questions
Static modeling: Define business concepts, objects, and rules	■ Perform in parallel with dynamic modeling of IT services. As business nouns are introduced, elicit and document definitions and rules.	**UML:** ■ System use-case model: System use cases, actors, Role Map, system use-case diagrams, system use-case descriptions **Alternatives to UML:** ■ DFDs ■ BPDs ■ Flowcharts	■ Business rules ■ Data dictionary **UML:** ■ Entity classes ■ Business-perspective class diagrams **Alternatives to UML:** ■ Business-perspective ERDs	*Refer to the "Define Business Concepts, Objects, and Rules" section in the Meeting Guide for a more comprehensive list of questions. Key questions include:* ■ What are the primary people, transactions, products, and services that the business needs to track with the aid of the software system? *For each entity (class) included in the model, ask stakeholders:* ■ Briefly explain the term. ■ Provide a typical example. ■ What type of information (attributes) does the business track about it? ■ Does the business need to link it to any other business objects and, if so, how many of each type?
Requirements Management: Reuse user requirements	■ After user tasks and users have been identified ■ Review periodically as user requirements are elaborated	■ User requirements ■ Business rules **UML:** ■ System use-case model: System use cases, actors, system use-case diagrams, system use-case descriptions **ITIL:** ■ Service Portfolio ■ S(L)Rs	■ Updated user requirements ■ Business rules **UML:** ■ Updated system use-case model: Included use cases, extending use cases, generalized use cases and their base use cases, system use-case diagrams, system use-case descriptions **ITIL:** ■ Interim updates for Service Portfolio, S(L)Rs	*Meet with team members to review user requirements (system use-case model) and find opportunities for reuse. Refer to the "Reuse User Requirements" section in the Meeting Guide for list of questions. Questions include:* ■ Do any requirements appear more than once in the documentation? ■ Do they include any sub-goals that have already been documented (for example, as included use cases)? ■ Are any existing static modeling rules relevant to this user task?

Table 1.2 Discovery Phase (continued)

Objective	Predecessors, Timing	Input Documents	Deliverables	Interview Questions
Analyze the life cycle of key business objects	A business object has been identified that is key to the business area.	■ User requirements ■ Static model **UML (extended):** ■ Business use-case model (diagrams and text) ■ System use-case model ■ System use-case briefs ■ Role Map ■ Entity classes and class diagrams	■ State diagrams/ state charts ■ Static model **UML:** ■ State-machine (Harel statechart) diagrams ■ Updates to entity classes and class diagrams **Alternatives to UML:** ■ State transition tables ■ Updates to data model	*Refer to the "Analyze the Life Cycle of Business Objects" section in the Meeting Guide for a more comprehensive list of questions. Questions include:* ■ Is there a business object (or objects)—such as a transaction, incident, artifact, product, or service—that is key to the business process? ■ Are there any business objects whose status must be tracked by the business area? *For each key business object:* ■ What statuses can it have? ■ Describe the life cycle of the object, starting from the time it becomes known to the business. ■ What triggers the transition from one status to another?
Requirements Management: Monitor requirements	■ Requirements attributes table (or equivalent) has been set up ■ Performed whenever requirements are identified or changed	New or changed requirements **UML:** ■ System use-case model **ITIL:** ■ RFCs, interim IT S(L)Rs, CMS	■ Requirements attributes table ■ Requirements traceability matrix **ITIL:** ■ Updates for Service Portfolio, S(L)Rs, CMS	*Meet with stakeholders and team members to review and update requirements attributes, the relationships between new or changed requirements and other artifacts, and Configuration Items.*

Table 1.2 Discovery Phase (continued)

Objective	Predecessors, Timing	Input Documents	Deliverables	Interview Questions
Define non-functional IT service level requirements[28]	■ May occur at any time	Features, existing requirements **UML:** ■ System use-case model **ITIL:** ■ IT Service Portfolio ■ Interim S(L)Rs	Non-functional IT requirements (quality attributes) **ITIL:** ■ Interim IT SLRs ■ Interim updates to service pipeline	*Refer to the "Define Non-Functional SLRs" section in the Meeting Guide for a more comprehensive list of questions. Key questions include:* ■ What volume of transactions/customers must be accommodated? ■ How available must the IT services be? 24/7? ■ What are the security requirements? ■ Are there any accessibility guidelines that apply?

Table 1.2 Discovery Phase (continued)

Objective	Predecessors, Timing	Input Documents	Deliverables	Interview Questions
Service Validation and Testing[29]: Review test plans and scripts	QA has prepared test plans and scripts	■ Test Strategy ■ Test Plan ■ Test Scripts ■ Requirements Work Plan ■ Functional requirements ■ Non-functional requirements *UML:* ■ System use-case model and documents *ITIL:* ■ S(L)Rs ■ Service Catalogue (pipeline)	■ Updates to Test Strategy, Test Plan, and Test Scripts	*Review test plan and test scripts with QA team:* ■ Will the testing ensure that the solution does what the client expects it to? 　■ Is every user task (system use case) and scenario (flow) covered in the test plan? 　■ Do the expected test results conform to the user requirements (system use case)? ■ Will the testing ensure that the solution is "fit for use" (performs well according to specified terms)? 　■ Do test plans include testing of service level targets, usability, and accessibility requirements? 　■ Are there tests for service level guarantees with respect to availability, volume, continuity, and security? 　■ Are there tests to verify whether suppliers and processes comply with industry standards and guidelines? 　■ Does the plan include appropriate regression testing (tests to ensure that services that were not supposed to have changed remain unaffected by the solution)?

Table 1.2 Discovery Phase (continued)

Objective	Predecessors, Timing	Input Documents	Deliverables	Interview Questions
Review and sign off on requirements	**Walkthroughs:** ■ At regular intervals, as artifacts become available **Sign-off:** ■ Requirements may be signed off iteratively, as they are developed OR ■ One big sign-off is performed at the end of the phase	Any changed requirements artifacts: ■ Vision Document ■ Risk analysis ■ Features ■ Business services/ processes ■ User requirements (tasks identified) ■ Requirements attributes tables and traceability matrices ■ Non-functional requirements **UML (extended):** ■ Business use-case model ■ System use-case model ■ Role Map ■ Class diagrams	**Walkthroughs:** ■ Verified requirements documents **Sign-off:** On waterfall projects, the following items are baselined and finalized; on iterative projects, requirements are subject to change at any time as long as they are not being implemented. ■ Risk analysis ■ User requirements (details) ■ Requirements attributes tables and traceability matrix ■ Non-functional requirements ■ Requirements Work Plan	Meet with business stakeholders, developers, QA, and the project manager to review requirements. For a compete list of questions see the "Review Meeting" section in the Meeting Guide. Key questions include: ■ Are the requirements complete, correct, realistic, testable, and within scope? ■ Have all the necessary documentation and modeling elements been created or updated? Classes? Traceability tables?

Table 1.2 Discovery Phase (continued)

Objective	Predecessors, Timing	Input Documents	Deliverables	Interview Questions
Review and sign off on requirements		***Alternatives to UML:*** ■ Interim functional decomposition, DFD, BPD, ERD ***ITIL:*** ■ RFC (initial Request for Change) ■ Interim Service (Level) Requirements	***UML:*** ■ System use-case model (system use-case diagrams, modeling elements, and descriptions) ■ Class diagrams ■ Entity classes[30] ■ State-machine diagrams ***Alternatives to UML:*** ■ Finalized or baselined functional decomposition BPD, DFD, ERD, state transition diagrams ***ITIL:*** ■ Finalized or baselined BIA, S(L)Rs, RFCs, CMS updates, Service Design Package, Service Model, Process Interface Definition	

Table 1.2 Discovery Phase (continued)

Objective	Predecessors, Timing	Input Documents	Deliverables	Interview Questions
Review design	Selected user requirements (system use-case flows) have been verified or signed off[31]	▪ UI prototypes ▪ Proof of concepts ▪ Other design specifications ▪ Requirements traceability matrix **UML:** ▪ Sequence diagrams, technical class diagrams, communication diagrams **Alternatives to UML:** ▪ Design DFDs, ERDs	Verified UI prototypes, proof of concepts, other design specifications **UML:** ▪ Verified sequence diagrams, class diagrams, communication diagrams	*Some requirements (system use cases) may move into design and development at this point. Participate in structured walk-throughs with the technical team to review UIs (User Interfaces), prototypes, proof of concepts, and so on as they become available to ensure the requirements are supported. For example, reviewing a UI:* ▪ Does the interface support the user requirements documented in the corresponding system use case? ▪ Are all alternate and exception flows supported by the UI? ▪ Is the sequence of steps the same in the UI as in the user requirements (use case)? ▪ Does each requirement targeted for this iteration trace forward to a design item?
Evaluation[32]: Assess the results of each iteration	End of each iteration	▪ Test reports ▪ Project Plan (iteration plan) ▪ Risk list ▪ List of defects **ITIL:** ▪ Service Acceptance Criteria (SAC) ▪ Incident Management reports	Evaluation report	*Meet with project manager, team, and customer to evaluate the performance of any changes. (On an iterative project, these may include implementation of some of the requirements.) For a list of questions, see the "Assess the Results of an Iteration" section in the Meeting Guide. Questions include:* ▪ Did the change create any unintended effects? ▪ Have the targeted scenarios been implemented? ▪ Have the risks been eliminated or mitigated?

[26]Use-case briefs should be two to six sentences in length. For more on use-case briefs, see *Writing Effective Use Cases* by Alistair Cockburn (Addison-Wesley Professional, 2000), p. 38.

Table 1.2 Discovery Phase (continued)

27Augmentation of text with an activity diagram is recommended for complex use cases where the flows connect to each other in complex ways.

28Please note that in this handbook, when the words "service level" qualify a noun, they are not hyphenated, despite the book's practice of hyphenating other two-word qualifiers. As explained in the Introduction, this exception was made to conform with the spelling used in ITIL publications.

29In ITIL V3, Service Validation and Testing is listed as a process under Service Transition.

30Entity classes only are listed, as these are the responsibility of the BA.

31The degree to which the user requirements (system use cases) must be approved before design begins depends on how iterative the process is. In a highly iterative process, user requirements (system use cases) and design items, such as UI prototypes, are developed over a number of iterations; in a non-iterative process, the use cases are all signed off before any design is done.

32Evaluation is categorized by ITIL as a process within Service Transition. This step focuses on the BA contribution to the process.

Construction Phase

ITIL Service Life Cycle Phase: Service Design

The main objective of this phase is to finish the analysis and design, code, integrate, and test the software (see Table 1.3). On iteratively developed projects, these activities appear in all phases, including Discovery, but peak during this phase. Also on such projects, the remaining requirements are gathered during each iteration for the user interactions (system use-case flows) selected for that iteration.

The creation of design specifications and the code that occurs during construction is included as part of ITIL Service Design.

Final V & V Phase

ITIL Service Life Cycle Phase: Service Transition

The main objective of this phase is to perform final testing before the product or service is transitioned into production (see Table 1.4). The BA assists by reviewing test plans and ensuring that all requirements have been tested. (While final testing occurs in this phase, testing activities may occur throughout the life cycle, for example, before design or as a replacement for it. Also, see "Testing Throughout the Life Cycle with the Service V-Model" in the Tips and Checklists chapter of this book for a graphic that summarizes the steps in delivering a service capability and relates them to corresponding testing activities.)

Testing is included in the ITIL Service Life Cycle phase: Service Transition (specifically, the Service Validation and Testing process).

Table 1.3 Construction Phase

Objective	Predecessors, Timing	Input	Deliverables	Interview Questions
Business Impact Analysis: Analyze risk	Analyze risk at the start of each iteration; reassess regularly	▪ Risk analysis ▪ Project Plan ▪ Design specifications *ITIL:* ▪ Schedule of Changes ▪ RFCs ▪ BIA	▪ Risk Analysis (see BRD template) *ITIL:* ▪ Interim BIA	*Meet with business and technical stakeholders. Refer to the "Analyze Risk" section in the Meeting Guide for a more comprehensive list of questions. Key questions include:* ▪ Are there any threats that could have a negative impact on the outcome of this project? ▪ Are there any desirable events (opportunities) that would have a positive impact? *For each identified risk:* ▪ What is the likelihood it will occur? ▪ What is the impact on the business if it occurs? ▪ What is the best strategy for dealing with this risk?

(continued)

Objective	Predecessors, Timing	Input	Deliverables	Interview Questions
Gather remaining user requirements	Perform during each iteration, for user tasks (system use cases) selected for further analysis and/or implementation	■ Project Plan ■ Business Process Models ■ High-level user requirements (user tasks identified) *UML (extended):* ■ Business use-case workflows (text and/or activity diagrams) ■ System use-case model ■ System use-case briefs ■ Role Map *ITIL:* ■ RFCs, S(L)Rs	■ Interim user requirements *UML:* ■ Remaining system use-case descriptions and flows *ITIL:* ■ Interim S(L)Rs, RFCs	*Gather any remaining requirements for the user interaction (use-case flows) selected for the iteration at the start of the iteration. Refer to the "Gather Detailed User Requirements" section in the Meeting Guide for a list of questions.*
Gather Service Desk requirements	At any time but must be complete before product or service is put into production	*ITIL:* ■ Services Support Model ■ IT Service Continuity plan ■ Business Continuity Plan (BCP)	■ Non-functional Service Level requirements *ITIL:* ■ Services Support Model ■ Service Desk procedures ■ Incident escalation procedures ■ SLRs *UML:* ■ Role Map (Service Desk Agent actors) ■ System use-case model	*Refer to the "Gather Service Desk Requirements" section in the Meeting Guide for a more comprehensive list of questions. Key questions include:* ■ What new (or revised) types of incidents and service requests will the Service Desk have to contend with due to the changes? ■ What are the known errors? ■ How many incidents and events must the system be able to handle per hour/month/day?

Table 1.3 Construction Phase (continued)

Objective	Predecessors, Timing	Input	Deliverables	Interview Questions
Review and sign-off of requirements	■ Conduct walkthroughs regularly to validate requirements discovered during this phase. ■ Sign off at scheduled points during each iteration requirements or in one sign-off before design begins.	■ Changed functional and non-functional requirements ■ Requirements attributes tables and traceability matrices ■ Requirements Work Plan *UML:* ■ System use-case model, static model (classes, class diagrams), state-machine diagrams *ITIL:* ■ RFCs, S(L)Rs, CMS, SOC (Schedule of Changes), PSO (Projected Service Outages)	***After Walkthrough:*** ■ Verified requirements documents and plans ***After Gate Review:*** On waterfall projects, the following items are baselined and finalized; on iterative projects, requirements are subject to change at any time as long as they are not being implemented. ■ Functional and non-functional requirements *UML:* ■ System use-case model ■ Static model (classes) ■ State-machine diagrams *ITIL:* ■ Approved RFCs, new or changed services, CIs, assets ■ Updated Schedule of Changes ■ Finalized S(L)Rs, updates to CMS, Service Design Package (Service Model, Process Interface Definition)	*Meet with business stakeholders, developers, QA, and the project manager to review requirements. For a compete list of questions see the "Review Meeting" section in the Meeting Guide. Key questions include:* ■ Are the requirements complete, correct, realistic, testable, and within scope? ■ Have operational requirements been considered? Capacity, stress, availability, bandwidth? ■ Have the needs of the Service Desk been considered?

Table 1.3 Construction Phase (continued)

Objective	Predecessors, Timing	Input	Deliverables	Interview Questions
Review design	Requirements for selected design items have been signed off	■ UI prototypes ■ Proof of concepts ■ Other design specifications **UML:** ■ Sequence or Communication diagrams[33] ■ Class diagrams **Alternatives to UML:** ■ Technical-perspective DFDs, structure charts, context diagram	■ Verified UI prototypes, proof of concepts ■ Other design specifications verified **UML:** ■ Verified Sequence or Communication diagrams ■ Class diagrams **Alternatives to UML:** ■ Technical-perspective DFDs, structure charts, context diagram	*Review design for user tasks (system use cases) that are to be implemented in this iteration/phase. Participate in structured walk-throughs with the technical team to review UIs (User Interfaces), prototypes, proof of concepts, and so on as they become available For example, reviewing a UI:* ■ Does the interface support the user requirements (system use case)? ■ Are all possible scenarios (alternate and exception flows) supported by the UI? ■ Is the sequence of steps the same in the UI as in the user requirements (system use case)?
Plan User Acceptance Testing (UAT)		User requirements **UML:** ■ System use-case model ■ Existing test plan **ITIL:** ■ RFCs, S(L)Rs, SOC (Schedule of Changes)	UAT (User Acceptance Testing) test plan	*Meet with business stakeholders, the PM, and QA team:* ■ What will be the acceptance criteria? ■ Who will perform the UAT? ■ Will a formal or informal UAT process be used?[34] ■ What user tasks (system use cases) will be included in the UAT? ■ Are the expected test results in line with user requirements (system use cases)?

Table 1.3 Construction Phase (continued)

Objective	Predecessors, Timing	Input	Deliverables	Interview Questions
Service Validation and Testing[35]: Review test plans and scripts	QA has prepared test plans and scripts	■ Test strategy ■ Test plan ■ Test scripts ■ Requirements Work Plan ■ Functional requirements ■ Non-functional requirements *UML:* ■ System use-case model (diagrams and text) *ITIL:* ■ S(L)Rs ■ Service Catalogue (pipeline)	Updates to test strategy, test plan, test scripts	*Review test plan and test scripts with QA team. See corresponding activity in Discovery phase for questions. Questions include:* ■ Is every user task (system use case) and scenario (flow) covered in the test plan? ■ Do the expected test results conform to the user requirements (system use case)? ■ Will the testing ensure that the solution is "fit for use" (performs well according to specified terms)?
Plan user training	■ User roles have been identified ■ User roles have been mapped to services	■ User profile ■ Business process model *UML (extended):* ■ Role Map ■ System use-case model and descriptions ■ Business use-case model *Alternative to UML:* ■ Business-perspective DFDs	■ End-user training plan ■ Service Desk training plan	■ Who will be responsible for training users? ■ Have all user groups been considered in the user training plan? ■ For each user group, have training needs been considered for each user task accessed by the group? ■ Does training include integration with the business process, including steps carried out manually and using external systems? ■ Does the training plan address the needs of the Service Desk?

Table 1.3 Construction Phase (continued)

Objective	Predecessors, Timing	Input	Deliverables	Interview Questions
Evaluation[36]: Assess the results of each iteration	End of each iteration	Test reports **ITIL:** ■ SAC (Service Acceptance Criteria) ■ Incident Management reports	Evaluation report	*Meet with project manager, team, and customer to evaluate the performance of any changes. (On an iterative project, these may include implementation of some of the requirements.) For a list of questions, see the "Assess the Results of an Iteration" section in the Meeting Guide. Questions include:* ■ Did the change create any unintended effects? ■ Have the targeted scenarios been implemented? ■ Have the risks been eliminated or mitigated?

[33]These two diagrams are semantically equivalent.

[34]In a formal UAT, test scripts and expected results are defined in detail. With informal UAT, only test objectives are predefined, with details left up to the tester.

[35]In ITIL V3, Service Validation and Testing is listed as a process under Service Transition.

[36]Evaluation is categorized by ITIL as a process within Service Transition. This step focuses on the BA contribution to the process.

Closeout Phase

ITIL Service Life Cycle Phase: Service Transition

The purpose of this phase is to manage and coordinate the processes, systems, and functions required for the deployment of a release into production and end project activities. Table 1.5 focuses the BA perspective leading up to and following the release.

This phase corresponds to the ITIL Service Life Cycle phase, Service Transition. (However, Service Validation and Testing, a process of Service Transition, has been included in the previous Final V & V phase.)

Table 1.4 Final V & V Phase

Objective	Predecessors, Timing	Input	Deliverables	Interview Questions
Business Impact Analysis: Analyze risk	Analyze risk at the start of each iteration; reassess regularly	▪ Risk analysis ▪ Project Plan ▪ Design specifications *ITIL:* ▪ Schedule of Changes ▪ RFCs ▪ BIA	▪ Risk Analysis (see BRD template)	*Meet with business and technical stakeholders. Refer to the "Analyze Risk" section in the Meeting Guide for a more comprehensive list of questions. Key questions include:* ▪ Are there any threats that could have a negative impact on the outcome of this project? ▪ Are there any desirable events (opportunities) that would have a positive impact? *For each identified risk:* ▪ What is the likelihood it will occur? ▪ What is the impact on the business if it occurs? ▪ What is the best strategy for dealing with this risk?

(continued)

Objective	Predecessors, Timing	Input	Deliverables	Interview Questions
Review and sign-off of non-functional test results	■ Conduct reviews regularly to review test results ■ Sign off on the tests at the end of testing and before changes are made or moved to production	■ Functional requirements ■ Requirements traceability matrices ■ Test plan *UML:* ■ System use-case model ■ Static model (class diagrams), state-machine diagrams ■ Use-case scenario test scripts *ITIL:* ■ RFCs, S(L)Rs, updates to CMS	*Documentation verified or finalized includes:* ■ Changes to requirements attributes tables and traceability matrices *UML:* ■ System use-case model, static model (class diagrams), state-machine diagrams *ITIL:* ■ Approved RFCs, approved changes to CIs and assets, approved Schedule of Changes, finalized S(L)Rs, updates to CMS, Service Design Package (service model, Process Interface Definition)	*Meet with business stakeholders and QA to review test result:* ■ Have all of the functional changes to services been tested? ■ Have all the targeted user tasks (system use cases) and scenarios been tested? ■ Have all of the business rules been tested? Have all multiplicity (cardinality) rules in the static model been tested? ■ Do actual test results match expectations? ■ Did any test create unintended effects? ■ For each failed test, what is the recommended action? Delay release until fixed? Workaround?

Table 1.4 Final V & V Phase (continued)

Objective	Predecessors, Timing	Input	Deliverables	Interview Questions
Review and sign-off of non-functional test results	▪ Conduct reviews regularly to review test results ▪ Sign off on the tests at the end of testing and before changes are made or moved to production	▪ Non-functional test results (tests of non-functional SLRs) ▪ Non-functional requirements *UML:* ▪ System use-case model ▪ Static model (class diagrams), state-machine diagrams ▪ Use-case scenario test scripts *ITIL:* ▪ Non-functional SLRs	Signed-off test results; evaluation report	*Review test results:* ▪ Have the requirements of the Service Desk been tested? ▪ Have operational requirements been tested? Capacity, stress, availability, bandwidth? Usability? ▪ Do actual test results match expectations? ▪ Did any test create unintended effects? ▪ For each failed test, what is the recommended action? Delay release until fixed? Workaround?
Conduct User Acceptance Testing (UAT) and sign off on results	▪ Functional and non-functional testing by QA team has been successfully completed ▪ UAT test plan, process, and acceptance criteria have been agreed upon	▪ UAT test plan ▪ UAT acceptance criteria	Signed-off UAT test results	▪ Have the criteria for a successful UAT been met? ▪ Have non-functional require-ments that were part of the UAT test plan been satisfied? ▪ Was the agreed-upon UAT process followed? ▪ Have the customer and solution providers agreed on acceptable workarounds for non-serious errors?

Table 1.5 Closeout Phase

Objective	Predecessors, Timing	Input	Deliverables	Interview Questions
Pre-implementation readiness review	■ All changes have been implemented and tested but not released into production ■ UAT, functional, and non-functional testing has been successfully completed and signed off	■ Transition plan ■ Test sign-offs ■ Requirements traceability matrices ■ Non-functional requirements *ITIL:* ■ SOC (Schedule of Changes) ■ PSO (Projected Service Outages) ■ S(L)Rs, S(L)As	Final evaluation report	■ Has customer signed off on all changes? ■ Have all requirements been implemented and tested? Can every requirement be traced forward to a test? *Review transition plans:* ■ Have Service Transition procedures been approved by management? ■ Have technical transition plans been coordinated with the needs of the business? ■ Is there an appropriate plan for readying the Service Desk? Training users? ■ Is there adequate planning for expected operational requirements (expressed in non-functional SLRs) regarding capacity, availability, human resources, and so on? ■ Are there adequate plans for data conversion? ■ Are all requirements (SLRs) covered in agreements with solution provider (SLAs)?

(continued)

Objective	Predecessors, Timing	Input	Deliverables	Interview Questions
Evaluation: Post-Implementation Review (PIR)	Changes have been made operational	■ Incident Management reports ■ Customer satisfaction reports ■ Critical success factors, KPIs (Key Performance Indicators)	Evaluation report	*Meet with project manager, team, and customer to evaluate the performance of the service change. Key questions include:* ■ Did the change create any unintended effects? ■ Did the implemented changes comply with the requirements? ■ Does actual performance match expectations? Does predicted performance match expectations? ■ Have all the targeted scenarios been implemented? ■ Have all the targeted architectural issues been addressed? ■ Have the risks been eliminated or mitigated? ■ Have new risks been identified? ■ Did the changes achieve their business objectives, critical success factors, KPI targets? For example, has there been a reduction in the number of service interruptions?

Placing the IT Project Life Cycle in Perspective: The Spectrum Diagram

An IT project life cycle (such as the one described by the Noble Path in this chapter) is itself part of the larger life cycle of the business initiative; this larger life cycle includes the business planning activities that precede the IT project and the operations support that follows it. Figure 1.2 is an overview diagram that pulls together the end-to-end spectrum of a business initiative, indicating the relationships between business planning, the IT Software Development Life Cycle (SDLC), and the ITIL Service Life Cycle.

The top row in the figure indicates stages along the end-to-end spectrum. During the Plan stage, annual planning occurs; criteria for defining, categorizing, and prioritizing a project are developed; and projects are approved. During the Initiate stage, a business project is begun. During Execute, the proposed changes are realized. During Transition, the solution is made operational. At some point during or after this time, Post-Implementation Review

(PIR) occurs. PIR may not be able to be properly evaluated until a couple of weeks after a change has been put into production and may result in further changes to the system. Once in operation, ongoing support is provided for the solution.

The next row indicates where the IT project SDLC lies within this overall spectrum. The figure indicates that the IT SDLC begins with the spectrum's Initiate stage and ends during the spectrum's Transition phase. (The IT SDLC referred to here is the generic SDLC described in the Noble Path.) As the project closes, Early Life Support occurs—a period of time during which a team is on standby should problems occur, after which the internal IT team signs off on the changes.

The last two rows indicate where ITIL Service Life Cycle phases fit into the overall picture and their correspondence with IT SDLC phases.[37] ITIL Service Strategy overlaps the Plan stage that precedes the IT project, as well as the Initiation SDLC phase that occurs once the project begins. ITIL Service Design covers the SDLC phases of Discovery, Execute. and Final V & V, while ITIL Service Transition overlaps the Closeout SDLC phase, Early Life Support, and the PIR. ITIL Continual Service Improvement (CSI) runs across the entire spectrum.

Plan	Initiate	Execute				Transition	PIR	Support
Business Value and Alignment	IT Project SDLC					Early Life Support	Ongoing Support and Maintanance	
	Initiation	Discovery	Construction	Final V & V	Closeout			
ITIL Service Strategy		ITIL Service Design			ITIL Service Transition		ITIL Service Operation	
ITIL Continual Service Improvement (CSI)								

Figure 1.2 Spectrum diagram

[37]Please note that the figure is a simplification of the correspondence between ITIL Service Life Cycle phases and those of other life cycles, since each of the ITIL Service Life Cycle phases contains ITIL processes that apply at various points throughout a project.

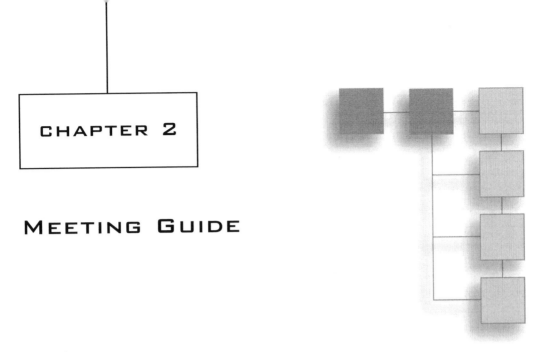

CHAPTER 2

MEETING GUIDE

T his chapter provides guidelines for meetings that a BA may be required to facilitate or participate in over the course of an IT project. For an overview of where each type of meeting fits into the life cycle, please see the Overview of BA Activities Throughout the Life Cycle chapter in this handbook.

Please note that not every requirements-gathering and verification event needs to be in the form of a group meeting. See the "Requirements Investigation Methods" checklist in the Tips and Checklists chapter for alternatives. The stakeholders, questions, and deliverables that appear in these guidelines apply regardless of which investigation method—or combination of methods—is chosen.

Planning for the Meeting

The following sections contain guidance for the BA regarding the planning of and preparation for meetings, including suggestions on the types of BA meetings to plan for, who to invite, and a standard meeting agenda.

Checklist: Who to Invite to Requirements Workshops

For more information about those listed in the following Roles and Participant checklists, see Tables 2.1 and 2.2 in this chapter.

Roles
- Facilitator
- Executive Sponsor

- Scribe
- Primary Participants
- Advisory Participants
- Observers

Participants

- Customers
- Users
- High-Level Management
- Line Management
- Product Champion
- Service Desk Agents
- Executive Sponsor and Approval Boards
- Business Process Owners
- Service Owner
- Service Manager
- Service Level Manager
- Product Manager
- Business Relationship Manager
- Project Manager
- Subject Matter Experts (SMEs)
- Business Architect
- Standards and Guidelines Organizations
- Internal Solution Providers (systems analysts/system architects/developers/vendors/IT service providers)
- External Service Provider organizations
- Testers
- Maintenance Programmers

Contribution to Meeting by Role and Stakeholder Type

This section describes the roles assigned for the meeting and the contributions sought from each type of stakeholder invited.

Responsibility by Role

Table 2.1 describes the responsibilities of each role in the meeting.

Table 2.1 Responsibility by Role

Role	Responsibility
Facilitator	Runs the meeting. Ensures meeting stays close to the agenda and meets its objectives. Must be seen as neutral.
Scribe	Documents results of the meeting.
Primary Participants	Have speaking and voting rights.
Advisory Participants	Have speaking rights but no voting rights.
Observers	Do not have speaking or voting rights.

Contribution by Stakeholder Type

Table 2.2 describes the contributions made by each type of stakeholder invited to the meeting.

Types of Meetings That a BA May Be Asked to Participate In[1]

- **Scope initiation**: Brainstorm opportunities, risks, features.
- **Requirements definition.**
- **Problem Log (PLOG) Resolution**: Resolve a problem or issue.
- **Structured walkthrough**: Review a project artifact, such as a section of the BRD.
- **Process modeling, workflow analysis**: Analyze the workflow of a business process.
- **Design reviews**: Review external design definitions, screen prototypes, etc.
- **Business process management**: Manage, improve a business process.
- **Gate review**: Review and sign off on deliverables at specified points in the project.
- **Confirmation of agreements.**
- **Post-implementation review**: Assess results of a change.

Facilitated Meeting Work Plan

A Facilitated Meeting Work Plan is a plan of activities to be carried out by the facilitator in order to prepare for and execute a facilitated meeting. The purpose of the Facilitated Meeting Work Plan is to identify all of the activities that a facilitator will need to engage in, in order to be able to estimate effort and resources required for the meeting and consider all the steps necessary for a successful outcome. The purpose of a *standard* (but customizable) Work Plan is to institutionalize lessons learned from previous engagements and entrench best practices—such as proper preparation for the meeting—within an organization.

---

[1]Thanks to Bob Smolkin for the initial draft of this list.

Table 2.2 Contribution by Stakeholder Type

Stakeholder Type	Contribution
Customers	Provide insight into problems with current service offerings. Know what new services or changes are desirable from the perspective of the person paying for the service.
Users	Ensure that requirements meet the needs of end users of the IT system. Ensure system supports all user tasks (goals) and workflow requirements and is easy to use. Understand day-to-day problems with current system.
High-Level Management	Ensures that business objectives (such as increased capacity, reduced costs, and improved efficiencies) are met and that management control, tracking, and reporting requirements are included.
Line Management (internal users)	Ensures that solution improves line operations for internal users; concerned with increasing efficiency, performance, throughput, turnaround, and so on of users under their control.
Product Champion	Has broad vision for the change. An agent of change, motivator.
Service Desk Agents	Have first-hand knowledge of customer complaints, interruptions of service, and other problems with current system. Have own requirements whenever a change occurs: new procedures, training, and so on.
Executive sponsor and steering group	Point of escalation for resolving conflicts that arise as service design progresses. Early and continuing involvement of sponsors and the steering group (approval boards) promotes buy-in.
Business Process Owners	Understand problems and issues with current business process. Ensure that IT changes are consistent with the end-to-end business process. Ensure that the proposed process is fit for purpose. Ensure continual improvement of the process and its metrics.
Service Owner	An executive position with hiring and firing authority. Ensures that business objectives (financial, etc.) for the service are addressed and realized.
Service Manager	Ensures tactical, operational needs for the service are met. Responsible for continual service improvement and for evaluating emerging needs of customers.
Service Level Manager	Ensures that Service Level Agreements (SLAs) are defined, agreed on, and met. Works with customers and suppliers of services.

(continued)

Stakeholder Type	Contribution
Product Manager	Provides input regarding the impact on the business if the proposed changes are made or not made. Provides insight regarding the impact of the change on existing services. Defines the overall risk profile and costs across lines of service.
Business Relationship Manager	Provides a consolidated view of costs and risks across customers and contracts. Provides insight into how proposed changes will impact other services currently supplied to customers.
Change Manager	Responsible for a final step in the approval process—ensuring that the Change Management process is followed. Primarily concerned with protecting the production environment and ensuring that the change does no harm (i.e., that change-related incidents are minimized). Reviews a checklist of items to ensure that the sponsor has agreed to the changes, that funding is available, and that resources have been allocated.
Project Manager	Ensures that requirements are within scope of project and well-managed and that the System Development Life Cycle (SDLC) is being properly followed.
SMEs	Provide deep knowledge in their area of expertise (business, technical, or other).
Business Architects	Ensure that business standards, guidelines, and so on are being followed and that the changes are consistent with the business model.
Standards and guidelines organizations	Representatives of (or experts in) standards and guidelines that constrain the project.
Internal Solution Providers (systems analysts/system architects/developers/vendors/IT service providers)	Provide a reality check to ensure that the requirements and requested warranties are realistic and that the requirements are of sufficient quality to be used for design and coding purposes.
External Service Provider organizations	Provide a reality check to ensure that the requirements and requested warrantees are realistic and that the requirements are of sufficient quality to be used for design and coding and/or for the selection and customization of an off-the-shelf solution.
Supplier Manager	Ensures that all contracts with suppliers support the needs of the business and that all suppliers meet their contractual commitments. Ensures that suppliers have acceptable plans for responding to failures of their components.

Table 2.2 Contribution by Stakeholder Type (continued)

Stakeholder Type	Contribution
Testers	Ensure that requirements are testable. Report on test plans and results.
Maintenance Programmers	Have first-hand knowledge of bugs in current system. Ensure that the changes will be maintainable in the future (proper documentation, standards followed, and so on).

Prerequisites, Timing Considerations

Create a Facilitated Meeting Work Plan once a need for a facilitated meeting has been identified. (See the previous section, "Types of Meetings," for objectives that might justify a facilitated meeting.) Be aware there may be guidelines, standards, and/or templates in use on the project that constrain the plan.

Standard Facilitated Meeting Work Plan

Following is a generic Facilitated Meeting Work Plan. If there is no standard or template for a plan on your project or organization, use this as a basis and customize according to your needs. If your plan uses an existing standard, use the following as a checklist to ensure all activities have been covered.

1. Prepare for the meeting.
    1.1 Assess meeting readiness.[2]
    1.2 Determine the purpose of the meeting.
    1.3 Determine the deliverables.
    1.4 Create agenda, meeting rules, and expectations.[3]
    1.5 Hold briefing sessions.
    1.6 Prepare and distribute materials: agenda, ground rules and expectations, input artifacts.
    1.7 Set up room.
2. Facilitate the meeting.
    2.1 Open meeting.
    2.2 Conduct meeting.
    2.3 Close meeting.
3. Follow up.

---

[2]See the next section, "Meeting Readiness Checklist."

[3]See "Standard Meeting Agenda," "Facilitated Meeting Rules and Guidelines," and "Facilitated Meeting Expectations" sections in this chapter.

Meeting Readiness Checklist

- Is there a vision for this project?   ❑ Yes   ❑ No
- Do the sponsor and users agree on scope? Is consensus possible?   ❑ Yes   ❑ No
- Will all impacted stakeholders be included in the process?   ❑ Yes   ❑ No
- Are they committed to the process?   ❑ Yes   ❑ No
- Is the deadline feasible?   ❑ Yes   ❑ No
- Will the participants work well with each other and with the facilitator?   ❑ Yes   ❑ No
- Will the participants include people who have long-term experience with the business area and with the IT system?   ❑ Yes   ❑ No
    - Are they open to new ideas?   ❑ Yes   ❑ No
    - Are they prepared to transfer their knowledge?   ❑ Yes   ❑ No
- Will a suitable location for the sessions be made available?   ❑ Yes   ❑ No

Standard Meeting Agenda

1. Open the session.
    1.1 Review administrative items: Schedule, rest rooms, phone calls, ground rules, introductions, etc.
    1.2 Review session objectives.
    1.3 Review agenda.
    1.4 Overview: Explain how we got here, overview of the business area, services, processes impacted by the project.
    1.5 Review action items from previous meetings that were due for this session.
2. Discuss assumptions.

    Review and verify assumptions.
3. Discuss requirements.

    Elicit and/or verify requirements. Use meeting deliverables to guide and structure the interview or review. For guidelines specific to each meeting type, see the following sections in this chapter: "Review Meeting (Structured Walkthrough and Gate Review)," "Meeting Objective: (Kick-Off Meeting) Identify Opportunities and Challenges," and so on.
4. Additional items.

    Open the floor to additional items not on the agenda.

5. Close the session.

    5.1 Review meeting minutes and deliverables.

    5.2 Review open and outstanding issues. Assign course of action, date, and responsible person for each issue.

    5.3 Approval and sign-off.

    5.4 Meeting follow-up procedures. Describe how stakeholders will be kept informed after the meeting and how they can contribute after the meeting.

    5.6 Next step(s).

Facilitated Meeting Rules and Guidelines

- One speaker at a time.
- One topic at a time.
- Stick to the agenda.
- No side conversations.
- Primary participants or substitutes must be present.
- Open to all ideas (as long as they are on topic).
- All persons are treated equally, regardless of job title.
- No complaint raised without a constructive suggestion for addressing it.
- Participants understand that the users who do the job have the best understanding of that job; the developers have the best understanding of the technology.

Facilitated Meeting Expectations

Participants agree to the following:

- Support the facilitator's role in the project.
- Be honest and open regarding the successes, problems, and risks associated with the current system and the project.
- Do preparatory work, as required, before the meeting, including reading the meeting agenda and input documents distributed prior to the event.
- If unable to attend, to provide a competent substitute.
- Be respectful of others and treat them as peers.
- Obey the rules of the meeting.
- Provide feedback to the facilitator in a timely manner.

Approvals Process Expectations

- An efficient approvals process will be in place that ensures decisions are made within prescribed timeframes.
- Someone will be assigned the authority to make decisions.
- Assistance will be requested in a timely manner if there is a problem getting approvals.
- All participants will support decisions and the team once approvals have been reached.

Review Meeting (Structured Walkthrough and Gate Review)

A review meeting, as referred to in the following sections, is a meeting held to review requirements artifacts, either periodically, as they are developed, or as part of a Gate Review prior to sign-off. This is also known as *Quality Review*. (For more tips on meetings involving the CAB (Change Advisory Board), please see the Tips and Checklists chapter of this handbook.)

Prerequisites, Timing Considerations

Walkthroughs:

At regular intervals, as artifacts become available.

Sign-offs:

Requirements may be signed off iteratively, as they are developed. In each iteration, the requirements selected for that pass are signed off prior to design and coding. Alternatively, one big sign-off may be performed at the end of requirements gathering with a diverse audience; the BRD is reviewed chapter by chapter with input and sign-off from affected stakeholders.

Who to Invite

- Customers
- Users
- High-Level Management
- Line Management
- Product Champion

- Service Desk Agents
- Executive Sponsor and Approval Boards
- Business Process Owner
- Service Owner
- Service Level Manager
- Product Manager
- Project Manager
- Change Manager
- Business Relationship Manager
- SMEs
- Business Architect
- Standards and Guidelines Organizations
- Solution Providers (systems analysts/system architects/developers/vendors/IT service providers)
- Supplier Manager
- Testers
- Maintenance Programmers

Checklist: Questions for the Interview

Questions for the client (customers, users, management):

- Does this represent your needs? (Are the requirements correct?)
- Did we miss anything? (Are the requirements complete?)
- Are all possible scenarios covered?
- Do IT services and workflows integrate well with manual and external workflows?
- Has the upstream impact of the change on the business been fully considered?

Questions for the developers:

- Can you build to it?
- Are there conflicting requirements?
- What is the downstream impact of the proposed change on technical components?

Questions for the testers:

- Can you test to it?

Questions for the PM:

- Are the requirements in scope?
- Is the project methodology being followed?
- Have all required deliverables been created or updated?
- Have requirements attributes and traceability matrices been updated?
- Have related documents and models been updated?
- Has an approval strategy been defined and is it being followed with respect to agreed-on roles and turnaround for approvals to documents?
- Have all required prior sign-offs occurred?
- Have plans been agreed on up front for managing documentation?
  - Have the roles of author(s), reviewers, approvers, and document owner (the executive who signs off at the end) been assigned to documents?
  - Has a naming convention for documentation been established? What naming convention will be used for version control? How will revision numbers be advanced.[4]
  - How will the requirements be packaged and linked—for example, in the BRD, SRS (Software Requirements Specification), and SLRs (Service Level Requirements), and who approves each of these on the business and supplier side?
- Is someone responsible for ensuring that the change causes minimal disruption to operations? (In organizations with a mature ITIL Change Management process implemented, this role should be filled by the change manager.)

Questions for the Supplier Manager:

If there is a Supplier Manager, the BA should ensure that the manager has asked his or her suppliers the following questions; otherwise, the BA should ensure that he or she has addressed these questions directly with suppliers:

- Have the following issues been addressed? If a service isn't working because one of your (supplier's) components is not working:
  - Do we know whom to speak to about the problem?
  - Have response time guarantees been agreed to?
  - Have penalties been agreed to?
  - Is there a contract?
  - Does the contract refer to Service Level Agreements (SLAs)?

---

[4]For example, there may be a standard meaning for each decimal revision number: ".1" for an initial draft, ".5" for reviewed and approved, and ".9" for a draft that is ready for approval by the owner, etc.

Questions for the Product Manager:

- What will be the cross-stream impact of the change on other services?
- What are the implications to the business if we implement the change and if we do not do it?

Questions for the Business Process Owner:

- Do the changes at the IT side mesh well with existing end-to-end business processes?
- Do the changes represent an improvement in the business process?

Questions for the Service Owner:

- Do the changes address the business objectives for the service?

Questions for the Service Manager:

- Have emerging needs of customers been taken into account?

Questions for the Service Level Manager:

- Have SLAs been defined and agreed on (between customers and suppliers)?

Questions for the Change Manager:

- Is there a Change Management process in place and is it being followed?
- Are there plans to minimize the impact of the change on the production environment?

Questions for Standards Bearers (Business Architect, Standards and Guidelines Organizations):

- Do the requirements conform to standards adopted for this business system and for this project (formats, templates, terminology, etc.)? If there is a discrepancy, which one is correct?
- Does the dynamic model (user requirements, system use cases, process model) conform to the static model (class diagrams, data model)?
- Are terms and business rules in the new requirements consistent with current usage?
- Are any requirements redundant (listed in more than one place)?
- Is the requirements documentation maintainable (easy to update)?

Questions for Operations:

- Have operational requirements been considered? Capacity, stress, availability, bandwidth? (See the section "Meeting Objective: Define Non-Functional SLRs" in this chapter for more details on what to look for.)
- Have requirements for the Service Desk been considered?

Structured Walkthrough Guidelines

- The author of the artifact (or artifacts) under review is the designated owner of the walkthrough and takes charge of booking the room, calling participants, and selecting scenarios with which to test the design.
- Before the session, the owner distributes the artifacts under review to participants; for example, data model.
- The participant list should include users, domain experts (those who understand the business well), and developers.
- The duration of the meeting should be 1½ to 2 hours. If you run out of time, schedule a follow-up session.
- The owner explains the process, the artifact under review, and runs the test scenarios through it. The participants should be looking for situations that are inaccurately handled or missing in the artifact.
- Keep egos out of it. Keep the focus on finding flaws in the artifact, not the author.

Meeting Objective: (Kick-Off Meeting) Identify Opportunities and Challenges

The purpose of this meeting is to brainstorm main issues, problems, and opportunities.

Prerequisites, Timing Considerations

Perform at start of project. Reconvene as necessary.

Input Documents

Initial RFC(s) where appropriate.[5]

Deliverables

Pareto chart, cause-and-effect graph, interim cost-benefit analysis (net annual benefits, ROI,[6] payback period, etc.)

ITIL:

Interim BIA

---

[5]Projects may begin with an initial request for a change, initiated by the business side or the technical team.

[6]Return On Investment (ROI) is calculated as (Net Benefits) / (Investment) × 100. Payback period is the number of years until investment is paid off.

Who to Invite

- Customers
- Users
- High-Level Management
- Line Management
- Product Champion
- Service Desk Agents
- Executive Sponsor and Approval Boards
- Business Process Owners
- Service Owner
- Service Manager
- Product Manager
- Business Relationship Manager
- Project Manager
- SMEs
- Maintenance Programmers

Checklist: Questions for the Interview

Table 2.3 is a checklist of questions to ask interviewees when brainstorming main issues, problems, and opportunities with business stakeholders and the technical team. The first column lists questions to ask during the interview; the second column identifies the artifacts (and components) that are updated based on their answers.

Meeting Objective: Identify Stakeholders and Interests

The objective of this meeting is to define the initial scope of the product/solution scope by identifying business and other stakeholders and their interests in the project and the key features they are looking for.

Prerequisites, Timing Considerations

A request for a change has been made, triggering the project.[7]

Input Documents

- Initial business case (opportunity evaluation)
- ITIL: High-level RFC(s) (Request for Change)

---

[7]For example, the request may have been a high-level RFC from sales and marketing to begin offering a new service.

Table 2.3 Identify Opportunities and Challenges

Questions	Where to Document the Answer
☐ What are the major problems with the way things are now? ☐ How often do they occur?	Pareto chart, BIA
☐ Why does each problem occur? ☐ Is this a root cause or is it, too, caused by something else?	Cause-and-Effect graph
☐ What is the cost to the business each time this problem occurs? ☐ What are the overall expected costs and savings? ☐ What are the annual (or monthly) costs and savings? ☐ What opportunities are we missing? ☐ What is this lost opportunity costing us? ☐ How much business are we losing?	Cost benefit analysis (BIA), payback period, ROI
☐ What services, products, or features do our customers want that we are not currently delivering? ☐ For each of these, why do they want it? ☐ What are they really looking for? (Continue until a root benefit is found.)	Cause-and-Effect graph
☐ What are the risks involved in making the change? In not making the change?	Risk Analysis

Deliverables

Vision Document Subsections:

- Problem Statement
- Problem Position Statement
- Stakeholders and Interest Table
- Objectives
- Features

Who to Invite

Invite representatives of a broad cross section of business areas and departments that have an interest in the change.

- Customers
- Users
- High-Level Management
- Line Management
- Product Champion
- Service Desk Agents
- Executive Sponsor and Approval Boards
- Business Process Owners
- Service Owner
- Service Manager
- Service Level Manager
- Product Manager
- Business Relationship Manager
- Project Manager
- SMEs
- Business Architect
- Standards and Guidelines Organizations
- Solution Providers (systems analysts/system architects/developers/vendors/IT service providers)
- Testers
- Maintenance programmers

Checklist: Questions for the Interview

Table 2.4 is a checklist of questions to ask interviewees in order to identify project stakeholders and their interests; the second column identifies the artifacts (and components) that are updated based on their answers.

Table 2.4 Identify Stakeholders and Interests

Questions	Where to Document the Answer
☐ Who will be affected by the success or failure of the solution?	Stakeholders (Stakeholders and Interests table)
☐ Who will receive reports and other output from the system?	
☐ Who are the users?	
☐ Who is the customer—the buyer of the end product or service?	
☐ Who is the sponsor—the funder of the project?	
☐ Has an approval strategy been defined?	
☐ Who is responsible for ensuring that the implementation of the change causes minimal disruption to operations?	
☐ What regulatory bodies and standards must the solution and project comply with?	
☐ Who will develop the system?	
☐ Who will test the system?	
☐ Who will maintain the system once it is deployed?	
☐ Who will support the users and the system once it is installed (Service Desk, etc.)?	
☐ Who will market and sell the system?	
☐ Is every affected business unit represented?	
☐ What is each stakeholder's interest (an addressed need or opportunity) in the solution?	Interests (Stakeholder and Interests table)
☐ What constraints (policies, standards, etc.) does the stakeholder place on the system?	
☐ What are the most important capabilities you would like to see in the solution?	Features (Vision Document)
☐ Prioritize them.	

Meeting Objective: Analyze Impact on Business Services and Processes

The objective of this meeting is to analyze the impact of the project on the business environment by identifying business services and processes affected by the change and exploring the impact of the change on interactions across the business boundary. If the initial request was for a change in an IT service or component (for example, to replace software or hardware), use this meeting to analyze the upstream impact of the change (for example, replacing an IT component) on the business.

Prerequisites, Timing Considerations

Stakeholders and interests have been identified.

Input Documents

Stakeholders and Interests table

UML (Extended):[8]

- As-Is business use-case model

ITIL:

- CMS (Configuration Management System)
- Business Service Catalogue, Technical Service Catalogue
- Existing S(L)As (Service Level Agreements)[9]

If the initial request was for a change in an IT service or component, use the Technical Service Catalogue to trace backward from IT component or IT service to business services and their customers. If the change is to a business service, analyze the cross-stream impact on other business services.

The CMS, if it exists, is invaluable in identifying the relationships of the various components involved in the proposed change or new service. The CMS defines the upstream and downstream relationships between Configuration Items (CIs)—items (such as services and components) that have been placed under configuration management. Figure 2.1 illustrates how the CMS can be used to trace the cross-functional impact of a new or changed business service through a combination of downstream and upstream relationships. The CMS first identifies the (downstream) IT components impacted by the new (or changed) service, then identifies the (upstream) existing business services that use those components.

---

[8]Artifacts marked "UML (extended)" are either part of the UML standard or a valid extension of it.

[9]Use existing SLAs in performing a gap analysis. As noted earlier, the parentheses in S(L)A and S(L)R are used to indicate that the term refers to any type of service level requirement or agreement (both functional and non-functional).

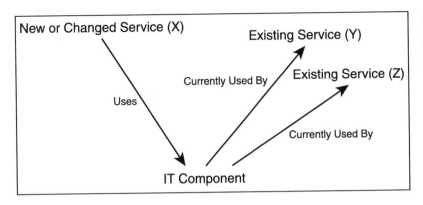

Figure 2.1
Using the CMS to trace the cross-stream impact of a new or changed business service

Deliverables

- Interim BIA (Business Impact Analysis)
- Impact of proposed changes on business services (BRD)

UML (Extended):

- To-Be business use-case diagrams, business use cases, actors, and business use-case descriptions.

Please note that a business use-case description (referred to in RUP as a *business use-case specification*) defines the interaction across the business boundary and is usually expressed using a text narrative; the text should be augmented with an activity diagram if the flows connect to each other in complex ways. (See the Business Use-Case Description Template in the Templates chapter.)

Alternatives to UML:

- Interim business-perspective DFDs

ITIL:

- Interim business SLRs
- Updates to Business Service Portfolio

The Business Service Portfolio consists of the Business Service Pipeline (services in development), Business Service Catalogue (current services), and Retired Services. New business services identified by the BA should be documented in the pipeline.

Who to Invite

- Customers
- High-Level Management
- Line Management

- Product Champion
- Business Process Owners
- Service Manager
- Product Manager
- Business Relationship Manager
- Project Manager
- SMEs
- Business Architect

Checklist: Questions for the Interview

Table 2.5 is a checklist of questions to ask stakeholders in order to identify the business services and processes impacted by the project and analyze changes to interactions across the business boundary; the second column identifies the artifacts (and components) that are updated based on their answers.

Table 2.5 Analyze Impact on Business Processes

Questions	Where to Document the Answer
☐ What existing business services and end-to-end processes will be affected by this project? ☐ What new business services or end-to-end processes will be introduced by this project? *For each identified business service or process:* ☐ What is the expected impact of the project? ☐ Who are the stakeholders? ☐ What is its priority? ☐ What event triggers the process? ☐ What are the inputs to the process? ☐ What are the outputs (reports, screens, files) created by the process? ☐ How is the desired functionality different from the current functionality (if a change)? ☐ What are the risks associated with changing the business process and with leaving it alone?	☐ Impact of proposed changes on business services (BRD) ☐ Risk analysis *UML:* ☐ Business use-case description (See the Business Use-Case Description Template in the Templates chapter.) *Alternatives to UML:* ☐ Updates to DFDs: Processes, inputs, and outputs

Meeting Objective: Analyze Risk

Risk is often defined to mean an uncertain outcome—a positive opportunity or a negative threat.[10] In practice, risk usually connotes a negative threat. The purpose of risk analysis is to analyze exposure to risk in order to support better decision-making and proper management of those risks.

The *BABOK*®[11] lists risk analysis under the BA Knowledge Area (KA) Enterprise Analysis. Risk analysis also plays a part in the *BABOK*'s Business Analysis Planning and Monitoring KA, principally with respect to the monitoring of mitigation plans and the updating of risk assessments as the project progresses.

Prior to the start of a project, the BA performs risk analysis as part of pre-project opportunity assessments (Feasibility Study, Business Case) when, typically, no project manager (PM) has yet been assigned. Once the project is in progress, the BA plays a supportive role, often working under the delegation of the PM, who is the primary person responsible for overall project risk. Throughout the project, the BA provides the PM with input, monitors the effectiveness of mitigation plans, and updates risk assessments for many types of risk, including product risk (such as that associated with a new service offering) and—in particular—risks associated with the quality of the requirements documentation (such as undetected gaps) and with the requirements-management process (such as risk related to the introduction of new requirements-management tools without proper training).[12]

Prerequisites, Timing Considerations

Analyze risk at the start of each iteration; reassess regularly. Risk analysis should occur periodically and frequently but may be combined with the iteration assessment. If faced with the choice between a process-heavy risk-management approach and frequent risk assessment, choose frequency; it is better to perform frequent assessments with a lean process than to have infrequent assessments and a detailed process.[13]

---

[10]Foundations of IT Service Management Based on ITIL V3, p. 65. The PMBOK has a similar definition.

[11]Refer to *The Guide to the Business Analysis Body of Knowledge*®, Version 2.0 Framework, p. 7, where, under Enterprise Analysis, it is listed as a purpose of the task, "develop a business case."

[12]From a clarification of the BA role in risk analysis in an e-mail to the author from Keith Sarre.

[13]These recommendations are from an e-mail to the author from Ken Clyne and an Agile Risk Management presentation by Clyne to the Rational Comes To You Conference in Chicago, Feb. 20, 2008.

Input Documents

- Vision Document
- Interim BIA (Business Impact Analysis)
- Impact of proposed changes on business services (BRD)

Deliverables

- Interim BIA (Business Impact Analysis)
- Interim Risk Analysis (See the Risk Analysis Table Template in the Templates chapter of this handbook.)

Who to Invite

Ideally, everyone should be invited to risk assessments. These include:

- Users
- High-Level Management
- Line Management
- Human Resources
- Product Champion
- Executive Sponsor and Approval Boards
- Business Process Owners
- Service Owner
- Service Manager
- Product Manager
- Business Relationship Manager
- Project Manager
- SMEs
- Solution Providers (systems analysts/system architects/developers/vendors/IT service providers)

Checklist: Questions for the Interview

Table 2.6 is a checklist of questions to ask interviewees in order to identify and evaluate risks that could impact the success or failure of the project; the second column identifies the artifacts (and components) that are updated based on their answers.

Table 2.6 Analyze Risk

Questions	Where to Document the Answer
☐ Are there any threats that could have a negative impact on the outcome of this project? ☐ Are there any unplanned events that could have a positive impact on the outcome?	Risks (in BIA, BRD)
Ask solution providers: ☐ Are there any technological issues that could impact the project? For example, is this the first time new technology is being used?	Technological Risks (a subsection of Risk Analysis)
Ask management and HR: ☐ Is there a risk we will be unable to obtain staff with the right skills for the project?	Skills Risks (a subsection of Risk Analysis)
Ask business stakeholders: ☐ Are there any internal, political forces that could impact the project? For example, are some stakeholders already committed to a specific solution? Are there conflicting visions? Are there power struggles or reorganizations that could undermine the project?	Political Risks (a subsection of Risk Analysis)
Ask project sponsor: ☐ Is there a risk the project will be canceled, and if so, what are the implications?	Business Risks (a subsection of Risk Analysis)
Ask users and other business stakeholders: ☐ How well do business stakeholders understand their own requirements? Do they know what they need?	Requirements Risk (a subsection of Risk Analysis)
For each identified risk: ☐ Who owns the risk? The client? The service provider? What risks will service providers take on the client's behalf? ☐ What is the likelihood of the risk occurring? ☐ What is the impact on the business if it occurs? ☐ What is the best strategy for dealing with this risk? Is there anything that can be done to prevent it from happening or to mitigate (lessen) the damage if it does occur? Should the risk be transferred (up the chain of command)? Or do we just accept the risk?	Risk Analysis (See "Tips: Managing Risk" in the Tips and Checklists chapter for tips on categorizing and managing risk.)

Meeting Objective: Requirements Management—Setup and Planning

The objectives of this meeting are to develop a Requirements Work Plan and to configure requirements management tools (requirements traceability matrices, automated tools, and so on).

Prerequisites, Timing Considerations

Initial cost-benefit, BIA reviewed; approval to proceed.

Input Documents

- Vision Document

ITIL:

- BIA

Deliverables

- Requirements Work Plan
- Requirements attributes table templates
- Requirements traceability matrix templates

ITIL:

- CMS Framework: For each CI impacted by the change (SLRs, IT services, etc.), define attributes and relationships with other CIs.
- Updates to Service Portfolio: Update relationships between items in the Service Portfolio to allow for upstream (tracing backward) and downstream (tracing forward) analysis.

Who to Invite

- Project Manager
- SMEs
- Team Leads
- Discipline Leads

Checklist: Questions for the Interview

Table 2.7 is a checklist of questions to ask interviewees when planning for requirements-management activities for the project; the second column identifies the artifacts (and components) that are updated based on their answers.

Table 2.7 Requirements Management Setup and Planning

Questions	Where to Document the Answer
☐ What facts need to be tracked about each requirement? Its author? Verification method? Priority?	Requirements attributes table *ITIL:* ☐ CMS Framework, Service Portfolio
☐ What level of requirements tracking is appropriate? For example, every use case? Every flow? Every step? ☐ What artifacts will each type of requirement be traced to?	Requirements traceability matrices *ITIL:* ☐ CMS Framework, Service Portfolio
☐ What are the business analysis activities for this project and what are their timelines? ☐ What assets (people, tools, etc.) are needed to manage (monitor, control changes, trace) the requirements? ☐ How will changes in the requirements and their status be communicated to stakeholders and team members? (Newsletter? Meeting?) ☐ What will be the procedures and acceptance criteria for signing off on the requirements? What is the timeline for doing so? ☐ How will the success of the requirements management process be measured? What are the Critical Success Factors (CSFs) and KPIs (Key Performance Indicators)? (For example, decrease in percent unauthorized requirements.) *For each KPI:* ☐ Why is the data being collected? ☐ How will the data be analyzed and used? ☐ Who will collect the data? ☐ Who will analyze the data? ☐ Who will act on the analysis?	Requirements Work Plan
☐ What questions about the requirements must requirements management be able to answer (status reports, dependencies, etc.)? ☐ Will you need to be able to determine the downstream impact of a business change on IT services and components? On clients? On suppliers? ☐ Will you need to be able to determine the upstream impact of an IT change on business services and clients? Of an IT project cancellation?	☐ Requirements attributes table ☐ Requirements traceability matrices *ITIL:* ☐ CMS Framework, Service Portfolio

Meeting Objective: Define Internal Workflow for End-to-End Business Processes

The objective of this meeting is to analyze the workflow of end-to-end, cross-functional business processes. Begin by examining the As-Is workflow. Use the As-Is model as the basis for examining pain points and opportunities for change and develop it into a To-Be model. This meeting objective may be the main point of a project to improve business processes, or it may be a preliminary step for an IT project.

Prerequisites, Timing Considerations

Business services and processes impacted by the change have been identified.

Input Documents

- Impact of proposed changes on business services. (See the BRD template in the Templates chapter.)

UML (Extended):

- Business use-case diagrams
- Business use cases
- Actors
- Business use-case descriptions

Assemble list of invitees from the business actors and internal workers tied to the business use case(s) under discussion.

ITIL:

- Business Service Portfolio
- BIA

Deliverables

- Business process cross-functional workflow for each business process, excluding technology.

UML (Extended):

- Business use-case realizations

(A business use-case realization is a description that includes internal workflow and is usually expressed using activity diagrams with a partition for each actor and worker.)

Alternatives to UML:

- Text, BPD

ITIL:

- Interim S(L)Rs

Who to Invite

Invite representatives from each of the internal and external participants involved in executing the end-to-end business process. Participants should represent the following groups:

- Customers
- Users
- Business Process Owners
- Service Owner
- Service Manager
- Product Manager
- Project Manager
- SMEs
- Business Architect

Checklist: Questions for the Interview

Table 2.8 is a checklist of questions to ask interviewees in order to define the internal workflow for a business process; the second column identifies the artifacts (and components) that are updated based on their answers.

Meeting Objective: Describe Users

The objective of this meeting is to define human and automated users of the system.

Prerequisites, Timing Considerations

Impact of changes on business services and end-to-end processes has been analyzed. To-Be cross-functional workflow of business process(es) impacted by the change has been determined.

Input Documents

- Stakeholders and Interests Table
- Business process model: Participants (actors and workers), workflow
- User profile

Table 2.8 Define Internal Workflow for End-to-End Business Processes

Questions	Where to Document the Answer
For each end-to-end business process or service: ☐ What is the current (As-Is) workflow (if applicable)? ☐ What are the problems, bottlenecks, or inefficiencies with the current workflow? ☐ What is the desired (To-Be) workflow (without focusing on who does what)? ☐ Are there any activities that could be carried out concurrently?	Business process cross-functional workflow for each business process, excluding technology. *UML:* ☐ Business use-case realizations[14] ☐ To-Be business use-case workflow using activity diagrams and/or textual documentation. (If business use-case realizations are employed, then the description of the internal workflow resides within the business use-case realization.) *Alternatives to UML:* BPD
☐ Are all participants in the end-to-end process accounted for? ☐ What is the role of each participant? ☐ Which participant carries out each activity in the workflow?	Model participants in the process are referred to as *swimlanes* (also referred to as *partitions* on a UML activity diagram) in the business process model. Depict swimlanes as horizontal rows or vertical columns on workflow diagrams, with one swimlane per participant. Depict each activity within the swimlane of the participant who carries it out. Use this technique to document the As-Is process and to document the evolving consensus regarding how these activities will be apportioned among participants in the To-Be process. *UML:* ☐ Updates to business actors and workers in business use-case model ☐ Activities moved to appropriate partitions on activity diagram *Alternatives to UML:* ☐ Updated BPD; participants indicated as swimlanes and pools (BPMN)

[14]A *business use-case realization* is the name given in some methodologies for the modeling element ("container") for business internal processes, while the *business use case* itself (and its description, known in RUP as a business use-case *specification*) describes business façade functionality only (the interface between a customer and the business).

UML (Extended):

- Business use-case model: Business actors and workers, business use cases, business use-case diagram, business use-case realizations
- Role Map (if there is an existing one)

(*Role Map* is a term popularized by Larry Constantine.[15] It is a limited form of a use-case diagram containing only actors and their relationships to each other.)

Alternative to UML:

- DFD
- Updated BPD

ITIL:

- CMS

ITIL:

- Updates to user CIs (Configuration Items) by CMS

Deliverables

- User profile (see the "Actors" section of BRD template in the Templates chapter).

UML:

- Role Map

Alternatives to the UML:

- External entities/agents (DFD), updated BPD

ITIL:

- Updates for CMS: User CIs

Who to Invite

Use input documents to draw up initial list of invitees. Consider stakeholders and their interests. Examine workflow models: swimlane, pools,[16] or partitions may indicate user

---

[15]See preprint of *Users, Roles, and Personas* by Larry Constantine, IDSA, Chief Scientist (Constantine & Lockwood, Ltd., 2005) p. 9, http://www.foruse.com/articles/rolespersonas.pdf.

[16]On a BPD, *pools* represent independent organizations involved in a process, such as a B2B (business-to-business) process. Each organization is represented as a pool; each pool can be further divided into lanes, each representing a business area within the organization. Communication between pools is achieved through messages; sequence flows are used between activities in the same pool. A sequence flow may cross lanes within the same pool but may not cross pools.

groups. If using the business modeling extension to UML, consider the business actors and workers associated with the business use cases under discussion. Invite both those who will be direct users and others who have an interest in the definition of user groups.

Invitees should represent the following:

- Customers
- Suppliers
- IT Service Providers
- Existing Users (UML: see existing Role Map)
- High-Level Management
- Line Management
- Service Desk Agents
- Business Process Owners
- Project Manager
- SMEs
- Business Architect

Checklist: Questions for the Interview

Table 2.9 is a checklist of questions to ask interviewees in order to identify user groups impacted by the IT project. Use the input documents (listed in the preceding "Input Documents" section for this meeting) as a basis for review and discussion. For example, consider business actors, workers, and partitions in the business use-case (business process) model as candidate end users.

Meeting Objective: Identify User Tasks

The objective of this meeting is to identify user tasks (goals) that will need to be changed or added as a result of this project—with each user task representing a piece of meaningful work that a user accomplishes with the assistance of an IT system in a single interaction.

Prerequisites, Timing Considerations

Impacted business services and end-to-end processes have been analyzed; To-Be end-to-end processes have been analyzed.

Input Documents

- Business process model: cross-functional workflow
- Existing IT services model

Table 2.9 Describe Users

Questions	Where to Document the Answer
☐ Will any of the currently known user groups referred to in the Input Documents access the new or changed services? (See the preceding "Input Documents" section for this meeting for a list of inputs, such as the user profile and Role Map.) ☐ Which of the players involved in the business process will be direct users of the system? ☐ Will any others receive messages or reports from the system? ☐ Who are the customers of Web services and applications? ☐ Will any of the communication to other organizations or systems be automated (e.g., by sending electronic messages and transactions)? ☐ Which external computer systems will the system communicate with?	*UML:* ☐ Role Map *Alternatives to the UML:* ☐ External entities/agents (DFD), updated BPD *ITIL:* ☐ Updates for Configuration Management System (CMS): User CIs
☐ Is there any overlap between the roles of the various user groups?	User profiles *UML:* ☐ Generalization relationships between actors in the Role Map

UML (Extended):

- To-Be business use-case model:
  - Business use-case diagrams
  - Business use-case realizations
- As-Is system use-case model

ITIL:

- RFCs (Requests for Change)
- Business Service (Level) Requirements
- Technical Service Catalogue: Use the catalogue to trace a change at one level to other levels (such as from a business service to IT service)

Deliverables

- Functional requirements: User tasks

UML:

- System use-case diagrams
- System use cases
- Actors
- System use-case briefs (short textual descriptions)

Alternatives to the UML:

- DFDs

ITIL:

- Interim IT SLRs
- RFCs

Who to Invite

- Customers
- Users
- Line Management
- Product Champion
- Business Process Owners
- Project Manager
- SMEs
- Solution Providers Technical Architect, Systems Analyst (for input regarding communication with external systems)

Checklist: Questions for the Interview

Table 2.10 is a checklist of questions to ask interviewees in order to identify the user tasks that need to be supported by the solution; the second column identifies the artifacts (and components) that are updated based on their answers. If the use-case approach is being used, each user task is modeled and documented as a *system use case*; if a structured-analysis approach is being used, each user task is modeled and documented as a *process.*

Meeting Objective: (Static Modeling) Define Business Concepts, Objects, and Rules

The objective of this meeting is to create an initial draft of the static model. The model defines and documents rules related to business nouns, such as business concepts and business object types. The purpose of the static model is to promote consistency by providing a single place to define rules and definitions that cut across the functional requirements.

Table 2.10 Identify User Tasks

Questions	Where to Document the Answer
General questions for finding system use cases: ☐ What menu options/tools would you like to see? ☐ What tasks will you be doing with the assistance of the IT system? ☐ What events must the system respond to? ☐ What automated transactions/requests/messages from other systems must the proposed system be able to handle?	*UML:* ☐ System use cases *Alternatives to UML:* ☐ Processes (DFDs)
For each system use case you discover: ☐ Which user groups use this option? ☐ Can the task be triggered automatically by an electronic request? If so, what computer system is the source of the request? ☐ Is it a scheduled event? (If so, model "Time" as the primary actor.) ☐ Do any organizations, people, or systems receive electronic messages or reports as a result of the interaction? ☐ Does the system need to communicate with any external systems during this process? For example, does it issue queries or send electronic transactions?	*UML:* ☐ Communication associations between actors and system use cases *Alternatives to UML:* ☐ Data flows between external entities/agents and processes (DFDs).

Prerequisites, Timing Considerations

Perform in parallel with dynamic modeling of IT services. As business nouns are introduced, elicit and document definitions and rules.

Input Documents

- **Business process model**: Compile a list of candidate entity classes from noun phrases that appear in the model, such as those that appear as participants in the process and business objects that are manipulated by the process.

UML (Extended):

- **Business use-case model**: Business use cases, business actors and workers, business use-case diagrams, business use-case descriptions, business use-case realizations.

Compile a list of candidate entity classes from noun phrases that appear in the business use-case model (diagrams and text), such as business actors, participants responsible for carrying out the process and business objects that are manipulated by the business use case.

▪ **System use-case model:** System use cases, actors, Role Map, system use-case diagrams, system use-case briefs, system use-case descriptions.

Compile a list of candidate entity classes from actors in the Role Map. Compile a list of candidate entity classes from actors and from nouns appearing in system use-case names and system use-case briefs and descriptions.

▪ **Activity diagrams:** Compile a list of candidate entity classes from partition names, objects (when object flows are included), and nouns appearing in activity names and elsewhere on the diagram (guards, events, and so on).

Alternatives to UML:

▪ **DFDs:** Compile a list of candidate entities from external agents (actors), data stores, data flows, and from nouns appearing in process names

▪ **BPDs, flowcharts:** Compile a list of candidate entities from swimlanes, objects and pools, and nouns appearing in task and event names and elsewhere on the diagrams (gateways, decisions, and so on).

Deliverables

BRD subsections:

▪ Business rules
▪ Data dictionary

UML:

▪ Entity classes
▪ Business-perspective class diagrams

Alternatives to the UML:

▪ Business-perspective ERDs

Who to Invite

▪ Customers
▪ Users
▪ High-Level Management
▪ Business Process Owners

- Project Manager
- SMEs
- Business Architect

Checklist: Questions for the Interview

Meet with stakeholders to identify the candidate entities (classes). Review any new or changed requirements documentation. See the preceding "Input Documents" section for this meeting for guidance on reviewing existing documentation. Use the questions in Table 2.11 to elicit more key candidate classes.

For each candidate class found with the questions in Table 2.11 and a review of the input documents, determine whether to include it in the model by asking stakeholders the questions in Table 2.12. Include those candidate classes that elicit a "yes" response to either question in the table.

For each entity class included in the model, ask stakeholders the questions in Table 2.13.

For every linked pair of business objects discovered in the last question of Table 2.13, ask stakeholders the questions in Table 2.14.

Table 2.11 Elicit New Candidate Classes

Questions	Where to Document the Answer
☐ What are the primary 　o People and organizations 　o Transactions and events 　o Products and services 　o Locations that the business needs to track with the aid of the software system? ☐ What business concepts apply to this area of the business?	☐ Static model ☐ Data dictionary *UML:* ☐ Candidate entity classes *Alternatives to UML:* ☐ Candidate entities (ERD)

Table 2.12 Evaluate Candidate Classes

Questions	Where to Document the Answer
☐ Will the business rely on the IT system to keep track of each business object of this type? ☐ Will the IT system be used to bring up any details about this object after the interaction that introduced it is over?	☐ Static model *UML:* ☐ Entity classes *Alternatives to UML:* ☐ Entities (ERD)

Table 2.13 Analyze Entity Classes

Questions	Where to Document the Answer
□ Briefly explain the term.	□ Static model
□ Provide a typical example.	□ Data dictionary
□ What volume of this type of business object must the system be able to handle? For example, how many customers, products, and so on must the system be able to serve?	*UML:* □ Entity class documentation *Alternatives to UML:* □ Entity documentation (ERD)
□ What is the expected rate of increase in volume? For example, how many new customers, products, and so on are expected each year?	
□ What type of information (attributes) does the business track about it?	Data dictionary *UML:* □ Class attributes *Alternatives to UML:* □ Entity attributes □ Data dictionary
□ Does the entity (class) have subtypes? For example, are there types of customers? □ Do the business rules differ according to type?	*UML:* □ Model subtypes as specialized classes
□ Does the business need to link it to any other business objects? (For example, policies may be linked to benefits.)	*UML:* Model as associations on class diagrams *Alternatives to UML:* Model as relationships on ERDs

Table 2.14 Analyzing Cardinalities

Questions	Where to Document the Answer
□ How many of [the 2nd object in the relationship] would be linked to each of [the 1st object]? Must there be at least one? What is the maximum? □ Repeat the previous questions, reversing the objects.	Business rules *UML:* □ Model as multiplicities on class diagrams *Alternatives to UML:* □ Model as cardinalities on ERDs

Meeting Objective: Define Non-Functional SLRs

The purpose of this meeting is to ensure that non-functional requirements are considered as part of the analysis before a solution is designed (or selected), developed, and put into production. The requirements may be defined at the business level (for business services) or at the IT level (for IT services). Non-functional requirements, also referred to as quality attributes or SLRs (Service Level Requirements),[17] are any requirements other than functional requirements. Functional requirements describe the functionality that the system must provide (what the system must do). Non-functional requirements include security and auditing requirements and operational requirements, such as response time and throughput.

Prerequisites, Timing Considerations

May occur at any time.

Input Documents

- Vision document, features, existing requirements
- Architectural documents: Enterprise architecture, business architecture, product line architecture, information system architecture. The architecture of a system (enterprise, business, product line, and so on) defines its components, the relationships between them and between the system and its environment, as well as design principles that "inform, guide, and constrain its structure and operation and future development."[18] The enterprise architecture shows how all the components are integrated. The requirement to comply with existing architectures should be documented in the SLRs and any architectural documents that apply must be adhered to by them. Architectural documentation used as input to this meeting includes:
  - Roles and responsibilities
  - Policies (business, IT, etc.)
  - Designs
  - Infrastructure

UML (Extended):

- Business use-case model

---

[17]As explained elsewhere in this book, there is some confusion over the term SLR, with some reserving it for non-functional requirements and some for both non-functional and functional requirements. This meeting refers primarily to non-functional requirements and to system-wide requirements (some of which might be categorized either way).

[18]ITIL V3 Core Book: Service Design, 2007, OMG, p. 36.

ITIL:

- Service Portfolio
- Interim S(L)Rs (drafts)

Deliverables

BRD subsections:

- Interim non-functional requirements

ITIL:

- Interim SLRs (Service Level Requirements)
- Interim updates to service pipeline

Who to Invite

- Customers
- Users
- High-Level Management
- Line Management
- Service Desk Agents
- Executive Sponsor and Approval Boards
- Business Process Owners
- Service Manager
- Service Level Manager
- Project Manager
- SMEs
- Business Architect
- Standards and Guidelines Organizations
- Solution Providers (systems analysts/system architects/developers/vendors/IT service providers)
- Testers (for input on testability requirements)
- Maintenance Programmers (for input on maintainability requirements)

Checklist: Questions for the Interview

Table 2.15 lists questions for eliciting non-functional requirements and identifies where to document them within the non-functional Service Level Requirements (SLRs). See the Service Level (Non-Functional) Requirements Template in the Templates chapter for a full description of the SLR and its subsections.

Table 2.15 Define Non-Functional SLRs

Questions	Where to Document the Answer
☐ What types of reports and records are required by auditors?	☐ Auditing and reporting requirements (This item is listed in the "System-Wide Capabilities" section of the SLR template in the Templates chapter.)
☐ What types of activity logs (histories) are required?	☐ Activity logging requirements (This item is listed in the "System-Wide Capabilities" section of the SLR template in the Templates chapter.)
☐ Will the business or system be required to manage licenses? If so, what are the requirements for installing, tracking, and monitoring of licenses?	☐ Licensing requirements (This item is listed in the "System-Wide Capabilities" section of the SLR template in the Templates chapter.)
☐ Describe any security requirements related to access to data, privacy restrictions, homeland security, and so on.	☐ Security requirements (This item is listed in the "System-Wide Capabilities" section of the SLR template in the Templates chapter.)
☐ Describe any precedence and concurrency rules regarding the performing of services and processes, the movement of work items, approvals, and so on. Do some processes have to occur in a specific sequence with respect to each other? Can some processes occur at the same time?	☐ Dependencies and Rules of precedence (This item is listed in the "System-Wide Capabilities" section of the SLR template in the Templates chapter.)
☐ What is the maximum number of users that must be able to be engaged in the same operation at the same time?	☐ Concurrency Requirements (This item is listed in the "System-Wide Capabilities" section of the SLR template in the Templates chapter.)
☐ Describe any requirements regarding the nature of the user interface. ☐ Are there requirements related to ease of use of the service? How will compliance be measured? ☐ Are there any standards and guidelines that the user interface must comply with? ☐ Describe accessibility requirements for users with special needs, such as those with disabilities.	☐ Usability requirements (This item is listed as a section of the SLR template in the Templates chapter.)
☐ What level of fault tolerance must the business or system guarantee? (See the rest of this table for more specific reliability questions.)	☐ Reliability requirements (This item is listed as a section of the SLR template in the Templates chapter.)
☐ How correct must the metrics generated by the services covered in this project be? 100% accurate? 90%?	☐ Accuracy requirements (This item is listed in the "Reliability Requirements" section of the SLR template in the Templates chapter.)
☐ How precise must amounts be? Dollar amounts to the nearest cent? 1/10 of a cent?	☐ Precision requirements (This item is listed in the "Reliability Requirements" section of the SLR template in the Templates chapter.)

(continued)

Questions	Where to Document the Answer
☐ How available must business services be? Business hours? 24/7?	☐ Availability requirements (This item is listed in the "Reliability Requirements" section of the SLR template in the Templates chapter.)
☐ What is the minimum allowable mean time between an occurrence of a service failure and a second failure of the same service?	*ITIL:* ☐ Mean Time Between Failures (MTBF) (This item is listed under the "Availability Requirements" section of the SLR template in the Templates chapter.)
☐ What is the minimum allowable mean time between an occurrence of a system or service failure and an occurrence of the next failure?	*ITIL:* ☐ Mean Time Between System/Service Incidents (MTBSI) (This item is listed under the "Availability Requirements" section of the SLR template in the Templates chapter.)
☐ What is the maximum allowable mean elapsed time to fix and restore a service, from the time an incident occurs until it is available to the customer?	*ITIL:* ☐ Mean Time Between System/Service Incidents (MTBSI) (This item is listed under the "Availability Requirements" section of the SLR template in the Templates chapter.)
☐ What is the maximum allowable mean time between the occurrence of an incident and its detection by the business/system?	☐ Detection and recording (This item is listed under the "Availability Requirements" section of the SLR template in the Templates chapter.)
☐ What is the maximum allowable mean time to repair a Configuration Item or IT service after a failure, from when the CI or IT service fails until it is repaired (not including the time required to recover or restore)?	*ITIL:* ☐ Mean Time to Repair (MTTR) (This item is listed under the "Availability Requirements" section of the SLR template in the Templates chapter.)
☐ What extra assets (redundancies) are required to support reliability and sustainability requirements? (See the rest of this table for more directed questions regarding various types of redundancy.)	☐ Redundancy (This item is listed under the "Reliability Requirements" section of the SLR template in the Templates chapter.)
☐ What extra assets are required to support continuous operation of non-interruptible services?	☐ Active redundancy (See the "Redundancy" section of the SLR template in the Templates chapter.)
☐ What duplicated assets are required to operate simultaneously and always be ready to replace their counterparts?	☐ Active redundancy (See the "Redundancy" section of the SLR template in the Templates chapter.)
☐ What duplication of assets is required to support reliability of interruptible services? ☐ What redundant assets will be kept off-line (on standby) until required?	☐ Passive redundancy (See the "Redundancy" section of the SLR template in the Templates chapter.)
☐ For which services and assets, should the risk be spread by using different types of assets to provide the same service (for example, using different service delivery mechanisms)?	☐ Heterogeneous redundancy (See the "Redundancy" section of the SLR template in the Templates chapter.)

Table 2.15 Define Non-Functional SLRs (continued)

Questions	Where to Document the Answer
☐ For which services and assets should duplicated assets be of the same type?	☐ Homogeneous redundancy (See the "Redundancy" section of the SLR template in the Templates chapter.)
☐ What types of errors should the system be able to handle and how should it respond? ☐ What types of errors should the system prevent from happening?	☐ Error-Handling (See the "Reliability Requirements" section in the SLR template in the Templates chapter.)
☐ How many users must be able to use the service at the same time?	☐ Stress Requirements (See the "Performance Requirements" section in the SLR template in the Templates chapter.)
☐ What is the maximum allowable wait time from service request until delivery?	☐ Turnaround-Time Requirements (See the "Performance Requirements" section in the SLR template in the Templates chapter.)
☐ What is the maximum allowable wait time that a user of the service(s) must wait for a response after submitting input?	☐ Response-Time Requirements (See the "Performance Requirements" section in the SLR template in the Templates chapter.)
☐ How many transactions per unit of time must the solution be able to handle?	☐ Throughput Requirements (See the "Performance Requirements" section in the SLR template in the Templates chapter.)
☐ How much data transfer per unit of time must the solution be able to support?	☐ Bandwidth (See the "Throughput Requirements" section in the SLR template in the Templates chapter.)
☐ Are there any requirements related to startup and shutdown? Timing constraints?	☐ Startup and Shutdown Requirements (See the "Performance Requirements" section in the SLR template in the Templates chapter.)
☐ How scalable must the solution be? ☐ Must it be able to be easily enlarged, for example, by increasing maximum number of simultaneous users or throughput?	☐ Scalability (See the "Supportability Requirements" section in the SLR template in the Templates chapter.)
☐ What changes in service requirements are expected down the road? ☐ Are there any changes expected due to regulations or changing market conditions? ☐ How will these changes be accommodated?	☐ Expected changes (See the "Supportability Requirements" section in the SLR template in the Templates chapter.)
☐ How easy should it be to change process(es) in order to improve them, for example, by clearing bottlenecks, maximizing efficiencies, or correcting deficiencies?	☐ Maintainability (See the "Supportability Requirements" section in the SLR template in the Templates chapter.)

Table 2.15 Define Non-Functional SLRs (continued)

Questions	Where to Document the Answer
☐ What aspects of the service(s) need to be configurable, that is, changeable, without requiring reprogramming?	☐ Configurability (See the "Supportability Requirements" section in the SLR template in the Templates chapter.)
☐ To what extent must the solution be able to be geared to local conditions and requirements? ☐ For example, must multiple languages be supported? Different tax systems? Different addressing standards? Different marketing campaigns? Different catalogues of products and services based on location?	☐ Localizability (See the "Supportability Requirements" section in the SLR template in the Templates chapter.)
☐ How easy must it be to install the system? What skill level is required of the installer?	☐ Installability (See the "Supportability Requirements" section in the SLR template in the Templates chapter.)
☐ What other systems, software, and hardware (devices, operating systems, and so on) must the solution be compatible with?	☐ Compatibility (See the "Supportability Requirements" section in the SLR template in the Templates chapter.)
☐ Describe the level of testing (such as regression testing) required of various types of services and components and the planning information for setting up and conducting these tests.	☐ Testing Requirements (See the "Testing Requirements" section of the SLR template in the Templates chapter.)
☐ Describe the level of training required. ☐ Which organizations will be required to develop and deliver training programs? ☐ Which organizations will be tasked with planning for the delivery and execution of the training? ☐ Which organizations will be tasked with providing the training? The client? The solution provider? Third party? Internal staff?	☐ Training Requirements (See the "Training Requirements" section of the SLR template in the Templates chapter.)
☐ What are the maximum volumes that the solution must be able to support? ☐ What is the maximum number of accounts, customers, and so on? ☐ What are growth requirements? What growth is forecasted with respect to numbers of accounts, customers, simultaneous users, required bandwidth, and so on?	☐ Capacity Requirements[19] (See the "Capacity Requirements" section of the SLR template in the Templates chapter.)

Table 2.15 Define Non-Functional SLRs (continued)

Questions	Where to Document the Answer
☐ What backup and recovery facilities are required? ☐ Which components must be restorable in case of failure? ☐ What is the required recovery point?	☐ Backup/Recovery Requirements (See the "Backup/Recovery Requirements" section of the SLR template in the Templates chapter.)
☐ Are there any design constraints on the solution?	☐ Design Constraints (See the "Other Constraints" section in the SLR template in the Templates chapter.)
☐ Are there any constraints on the coding and construction of the solution? For example, must a specific programming language be used?	☐ Implementation Constraints (See the "Other Constraints" section in the SLR template in the Templates chapter.)
☐ What protocols, formats, and so on must be followed when interfacing with external organizations or systems?	☐ Interface Constraints (See the "Other Constraints" section in the SLR template in the Templates chapter.)
☐ What are the physical constraints on the hardware? Are there constraints related to size, temperature control, materials, and so on?	☐ Physical Constraints (See the "Other Constraints" section in the SLR template in the Templates chapter.)
☐ Are there any legal or regulatory requirements, existing or pending legislation, governing bodies or standards that constrain the system?	☐ Legal and Regulatory Requirements (This item is listed as a section of the SLR template in the Templates chapter.)
Negotiate contingency expectations and plans with business stakeholders and service providers (or supplier manager, if one exists): ☐ What is the contingency plan in case of full or partial failure of a service? ☐ If an incident occurs, how long can the customer live with it before the contingency plan kicks in? ☐ How long will it take to transition to the contingency site? What is the acceptable amount of time? ☐ What is the time-share allocated for the contingency? (How long will we be able to use the contingency solution?) ☐ How long will it take to transition back from contingency to normal operations? What is an acceptable amount of time? ☐ If the timeshare for the contingency is up, is there an alternate and what is the time required to transition to and back from the alternate?	☐ IT Service Continuity Requirements (This item is included under the "Backup/Recovery Requirements" section of the SLR template in the Templates chapter.)

[19]Growth forecasts assist Demand Management. Poorly anticipated demand results in insufficient capacity, which, in turn, limits the growth of the service and degrades its quality. (See ITIL V3 Core Book Service Strategy, 2007, p. 129.)

Table 2.15 Define Non-Functional SLRs (continued)

Questions	Where to Document the Answer
☐ What are the essential business functions that must be kept on life support when a contingency plan kicks in due to a full or partial service failure?	*ITIL:* ☐ Vital Business Functions (VBF) (This item is included under the "Backup/Recovery Requirements" section of the SLR template in the Templates chapter.)

Meeting Objective: Gather Detailed User Requirements

The objective of this meeting is to elicit and document detailed user requirements. Define the flow of the user-system interaction from the point of view of the user without regard for technical design. (These requirements will then be input to design.)

Prerequisites, Timing Considerations

User tasks (within functional requirements); IT services have been identified.

UML:

System use cases have been identified.

Input Documents

- **Project plan:** On an iterative development project, the plan will address which user tasks (system use cases and flows) are to be analyzed and realized in each iteration.
- **Business process models, high-level user requirements (user tasks identified):** To determine triggers and pre-conditions for user tasks.

UML:

- Business use-case realizations: To determine triggers and pre-conditions
- System use cases
- Actors
- Role Map
- System use-case diagrams
- System use-case briefs[20] (A *use-case brief* is a short paragraph describing the use case.)

Alternatives to UML:

- **BPDs:** To determine triggers and pre-condition.
- **DFDs:** Use input data flows to help determine pre-conditions (input data must be available); derive triggers from data flows originating from external entities.

---

[20]Use-case briefs should be two to six sentences in length. For more on use-case briefs, see *Writing Effective Use Cases* by Alistair Cockburn (Addison-Wesley Professional, 2000), p. 38.

ITIL:

- RFCs, S(L)Rs

Deliverables

BRD Subsections:

- Interim user requirements

UML:

- **System use-case descriptions**: A system use-case description (referred to in RUP as a *use-case specification*) defines the interaction between actors and the business and is usually expressed using a text narrative. (See the System Use-Case Description Template in the Templates chapter.) The text may be augmented with an activity diagram with one partition for the system and one for each actor. (Augmentation of text with an activity diagram is recommended for complex use cases where the flows connect to each other in complex ways.) The description defines triggers, pre-conditions, post-conditions, and flows.

ITIL:

- Interim S(L)Rs

Who to Invite

- Users
- High-level management
- Line Management
- Business Process Owners
- Project Manager
- SMEs

Checklist: Questions for the Interview

Meet with stakeholders to discuss user requirements. Ask the questions in Table 2.16 for each user task (system use case).

For each user task, ask the questions listed in Table 2.17. Document answers in the user requirements. If the use-case approach is being used, the user requirements are documented as system use-case descriptions (referred to in RUP as use-case *specifications*). The precise location of the documentation will depend on the template. The second column of the table indicates where to document answers within the System Use-Case Description Template provided in the Templates chapter of this handbook.

Table 2.16 Gather Detailed User Requirements

Questions	Where to Document the Answer
☐ How important is it that this user task (system use case) be supported by the solution? ☐ Would the solution be acceptable if it did not include it? ☐ Would you accept a workaround, if you knew it would be added in a later release?	☐ Priority Ideally, the *priority* of a requirement should be documented externally (outside of the requirement)—for example, as an attribute of the Requirements Attributes table. (For more information, see the section "Requirements Attributes Table" in the BA Toolkit chapter. See also the "Requirements Repository" section in the Requirements Work Plan Template in the Templates chapter.)
☐ What event triggers the interaction?	☐ Trigger (This item is documented under the "User Requirements" section in the BRD template in the Templates chapter. If the use-case approach is being used, the User Task Description takes the form of a system use-case description [referred to in RUP as a use-case *specification*], and the trigger is documented within it. Also see the "Trigger" section of the System Use-Case Description Template in the Templates chapter.)
☐ Are there any activities or events that should already have taken place before the interaction begins?	☐ Pre-conditions (This item is documented under the "User Requirements" section in the BRD template in the Templates chapter. When the use-case approach is being used, this item is documented within the system use-case description. Also see the "Pre-Conditions" outline entry of the System Use-Case Description Template in the Templates chapter.)
☐ What is the net effect of the interaction once it has completed successfully?	☐ Post-conditions on success[21] (This item is documented under the "User Requirements" section in the BRD template in the Templates chapter. If the use-case approach is being used, document within the system use-case description. Also see the "Post-Conditions on Success" outline entry of the System Use-Case Description Template in the Templates chapter.)
☐ What should the net effect of the interaction be when it is not completed successfully (for example, because the user cancelled, invalid input, or a requested IT service was not available)? ☐ Should any audit trails or logs of the failed attempt be produced?	☐ Guaranteed post-conditions[22] (This item is documented under the "User Requirements" section in the BRD template in the Templates chapter. If the use-case approach is being used, document within the system use-case description. Also see the "Post-Conditions" outline entry in the System Use-Case Description Template in the Templates chapter).

[21]May also be documented as Success Guarantees. See *Writing Effective Use Cases*, Cockburn.

[22]May also be documented as Minimal Guarantees. See *Writing Effective Use Cases*, Cockburn.

Table 2.17 Describe Interactions Between the User and the IT System

Questions	Where to Document the Answer
☐ Describe a typical, successful interaction. ☐ What is the user doing at each step? ☐ What should the system do in response?	☐ Basic Flow steps
☐ What kinds of options, tool icons, and so on would be useful to the user while performing this task? ☐ Do users need to be able to refresh the screen with real-time information at any time during the task? ☐ Will they need to be able to do searches?	☐ Alternate Flow triggers
Review each step in the basic flow with stakeholders: ☐ Is there any other way it could play out? ☐ Is there anything that could go wrong? ☐ Are there any editing or verifications that might fail? ☐ Could a user or system timeout occur a this point? ☐ Are these events correctable or do they lead to cancellation?	☐ Alternate Flow triggers (names)[23]
Review the user requirements for this task: ☐ When should the user be allowed to cancel the transaction? ☐ Is there anything else that could happen that could result in the task being cancelled?	☐ Alternate Flow triggers (names)[24]
Once all flows have been identified, ask stakeholders to describe the interaction for each flow. Review each new step as previously described for the basic flow.	☐ Alternate Flow steps

[23]Non-correctable errors may be documented as Exception Flows rather than grouping them with other Alternate Flows. (All flows other than the Basic Flow are listed as Alternate Flows in the System Use-Case Description Template that appears in the Templates chapter of this handbook).

[24]If using a template that includes a section for Exception Flows (as described in the previous footnote), list events resulting in cancellation as Exception Flows.

Meeting Objective: Reuse User Requirements

The purpose of this meeting is to investigate opportunities for reorganizing the user requirements for minimum redundancy and maximum reuse.

Prerequisites, Timing Considerations

After user tasks and users have been identified; review as user requirements are elaborated.

Input Documents

- User requirements
- Business rules

UML:

- **System use-case model**: System use cases, actors, system use-case diagrams, system use-case descriptions.

ITIL:

- Service Portfolio
- S(L)Rs

Deliverables

- Updated user requirements
- Business rules

UML:

- Updated system use-case model:
    - Included use cases, extending use cases, generalized use cases and their base use cases
    - System use-case diagrams
    - System use-case descriptions

ITIL:

- Interim updates for Service Portfolio, S(L)Rs

Who to Invite

This is an internal meeting for team members.

- Other BAs on the team
- Project Manager
- Owner of user requirements model (system use-case model)
- Business Architect

Checklist: Questions for the Interview

Table 2.18 is a checklist of questions to ask interviewees in order to identify opportunities for the reuse of requirements documentation and models; the second column identifies the artifacts (and components) that are updated based on their answers.

The questions in Table 2.19 apply when the use-case approach is being used to document user requirements.

Table 2.18 Reuse User Requirements

Questions	Where to Document the Answer
☐ Have we already partially implemented functionality like this?	Reuse existing requirements artifacts; refer to them from new requirements documentation produced for this project. (For example, in the UML, a new extending use case might add functionality to an existing system use case; a new system use case might refer to an included use case that already exists in the model.)
☐ Are there any standards that the requirements must comply with?	Non-functional (compliance) requirements. Standards constrain and guide the management and specification of requirements documents.
☐ Do any requirements appear more than once in the user requirements documentation? ☐ Do they include any sub-goals that have already been documented?	User requirements: Sub-goals documented and referenced.
☐ Do the user requirements refer to any business rules (validation rules, adjudication rules, derivation rules, decisions tables, etc.) that are already documented in the business rules repository?	Replace the redundancy in the user requirements with a reference to the relevant business rule(s).
☐ Are there any business rules expressed in one of the user requirements that apply in a number of contexts (for example, across a number of user tasks)?	Add the business rules to the business rules repository and replace the redundancy in the user requirements with a reference to the relevant rule(s).

Table 2.19 Reuse System Use-Case Documentation and Modeling Elements

Questions	Where to Document the Answer
☐ Are there any system use cases that share some sub-goal?	Model the sub-goals as included use cases on system use-case diagrams. Update text documentation.
☐ Does any set of steps appear in more than one system use case?	Model common steps as an included use case on system use-case diagrams. Create text documentation for included use cases; replace original steps in base (including) use case with a reference to the included use case.
☐ Are there any included use cases already in the model that can be used by the new or changed system use cases?	Refer to the included use cases from the new or changed base (including) system use case on system use-case diagrams and in the text documentation.
☐ Looking at one use case, does it contain a number of alternate flows that are triggered by the same condition?	If the original use case has too many flows, model the commonly triggered flows as an extending use case and remove them from the original use case. Update system use-case diagrams and text.
☐ Looking at one use case, will it be released in a basic ("vanilla") version as well as enhanced or customized versions?	Model the requirements for the basic version as a base system use case; model the enhanced or customized versions as extending use cases. Update system use-case diagrams and text.
☐ Is there a generic workflow or common flows that apply across a set of system use-cases?	Model the generic workflow and/or common alternate flows in a generalized use case; model specifics in specialized use cases. (Alternative option[25]: Model common steps as included use cases.)

[25]This alternative is provided because generalized use cases, despite being advisable here from a redundancy point of view, are not used widely.

Meeting Objective: Analyze the Life Cycle of Business Objects

The objective of this meeting is to analyze the life cycle of business objects from the time the business area or system becomes aware of them in order to understand the rules that govern the progress of business objects across IT services. These rules include those that govern the sequence in which an object's status changes and the different ways the business or system treats the object based on its status.

Prerequisites, Timing Considerations

A business object has been identified that is key to the business area or system and whose changes in status must be controlled.

Input Documents

- User requirements
- Static model

UML:

- Business use-case model (diagrams and text)
- System use-case model
- System use-case briefs
- Role Map
- Entity classes and class diagrams

Deliverables

BRD Subsections:

- Interim state diagrams
- Interim static model

UML:

- State-machine (Harel) diagrams
- Updates to entity classes and class diagrams

Alternatives to the UML:

- State transition tables, interim updates to data model

Who to Invite

Invite a diverse group of stakeholders that represent those who have an interest in this business object across its life cycle. Follow up with more focused groups if necessary. Invitees should represent the following:

- Customers
- Users
- High-Level Management
- Line Management
- Product Champion
- Business Process Owners
- Project Manager
- SMEs

- Business Architect
- Standards and Guidelines Organizations

Checklist: Questions for the Interview

Meet with stakeholders in order to analyze the life cycle of business objects. Table 2.20 is a checklist of questions to ask interviewees in order to identify key types of business objects for life-cycle analysis.

For each key business object you discover, ask the questions listed in Table 2.21 in order to analyze its life cycle.

For each state you discover, ask the questions listed in Table 2.22 in order to analyze the behaviour of the object while in the state.

Table 2.20 Identify Key Business Objects

Questions	Where to Document the Answer
□ Is there a business object (or objects)—such as a transaction, incident, artifact, product, or service—that is key to the business process? □ Are there any business objects whose progress within the business area must be well managed? □ Are there any business objects that are treated differently because of their status?	□ State transition diagram □ Static model (if new entities are discovered) *UML:* □ State-machine (Harel statechart) diagrams □ Class diagrams *Alternatives to UML:* □ ERDs

Table 2.21 Analyze States and Transitions

Questions	Where to Document the Answer within the State Model
□ What statuses can it have?	States
□ What is the object's initial status?	*UML:* Initial pseudostate
□ Describe the life cycle of the object, starting from the initial status.	*UML:* States and transitions
□ What triggers the transition from one status to another? □ What events or user tasks (system use cases or flow) cause it to change status?	*UML:* Transition names
□ What status does it have as a result of the change?	*UML:* Transitions

Table 2.22 Analyze State Behaviour

Questions	Where to Document the Answer within the State Model
☐ Is there any activity that must occur as soon as the object is assigned that status? ☐ Any messages, notifications, audit trails, or reports?	*UML:* entry activity
☐ Is there any activity that occurs while the object has that status?	*UML:* do activity
☐ Is there any activity that must occur whenever it moves out of that status?	*UML:* exit activity
☐ What event(s) affect the object while it is on this status? ☐ What is the required response to this event? ☐ Which operations are permitted while it has that status? ☐ Which operations are disabled (not allowed) when it has that status?	*UML:* event activities

Meeting Objective: Assess the Results of an Iteration[26]

This meeting is a review meeting held to assess the results of a change made during an iteration (pass) in the project.

Prerequisites, Timing Considerations

End of each iteration.

Input Documents

- Test reports
- Project plan (iteration plan)
- Risk list
- List of defects

ITIL:

- Service Acceptance Criteria (SAC)
- Incident Management reports

---

[26]Evaluation is categorized by ITIL as a process within Service Transition. This handbook focuses on the BA contribution to the process.

Deliverables

- Evaluation report

Who to Invite

- Customers
- Users
- High-Level Management
- Line Management
- Business Process Owners
- Project Manager
- SMEs
- Solution Providers (systems analysts/system architects/developers/vendors/IT service providers)
- Testers

Checklist: Questions for the Interview

Table 2.23 is a checklist of questions to ask interviewees in order to assess the results of an iteration.

Table 2.23 Assess the Results of an Iteration

Questions	Where to Document the Answer
☐ Did the change create any unintended effects?	Evaluation report
☐ Does actual performance match expectations? Does predicted performance match expectations?	
☐ Have the targeted scenarios been implemented?	
☐ Have the targeted architectural issues been addressed?	
☐ Have the risks been eliminated or mitigated	
☐ Have new risks been identified?	

Meeting Objective: Gather Service Desk Requirements[27]

The objectives of this meeting are to elicit and document requirements that impact the Service Desk (Help Desk) function. The purpose of this step is to ensure that requirements for user support are considered fully before changes are put into production.

Prerequisites, Timing Considerations

At any time; must be complete before product or service is put into production.

Input Documents

ITIL:

- **Services support model**
- **IT service continuity plans**: Include guidance that impacts the Service Desk's response to those incidents that result in partial or full failure of a service. The BA should research the IT service continuity plans to determine at what point during the outage the invocation of service continuity (contingency) plans should start and to understand guidelines for the transition to and back from contingency so that the new service requirements may be integrated with the existing continuity plans and provisions.
- **Business continuity plan (BCP)**: Guidelines for the invocation of contingency plans in the event of partial or full failure of a service must support the BCP and therefore have dependencies on it.

Deliverables

Subsection of the BRD:

- Non-functional Service Level Requirements

ITIL:

- **Services support model**
- **Service Desk procedures**

---

[27]The questions for this activity have been adapted from the ITIL Service Desk function as described in Foundations of ITIL Service Management Based on ITIL V3, p.302–305.

■ **Incident escalation procedures**: Incident escalation procedures describe the rules for handling incidents, 1st tier support, 2nd tier, etc. The BA should be aware that incidents related to security and those that disrupt continuity may have special requirements. They may differ from procedures for other types of incidents with respect to the duration of service outage that will be tolerated, escalation paths and notifications, and they may involve security, legal, and public relations, etc.

■ **SLRs**

UML:

■ Role Map (Service Desk Agent actors)
■ System use-case model

Who to Invite

■ Customers
■ Users
■ High-Level Management
■ Service-Desk Line Management
■ Service Desk Agents
■ Project Manager
■ SMEs
■ Business Architect
■ Standards and Guidelines Organizations
■ Solution Providers (systems analysts/system architects/developers/vendors/IT service providers)

Checklist: Questions for the Interview

Table 2.24 is a checklist of questions to ask interviewees in order to gather Service Desk requirements; the second column identifies the items that are updated based on their answers.

For each new or revised type of incident that the Service Desk will need to manage as a result of the project, ask the questions listed in Table 2.25.

Table 2.24 Gather Service Desk Requirements

Questions	Where to Document the Answer
☐ What are the service level targets for the Service Desk? For example, what is the required turnaround time for resolution of a service event? ☐ How many incidents and events must the Service Desk be able to handle per hour/month/day? Does this fluctuate during the day or day by day and, if so, how? What are the peak and slow times?	Non-functional requirements *ITIL:* ☐ Services support model ☐ Service Desk procedures ☐ SLRs
☐ What new (or revised) types of incidents will the Service Desk need to manage as a result of the project? (An incident is an unplanned disruption or reduction of service.) ☐ What new or changed types of service requests will the Service Desk be expected to handle? (A service request is a user request for support, delivery of a service, and so on.)	Non-functional requirements *ITIL:* ☐ Services support model ☐ Service Desk procedures ☐ Incident escalation procedures
☐ What are the known errors? Are there workarounds that the Service Desk should be made aware of?	*ITIL:* ☐ Input to problem management ☐ Services support model ☐ Service Desk procedures
☐ Are there any business users with deep knowledge of a business process or application who would be prepared to act as super-users, assisting the Service Desk and users in specialized areas? ☐ If the Service Desk is being outsourced, are the external organization's processes and tools consistent with those used internally? ☐ What new training will the Service Desk require in order to handle incidents (help calls, etc.) related to the new services? ☐ How will the Service Desk be kept up to date of new developments? ☐ Are there special procedures and guidelines in place for handling security incidents? ☐ Are there special procedures and guidelines in place for handling incidents that result in full or partial loss of a service? Is there an IT service continuity plan and/or a business continuity plan that must be complied with for such incidents?	*ITIL:* ☐ Services support model ☐ Service Desk procedures ☐ Incident escalation procedures

(continued)

Questions	Where to Document the Answer
☐ Will the Service Desk have access to the new services?	*ITL:* ☐ Services support model ☐ Service Desk procedures *UML:* ☐ Role Map ☐ System use-case diagrams

Table 2.25 Analyze the Required Response to an Incident

Questions	Where to Document the Answer
☐ How fast does the business need to respond?	*ITIL:* Urgency (used to determine priority)
☐ How severe is its impact? For example, how many users are impacted by a failure of an IT service?	*ITIL:* Impact (used to determine priority)
☐ How should this type of incident be escalated? Functionally, to a more specialized support team or, hierarchically, to higher-level management? ☐ What degree of first-line support is required of the Service Desk? Who will provide Tier 1 support? Tier 2?	*ITIL:* ☐ Services support model ☐ Service Desk procedures ☐ Incident escalation procedures

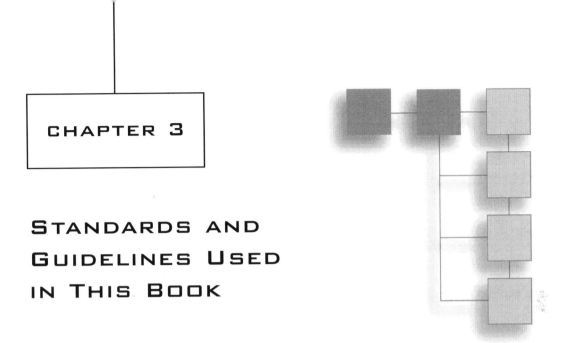

CHAPTER 3

Standards and Guidelines Used in This Book

This handbook contains best practices that derive from a variety of sources. The preferred approach to software development is iterative-incremental development, with an empirical, agile approach when it is appropriate for the project. (For a discussion of factors favouring an empirical approach see "Adapting the Noble Path" in the chapter Overview of BA Activities Throughout the Life Cycle.) Also, special emphasis is placed on specific frameworks, guidance, and standards that impact the BA role: Information Technology Infrastructure Library (ITIL), the *Business Analysis Body of Knowledge®* (*BABOK®*), and the Unified Modeling Language (UML). This chapter provides an overview of ITIL, the *BABOK®*, and the UML, and summarizes the BA's contribution to their implementation.

ITIL

One of the objectives of this book is to begin the process of integrating BA practice into ITIL (Information Technology Infrastructure Library) Service Management (ITSM)— a framework of publicly available best practices gaining broad international support. Until recently, the focus of ITIL has been more on service operations (handling of incidents, ensuring continuity of service, and so on) and less on the development of those services. The latest version, ITIL V3, introduced the Service Life Cycle—a process for analyzing, designing, and developing those services. With this change, ITIL has embraced the "front end" of service management: the analysis of what those services should be and their subsequent construction. The BA, who has always been instrumental in achieving the ITIL goal of services that match customer expectations, is now more crucial than ever in ITIL implementation.

Table 3.1 BA Role in Service Strategy

Life Cycle Phase	Function or Process	Purpose	BA Role
Service Strategy	(Overall)	Achieve superior performance versus competing alternatives. Guide the development of service management as a strategic organizational capability and asset.	The BA contributes to the strategic audit (analysis of currently available services and their value to the company and to customers) and helps determine services required by customers.
	Financial Management (FM)	Provide management information to ensure cost effectiveness of service delivery. FM helps the business and IT "identify, document, and agree on the value of the service being received and the enablement of service demand modeling and management."[1]	The BA works with FM, the business, and IT to answer questions about the cost of a proposed change and to explain how a change adds value to the business.
	Service Portfolio Management	Govern investments in Service Management. Document standardized services	BA assists in audit of inventory of existing services and their documentation in the Service Catalogue, and identifies new required services to be documented in the service pipeline.
	Demand Management	Predict the demand for services and align supply accordingly	The BA analyzes the business area to determine patterns of activity and predicted demand.

[1]ITIL V3 Core Book, Service Strategy, p. 97.

Tables 3.1 through 3.5 provide an overview of ITIL Service Life Cycle phases, their functions and processes, and the BA contribution to them. A *function* is a unit "of organizations specialized to perform certain types of work and responsible for specific outcomes."[2] A *process* is a structured set of activities designed to accomplish a defined objective.[3] The Purpose column in the tables describes the rationale for goals and objectives of the phase, function, or process; the last column describes the BA's involvement.

Table 3.2 provides an overview of the BA contribution to Service Design.

---

[2]ITIL V3 Core Book, Service Operation, 2007, p. 12.

[3]Foundations of ITIL Service Management Based on the ITIL V3, 2007, p. 172.

Table 3.2 BA Role in Service Design

Life Cycle Phase	Function or Process	Purpose	BA Role
Service Design	(Overall)	Analyze and design services and processes.[4] Ensure a holistic approach to all aspects of the design of new or changed services, including functional, management, and operational aspects.	This is a key ITIL Service Life Cycle phase from a BA perspective. The BA is heavily involved in the gathering, analysis, and documentation of functional, management, and non-functional requirements.
	Service Catalogue Management (SCM)	"The purpose of SCM is to provide a single source of consistent information on all of the agreed services" and their relationships.[5]	BA assists in the cataloguing of services and their dependencies in the Service Catalogue and develops functional and non-functional S(L)Rs. The BA also uses the Service Catalogue as input toward a Business Impact Analysis (BIA).
	Service Level Management	To ensure that the agreed level of IT service provision is attained for present and future services.	BA supports the Service Level Manager by identifying existing and future Service (Level) Requirements.[6]
	Capacity Management	Provide IT capacity that meets current and future needs against justifiable costs.[7]	BA gathers and documents capacity requirements and includes these with non-functional SLRs.
	Availability Management	Ensure that delivered and future availability meets or exceeds agreed requirements in a cost-effective manner.	The BA supports the Availability Manager by analyzing the customer and user perspective on availability, including expectations with respect to reliability, maintainability, and serviceability requirements and includes these with non-functional SLRs.
	IT Service Continuity Management (ITSCM)	Support business continuity by ensuring IT facilities can be resumed after a failure with the agreed timeframe.	The BA analyzes customer's continuity requirements and includes these with non-functional SLRs
	Information Security Management	Align IT and business security ensuring information security is managed in all service management activities.	The BA gathers business and user security requirements and includes these with non-functional SLRs.

(continued)

Life Cycle Phase	Function or Process	Purpose	BA Role
	Supplier Management	Manage suppliers and services to ensure consistent quality at the right price.	BA contributes to supplier evaluation. BA's SLRs serve as input to negotiation of SLAs with suppliers.

[4]The ITIL usage of the term *design* differs somewhat from its usage in other contexts. Elsewhere, the term often refers to the technical specifications for a solution and excludes business analysis activities, such as the gathering of business requirements. ITIL Service Design, in contrast, includes the gathering and analysis of requirements.

[5]ITIL V3 Core Book, Service Design, p. 60.

[6]Despite the possible connotation of the term *level* in Service Level Management, the process explicitly includes the identification of functional requirements. See Foundations of ITIL Service Management Based on ITL V3, p. 86, customer-based SLA discussion, p.196.

[7]Foundations of ITIL Service Management Based on ITIL V3, p. 200.

Table 3.3 provides an overview of the BA contribution to Service Transition.

Table 3.4 provides an overview of the BA contribution to Service Operation.

Table 3.5 provides an overview of the BA contribution to continual service improvement.

Table 3.3 BA Role in Service Transition

Life Cycle Phase	Function or Process	Purpose	BA Role
Service Transition	(Overall)	Manage processes, system, and functions required for implementing and releasing a change into production and establish the service specified in the requirements.	BA helps ensure that the transition process supports the change process of the business and that the service meets the requirements.
	Transition planning and support	Plan and coordinate resources and capacity to ensure Service Design specifications are realized.	The BA helps coordinate change plans of client, supplier, and business and implements and participates in quality reviews.
	Change Management	Control changes to services and related documentation. Ensure standardized methods and procedures are used for efficient and prompt handling of changes across the Service Life Cycle, that all changes are recorded, and that the risks for the business due to the change are minimized.	BA contributes heavily to this process by helping to ensure that all changes are authorized and follow the approved process, participating and contributing to the CAB (Change Advisory Board), reviewing and creating business and user-level RFCs, reviewing technical RFCs, tracing requirements to help identify upstream, downstream, and cross-stream CIs affected by the change, and contributing to updates to the Schedule of Changes.
	Service Asset and Configuration Management (SACM)	Account for and manage the integrity of service assets and CIs across the Service Life Cycle by ensuring only authorized components and changes are used. Define service and infrastructure components and their relationships.	Many of the BA deliverables are input to SACM. These include any items brought under SACM control and may include functional and non-functional requirements and requirements models. The BA provides input to the relationships and dependencies between CIs in SACM (for example, between business services, IT services, test scenarios, and IT components)

(continued)

Life Cycle Phase	Function or Process	Purpose	BA Role
	Release and Deployment Management	Define and agree on release and deployment plans. Build, test, and supply services according to requirements and design specifications. Ensure release and deployment packages are tracked and can be installed, tested, verified, and rolled back if required.	Ensure plans include adequate testing and training. Oversee release and deployment testing, including integration testing (service release) and pilots. Identify users in preparation for deployment.
	Service Validation and Testing	Validate that service meets or exceeds business and operational requirements and adds value to the business.	BA creates requirements that are the basis for service validation and testing. BA's functional user requirements are the basis for "fit for purpose" testing (ensuring the service performs its function correctly); BA's non-functional requirements are the baseline for "fit for purpose" testing (testing that the service is delivered in a manner appropriate for the operational conditions it is intended for). BA contributes to and may conduct "fit for purpose" testing and reviews results of "fit for use" testing
	Evaluation	Verify whether the performance of a service change met its objectives.	BA contributes to the formulation of acceptance criteria, risk assessment and Post-Implementation Review (PIR).
	Knowledge Management	Ensure that reliable and secure information is available throughout the Service Life Cycle.	Transfer knowledge between users, the service desk, and solution providers. Communicate needs of users and Service Desk to solution providers; assist in transfer of knowledge from providers back to stakeholders through user and Service-Desk training programs, technical risk assessments, cost-benefit analysis, and downstream impact analysis.

Table 3.4 BA Role in Service Operation

Life Cycle Phase	Function or Process	Purpose	BA Role
Service Operation	(Overall)	Provide and manage agreed services for business stake-holders within a specified level. Confirm IT service value and provide input to service improvements.	The BA helps ensure that service operations will be properly planned for by ensuring that operational (non-functional) requirements are taken into consideration up front and before deployment.
	Event Management	Detect random and planned events that have an impact on the delivery of IT services and take appropriate management action.	A number of BA deliverables serve as input to Event Management. These include events on activity diagrams and state-machine diagrams, system use-case triggers, alternate and exception flows (such as flows indicating the required response to log-on with an incorrect password or to user and system time-outs).
	Incident Management	Handle events that disrupt or might disrupt a service so that the regular state of affairs is resumed as quickly as possible.	The BA contributes to the development of the incident model (the procedures for handling incidents) by communicating between the business and service providers regarding new or changed incident types, identifying major incidents, and gaining agreement on their priorities and escalation procedures. The BA also gathers information from Incident Management regarding past incidents and their impact in contributing to the BIA, scope analysis, and prioritization of requirements.
	Request Fulfillment	Serve and manage requests from users for information, advice, a standard change, or access to a service.	The BA elicits and documents requirements with respect to self-service and standard changes. Required metrics for Request Fulfillment (such as request turnaround time and throughput) are documented by the BA in non-functional SLRs.

(continued)

Life Cycle Phase	Function or Process	Purpose	BA Role
	Problem Management	Manage knowledge about known problems and workarounds so that incidents can be diagnosed and corrective action taken if appropriate. Prevent problems and incidents from occurring.	Problem Management provides input to the BA in preparing the BIA, Cause-and-Effect diagramming, Five Whys, and in prioritizing requirements.[8] The BA elicits input from the Service Desk and users about known problems and workarounds and communicates these to Problem Management.
	Access Management	Grant authorized users the right to use a service; deny access to unauthorized users.	The BA defines user groups and the services they can access in the BRD (for example, in UML Role Maps and system use-case diagrams).
	Monitoring and Control	Provide continuous monitoring, reporting, and control of services.	The BA provides reporting and monitoring requirements in the non-functional SLR section of the BRD.
	IT Operations	Deliver services as agreed with the customer.	BA documents requirements with respect to scheduling, backup, restoring and archiving (how long records must be kept, required restoration point, and so on) in non-functional SLRs.
	Service Desk	A functional unit that aims to restore normal service as quickly as possible. It deals with all incidents and service requests. The Service Desk provides a single point of contact for IT users.	The BA gathers Service Desk requirements—such as expected volume of incidents, Service Desk availability requirements, and service level targets for the Service Desk, identifies those willing to serve as super users, and contributes to post-implementation client and user satisfaction assessment.

[8]When a requirement's objective is to fix an underlying problem, Problem Management can contribute to prioritization by providing information about the problem's impact on service delivery (for example, as the root cause of frequent incidents).

Table 3.5 BA Role in Continual Service Improvement

Life Cycle Phase	Function or Process	Purpose	BA Role
Continual Service Improvement (CSI)	(Overall)	Continually improve service management processes and services to ensure customer satisfaction. CSI activities are carried out through the entire Service Life Cycle.	Senior BA is responsible for setting and improving best practices with respect to requirements-gathering and documentation.
	CSI seven-step process	Define what is to be measured and the data that is to be gathered and processed to initiate corrective action.	BA SLRs and updates to the Service Catalogue serve as input to Service Improvement Plan and are used to determine service-level targets and priorities.
	Service Reporting	Generate reports about results achieved on delivering services.	BA helps attune reports (such as availability reports) to the needs of the business.

IIBA and *BABOK*®

The IIBA (International Institute of Business Analysis)™ is an independent non-profit professional association for business analysis. Its mission is "to develop and maintain standards for the practice of business analysis and for the certification of its practitioners."[9] The IIBA was formed in October 2003 with 28 founding members and became incorporated in 2006 as a non-profit association under the Canada Corporations Act with headquarters in Toronto, Canada. Two prime areas of IIBA activity are the development of the *BABOK*®, a collection of knowledge within the BA profession, and the professional certification of BAs through the creating and awarding of the CBAP (Certified Business Analysis Professional)™ designation.

The *BABOK*® divides knowledge required by BAs into KAs (Knowledge Areas). A BA must demonstrate knowledge and experience in these areas in order to qualify for the CBAP designation (see Table 3.6).

---

[9]See the Mission link under About the IIBA at www.theiiba.org.

Table 3.6 CBAP Qualification Requirements

Work Experience Requirement	7,500 hours (five years) business analysis work experience in the last 10 years engaged in tasks specifically related to the KAs as defined within the *BABOK®*.
Knowledge Areas Requirement	Demonstrate experience and expertise in at least four of the six knowledge areas.
Education Requirement	The minimum education requirement is high school or equivalent.
Professional Development Requirement	Twenty-one hours of professional development in the last four years. The professional development content must be directly related to business analysis or its underlying fundamentals and must be completed by the application date.
Reference Requirement	Two references from a career manager, client (internal or external), or Certified Business Analysis Professional. Each reference must complete a CBAP Candidate Reference Form and provide the applicant with the completed reference form in a sealed envelope that is signed by the reference across the seal.
Completed Application Package	Completed CBAP application form, two reference forms, a signed and dated CBAP Code of Ethical Conduct and Professional Standards Form, CBAP Exam Special Accommodation Form (if required), application, and exam fees.
Exam	Once an application has been accepted, the applicant must pass an extensive examination on the *BABOK®* Knowledge Areas.

Table 3.7 describes the KAs and relates them to tools and other items within this handbook that contribute to the carrying out of each KA. The last column of the table contains references to the handbook. Meeting Guide items listed in this column may be found in Chapter 2, tools listed under BA Toolkit may be found in Chapter 4, Tips and Checklists are in Chapter 5, and Templates are to be found in Chapter 6.

Table 3.7 KAs with Handbook References

KA	Description	Purpose	Tools and Techniques (by Chapter)
Business Analysis Planning and Monitoring	Describes how to determine which activities are necessary in order to complete a business analysis effort, including identification of stakeholders, selection of business analysis techniques, and approaches, including requirements management and monitoring techniques and software tools.	Plan the execution of business analysis tasks, change the approach as required, and monitor and continually improve business analysis practices.	*Meeting Guide chapter.* Analyze Risk (for pre-project opportunity assessments [Feasibility Study, Business Case]) *BA Toolkit chapter.* See Table 4.1 in the "BA Tools Overview" section. See also Activity Diagram (partitions), Business Process Diagram (BPD), Business Process Modeling, Business Use Case, Data Flow and Context Diagrams (DFDs), Functional Decomposition Chart, Role Map, System Use Cases, Requirements Traceability Matrix, Use-Case Analysis for Different Objectives *Tips and Checklists chapter.* Managing Risk, Planning Iterations, Determining How Much Static Modeling to Do *Templates chapter.* Business Requirements Document (BRD) template, Risk Analysis Table template, Vision Document template (Key Stakeholder and User Needs), Requirements Work Plan template

(continued)

KA	Description	Purpose	Tools and Techniques (by Chapter)
Enterprise Analysis	Describes how to translate a business need into a change that can feasibly be implemented by the business. Covers problem definition and analysis, business case development, feasibility studies, and the definition of a solution scope.	Identify and propose projects that meet strategic needs and goals.	*Meeting Guide chapter:* Analyze Risk *BA Toolkit chapter:* Business use cases, Context diagram, Cause-and-Effect diagram, class diagrams (static model), ERD (Data Model), The Five Whys, Functional Decomposition Chart, Pareto Analysis, Root-Cause Analysis, State-Machine Diagram *Tips and Checklists chapter:* Managing Risk *Templates chapter:* Business Use-Case Description template, Vision Document template, Business Case (a section of the BRD template), Risk Analysis Table template
Elicitation	Describes how to work with stakeholders to find out what their needs are and ensure that these needs are completely understood.	Explore, identify, and document stakeholder needs.	*Meeting Guide chapter:* The entire chapter deals with this KA. In particular, please see Who to Invite to Requirements Workshops checklist, Facilitated Meeting Work Plan, Meeting Readiness checklist, and Standard Meeting Agenda. Also see individual meeting guidelines for planning and executing elicitation events. *BA Toolkit chapter:* Role Maps and System use cases and diagrams (to identify users) and Structured Walkthroughs *Tips and Checklists chapter:* Requirements Investigation Methods *Templates chapter:* Stakeholders and Interests (a section of the Vision Document template), Actors (a section of the BRD template)

Table 3.7 KAs with Handbook References (continued)

KA	Description	Purpose	Tools and Techniques (by Chapter)
Requirements Analysis	Describes how to elaborate requirements so that the technical team is able to provide a solution that meets the needs of the business and stakeholders. Includes assessment of the current state of the business to identify and recommend improvements.	Elaborate stated requirements to right level of detail, validate that requirements meet the business need, verify requirements are of acceptable quality.	*BA Toolkit chapter.* Activity Diagram, BPD, Business Process Modeling, Business use cases, class diagram, Communication diagram, DFD, Decision Table, ERD (Data Model), Flowchart, Functional Decomposition diagram, FURPS+, Object diagram, Role Map, Sequence diagram, State-Machine diagram, Structured Walkthroughs, System use cases, and Use-Case Analysis *Tips and Checklists chapter.* SMART Requirements, Features, Naming a Process, How to Spot the Static Modeling Elements from the System Use-Case Model *Templates chapter.* BRD, Business Use-Case Description template, system Use-Case Description template, Service Level (Non-Functional) Requirements template

Table 3.7 KAs with Handbook References (continued)

KA	Description	Purpose	Tools and Techniques (by Chapter)
Solution Assessment and Validation	Describes how to assess proposed and deployed solutions to determine which solution best fits the business need and determine necessary workarounds or changes to the solution.	Assess solutions to ensure that strategic goals are met and requirements are satisfied.	*Meeting Guide chapter.* Review Meeting (Structured Walkthroughs and Gate Review) *BA Toolkit chapter.* Decision Table (to design tests and evaluate coverage), Role Map, Requirements Traceability (test coverage) Matrix *Tips and Checklists chapter.* Testing Throughout the Life Cycle with the Service V-Model, Test types, Structured Testing Guidelines *Templates chapter.* Actors (a section of the BRD template), Test Plan
Requirements Management and Communication	Describes how to manage conflict, changes, and approvals. Includes tracking and tracing of requirements.	Manage the requirements scope, facilitate communication of requirements to and from stakeholders, and ensure consistency of requirements by maximizing reuse.	*Meeting Guide chapter.* Requirements Management Setup and Planning, Reuse User Requirements *BA Toolkit chapter.* Data Flow and Context Diagrams (DFD), included and extending use cases, Requirements Attributes Table, Requirements Traceability Matrix, Class Diagrams and Static Model, Entity Relationship Diagram (ERD) and Data Model (for reusable business rules), Structured Walkthroughs *Tips and Checklists chapter.* ITIL Seven Rs of Change Management, Change Advisory Board, Five Keys to Requirements Management *Templates chapter.* Requirements Work Plan template

UML

The UML is a standard notation for the specification, visualization, and modeling of the structure and behaviour of business and software systems.[10] The UML is maintained by the OMG (Object Management Group). The current version at the time of printing is UML 2.1.2.

From the BA side, the standard governs the use of terms, concepts, and diagrams used to model the business and its requirements. Also, the BA must be able to review technical-perspective UML diagrams to ensure they are consistent with the requirements (for example, by verifying that sequence diagrams comply with the BA's system use cases.)

The following is a list of tools[11] in this handbook that conform to the UML standard or its business modeling extensions.[12]

- Activity Diagram
- Business Use Case (business modeling extension)
- Class Diagram
- Communication Diagram
- Object Diagram
- Role Map (a limited form of the UML use-case diagram)
- Sequence Diagram
- State-Machine Diagram
- System Use Cases (and Diagrams)
- Use-Case Analysis

---

[10]As noted in the Introduction, the UML contains diagrams (such as class diagrams) and modeling elements applicable to business systems, and it has been extended with business modeling diagrams and elements to further its use in that context.

[11]A reminder that the term *tool*, as used in this book, refers to any job aid that facilitates business analysis.

[12]Business modeling extensions do not form part of the UML standard but are UML-compliant extensions of it. Because they are not part of the core standard, their definitions are not consistently applied across the industry. Handbook entries related to business use-case modeling should be taken as a general guide.

CHAPTER 4

BA TOOLKIT

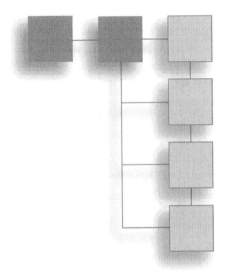

This chapter contains practical information on tools used by the BA over the course of a project. The tools are listed in alphabetical order. For an overview of which tools to apply to each type of project, see Table 4.1, "BA Tools by Project Type," in this chapter. For a description of the project phases (Initiation, Discovery, and so on) referred to in this chapter and for a chronological overview of when to use which tools as the project progresses, please refer to "Adapting the Noble Path" in Chapter 1. (Please note that the systems analyst [SA] referred to in this chapter is the role responsible for designing the software solution.)

BA Tools Overview

The tools described in this handbook were selected to cover the full range of BA activities. However, not all tools are used on every project. Table 4.1 provides an overview of the tools relevant to each type of project. Tools that conform with suggested best practices are marked X; alternatives are shown with parentheses (X) .

The projects are grouped into the following types:

- **BPI:** Business process improvement project, with no IT component.
- **Service change:** Add or update a service, where both business and internally supplied IT services are impacted. The assumption made in the table is that the change is to a non-legacy system where the accepted norm for modeling and coding is object-oriented. (Changes to legacy systems are described under the Legacy column.)

- **Third party**: Solution will be provided by an external party. This category includes COTS (Commercial Off-The-Shelf) solutions with and without customization and external service providers.

- **Minor IT change**: A small change to a system, such as changing a field or a report layout.

- **Legacy**: Changes to an old system, where the existing documentation uses structured analysis modeling techniques and relational database modeling.

Table 4.1 BA Tools by Project Type[1]

Tool	Project Type				
	Iteration	Service Change	Third Party	Minor IT Change	Legacy
Activity Diagram	(X)	X	X	X	(X)
Block Diagram	X	(X)	X		X
Business Process Diagram (BPD)	X	X	X	(X)	(X)
Business Use Case	(X)	X	X		
Cause-and-Effect Diagrams	X	X	X		X
Class Diagrams and Static Model	(X)	X	X	X	(X)
Communication Diagram	(X)	X	X		(X)
Context Diagram	X	X	X		X
Data Flow Diagram	X	(X)	(X)		X
Decision Table/ Tree	X	X	X	X	X

(continued)

Tool	Project Type				
	Iteration	**Service Change**	**Third Party**	**Minor IT Change**	**Legacy**
Entity Relationship Diagram (ERD) and Data Model	X	(X)	(X)	(X)	X
The Five Whys	X	X	X		X
Flowchart	X	(X)	(X)	(X)	X
Functional Decomposition Chart	X	(X)	(X)		X
FURPS+		X	X		X
Object Diagram		X			
Pareto Analysis	X	X	X		X
Requirements Attributes Table		X	X	X	X
Requirements Traceability Matrix	(X)	X	X	X	X
Role Map	(X)	X	X	X	
Root-Cause Analysis	X	X	X	(X)	X
Sequence Diagram		(X)	(X)		
State Diagram[1]	X	X	X		X
Structured Walkthroughs	X	X	X		X
System Use Cases (and Diagrams)		X	X	X	

[1]For UML projects (typically on non-legacy systems) use state-machine diagrams. Non-UML alternatives include Harel statechart diagram.

Activity Diagram

Table 4.2 Activity Diagrams at a Glance

What?	A diagram that describes the sequencing of activities in a process and (optionally) the participants responsible for each activity, as well as the objects used by the process. Example: Activity diagram describing the processing of a mortgage application through internal departments and an external credit bureau.
When?	• **Initiation:** BA creates activity diagrams to analyze impact of change on end-to-end business processes (as part of process improvement or in order to derive IT requirements). Business use-case descriptions are usually text narratives describing the consumer-business interaction for the business process; if the flows connect to each other in complex ways, however, the text should be augmented with activity diagrams showing one partition (swimlane) for the business area and one for each actor outside the business. Business use-case realizations include internal activities and should be documented using activity diagrams, with one partition for each participant in the process. (Refer to the "Business Use Case" section in this chapter for more on business use cases.) • **Discovery:** BA creates activity diagrams to model sequencing of system use cases (user tasks). System use-case descriptions (referred to in RUP as use-case specifications) are usually text narratives; if the flows connect to each other in complex ways, the text should be augmented with activity diagrams. (Refer to the "System Use Cases" section in this chapter for more on system use cases.) • **Construction:** Systems analyst (SA) uses the BA's activity diagrams as input to design. • **Final V & V:** Activity diagrams are used as input to design and testing; design specification and test scenarios must follow the workflow described in activity diagrams.
Where?	• **BRD:** Business services and processes/business use-case descriptions (included with text when flows connect in complex ways) and business use-case realizations[2]; IT services/user requirements/system use-case descriptions[3] (included with text when flows connect in complex ways).
Why?	• A picture is worth a thousand words, especially when process logic is complex.[4] • Picture format is well-suited to consolidating conflicting viewpoints. • Better than text for analyzing cross-functional business processes. • Enables BA to build a complete picture based on partial views supplied by each of the participants in a process. • Recommended as appendix to text for describing system use cases, where flows connect in complex ways. • For BA purposes, activity diagrams are preferable to their UML alternative, *sequence diagrams*, as they are more easily understood by business stakeholders.

[2]Business use-case descriptions are referred to in RUP as business use-case specifications.

[3]System use-case descriptions are referred to in RUP as use-case specifications.

[4]Use pictures only when they add clarity, not for the sake of making them. A picture that requires and contains a lot of text adds little value.

(continued)

Table 4.2 Activity Diagrams at a Glance

What to show stakeholders	Use basic symbol set only: Initial Node, Final Node, Control Flow, Activity, Decision, Guard, Fork and Join, Partitions. Add comments where necessary to clarify nuances not covered by basic set.
What to show team members	Full symbol set
Standard	UML
Complementary tools	Use-case text. (See templates for business use cases and system use cases.)
Alternatives	Flowchart, swimlane-workflow diagram, BPD (BPMN standard), sequence diagram (UML)

Activity Diagram Example

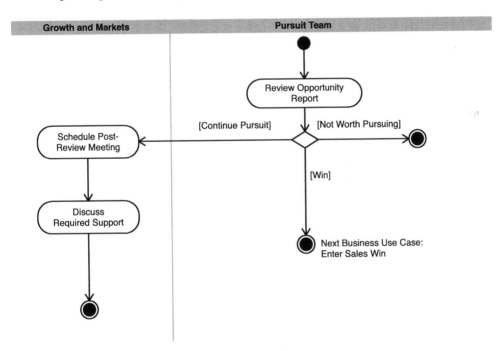

Figure 4.1 Activity diagram example: Review Pursuit

Notes on Figure 4.1:

The diagram describes workflow for the business process, Review Pursuit. The two participants in the process are represented by the partitions (columns), named "Growth and Markets" and "Pursuit Team."

Symbol Glossary: Activity Diagram—Key Modeling Elements

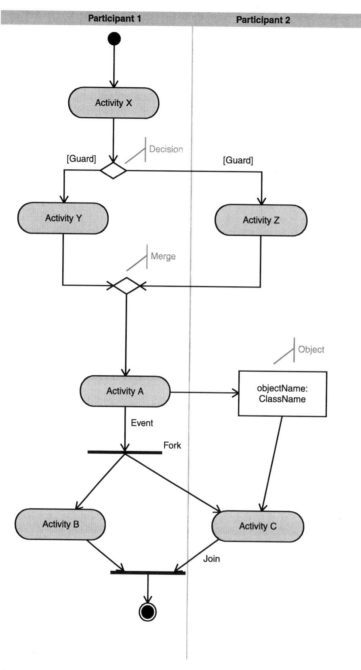

Figure 4.2 Symbol Glossary: Activity diagram—key modeling elements

Notes on Figure 4.2:

The figure contains the following modeling elements:

- **Partitions:** Also referred to in the UML as *swimlanes*. (Depicted as columns or rows; in Figure 4.2, these are the columns labeled "Participant 1" and "Participant 2.") See Figure 4.3 for an example of a Partition.

    - **Best BA practice:** Relax UML naming conventions. Formal UML naming convention: objectName:ClassName, where only one of the two names is required. objectName is the name of the business object (role, organizational unit, customer, etc.) responsible for carrying out the activities listed in its partition; ClassName is the name of the class (category) the object belongs to. For example:

        - primeContact:ServiceAgent   Both object and class are named.
        - primeContact   Only the object is named.
        - :ServiceAgent   Only the class is named.

Customer

Figure 4.3
Partition example

- **Initial node:** Begins the workflow. One per diagram. (See Figure 4.4.)

Figure 4.4
Initial node

■ **Control flow:** Solid-line arrow. Indicates direction of time. (See Figure 4.5.)

Figure 4.5
Control flow

■ **Activity:** A task. Also referred to as a *step*. (See Figure 4.6.)

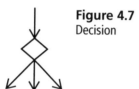

Figure 4.6
Activity

■ **Decision:** A choice.[5] Workflow will proceed along one and only one of the control flows exiting from the decision. (In the symbol glossary, either Activity Y or Z will occur, but not both.) There is no restriction on the number of control flows exiting the decision. (See Figure 4.7.)

Figure 4.7
Decision

■ **Guard:** Indicated in square brackets. A condition that may be added to a control flow. If the guard is true, the process flows along the control flow. (See Figure 4.8.)

[Guard]

Figure 4.8
Guard

■ **Event:** Indicated as a label (without brackets) on a control flow. A trigger. When the event happens, it interrupts the previous activity. (See Figure 4.9.)

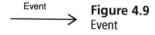

Event

Figure 4.9
Event

---

[5]A UML decision is equivalent to a BPD *exclusive-or*. Refer to the "Business Process Diagram" section in this chapter for more on BPD.

- **Merge**: Indicated as a diamond with more than one incoming flow and only one outgoing flow. Used to mark the point where alternative pathways merge (often following a previous decision). The merge symbol is not recommended for use with stakeholders; in this context, best BA practice is to bend UML 2 rules and indicate merging alternative flows by having them end at a common activity.[6] (See Figure 4.10.)

Figure 4.10
Merge

- **Object flow**: Indicated as a dashed arrow. Connects an activity to an object. When the object flow points from object to activity, the object is required as input to the activity. When the flow points from activity to object, the object is created or updated by the activity, or its status is changed. (See Figure 4.11.)

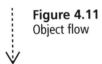

Figure 4.11
Object flow

- **Object**: The object required, created, or updated by an activity. Best practice: Use informal names when communicating with stakeholders. Formal UML naming convention is as follows (see Figure 4.12):

objectName:ClassName [stateName]

Either the objectName or ClassName may be specified, or both. The stateName is optional, for example, creditApplication123:Application [received].

Figure 4.12
Object

objectName:ClassName

---

[6]The formal UML 2 interpretation in these cases would be that both flows (logical AND) must have been triggered prior to the common activity, whereas the BA usually intends the meaning to be "either" flow (logical OR).

▪ **Fork and Join:** Also known in UML as *Synchronization Bars*. Indicated as vertical or horizontal bars. Used to mark beginning and end of parallel activities. In the symbol glossary in Figure 4.2, Activity B and C may begin in any sequence after the Fork, but both B and C must be complete before the flow can proceed past the Join. There is no limit to the number of control flows that may exit a Fork or to the number of incoming control flows that terminate at a Join. Each control flow exiting from a Fork may lead to any legal combination of modeling elements. (See Figure 4.13.)

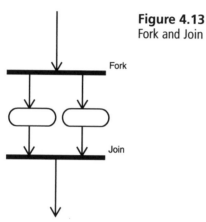

Figure 4.13
Fork and Join

▪ **Final node:** (Depicted as a bulls-eye; see Figure 4.14.) Marks the end of the process. There may be more than one final node. For example, when the diagram is used to describe a use case, there may be one final node to mark the end of the Basic Flow and one for each of the Exception Flows.

Figure 4.14
Final node

Symbol Glossary: Activity Diagram— Modeling Elements for Complex Diagrams

 If an activity diagram gets too big, break it up using a connector (see Figure 4.15) or using subactivities (see Figure 4.16).

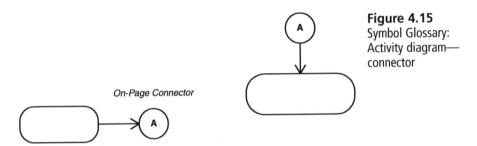

Figure 4.15
Symbol Glossary:
Activity diagram—
connector

A "rake" symbol indicates that an activity has subactivities, as shown in Figure 4.16.

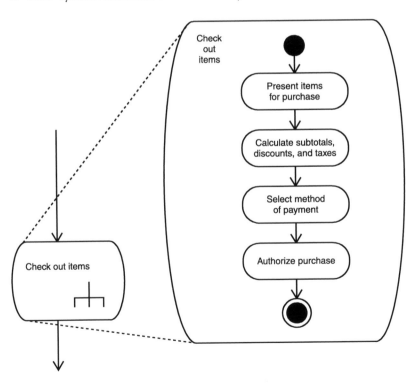

Figure 4.16
Symbol Glossary:
Activity diagram—
subactivities

Block Diagram

Table 4.3 Block/Swimlane Workflow Diagrams at a Glance

What?	A diagram showing a high-level view of a business process. Indicates steps, inputs, and outputs. Does not show decisions. A variant on the block diagram, the swimlane workflow diagram also shows participants responsible for carrying out each step.
When?	• **Initiation:** To analyze impact of a change on business processes; to identify opportunities for business process improvement. • **Discovery:** BA uses Block Diagrams as input to detailed flow analysis (See Tools: Flowcharts, BPD.)
Where?	• **BRD:** Business Services and Processes
Why?	• Ideal for working with stakeholders: Simple modeling elements make it easily understood. • Keeps focus on high-level issues, main activities, and who performs them; avoids getting into detailed process logic too soon.
What to show stakeholders	Full symbol set. (Standardization of modeling elements may be relaxed for the sake of clarity.)
What to show team members	Full symbol set.
Standard	
Complementary tools	Functional Decomposition chart (Structure chart), Data Flow diagrams
Alternatives	• Activity diagram (UML), using limited symbol set: Initial Node, Final Node, Activity, Control Flow, Partitions, and (optionally) Business Objects • Simple form of flowchart, BPMN

Block/Swimlane Workflow Diagram Example

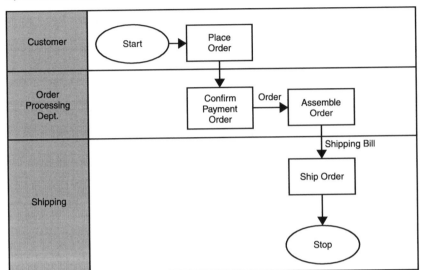

Process Name: Complete an Order

Input: Customer Profile

Customer — Start → Place Order

Order Processing Dept. — Confirm Payment Order → Order → Assemble Order

Shipping — Shipping Bill → Ship Order → Stop

Output: Shipping Bill

Figure 4.17
Block diagram example: Complete an order

Notes on Figure 4.17:

Figure 4.17 is an example of a block diagram with swimlanes for the end-to-end process of completing an order. The diagram indicates the participants in the process (Customer, Order Processing, and Shipping) as swimlanes (here depicted as rows). The process begins when a customer places an order. The order is sent to the Order Processing Department, which confirms payment and assembles the order, creating a shipping bill that goes to the Shipping Department, which ships the order.

Symbol Glossary: Block Diagram

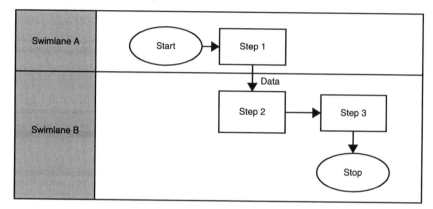

Figure 4.18
Symbol Glossary:
Block diagram

Notes on Figure 4.18:

The figure contains the following modeling elements:

- **Process name**: Indicated above the diagram. (If versioned, include version number.) Name should begin with a strong verb, if possible, e.g., *Book domestic flight* vs. *Process booking.* (See the "Tip: Naming a Process" section in the Tips and Checklists chapter of this handbook.)

- **Input**: Indicated just above the left corner of the box surrounding the diagram. Specifies artifacts and data required by the process.

- **Output**: Indicated just below the lower-right corner of the box surrounding the diagram. Specifies artifacts and data created or updated by the process.

- **Start (depicted as an oval)**: Indicates beginning of process.

- **Flow**: An arrow indicating the sequence in which steps are executed. If the flow line is labeled with a data or artifact(s), the arrow also indicates the direction of the data flow. A labeled arrow flowing out of a step indicates items created or modified by the step; a labeled arrow flowing into a step indicates items required as input to the step

- **Step (task; depicted as a rectangle)**: An activity (step) in the process. Name should begin with strong verb and end with a noun, for example, *Adjudicate loan application.* (Guidelines for naming steps are the same as those for naming processes, described in "Tip: Naming a Process" in the Tips and Checklists chapter.)
- **Stop (depicted as an oval)**: Indicates end of process.
- **Swimlanes (depicted as horizontal or vertical columns)**: Optional. Indicates a participant in the process.

Business Process Diagram (BPD)

Table 4.4 BPDs at a Glance

What?	A diagram that models the workflow of a business process. The notation is part of the BPMN (Business Process Modeling Notation) standard maintained by the OMG (Object Management Group).
When?	• **Initiation:** To model business processes impacted by the project. • **Discovery:** To model subprocesses and interactions with the IT system. • **Construction:** SA uses BA's models as input to interface and software design. • **Final V & V:** Input to integration test design.
Where?	• **BRD:** Business Services and Processes
Why?	• Popular standard for business process improvement projects. • Is able to capture nuances in sequencing rules better than the activity diagram.[7]
What to show stakeholders	Use any of the symbols included below in the glossary. Annotate liberally to clarify sequencing rules.
What to show team members	Full symbol set.
Standard	BPMN
Complementary tools	Functional Decomposition charts
Alternatives	Activity diagram (UML), IDEF3 Process Schematic diagram (IDEF),[8] flowchart

[7]For example, BPD includes a symbol for an Inclusive-OR, whereby one or more of the pathways exiting from a decision may execute. The activity diagram has no simple equivalent (though the effect can be achieved through a cumbersome combination of modeling elements, as described later in this section).

[8]The IDEF standard is not covered in this handbook.

BPD Example

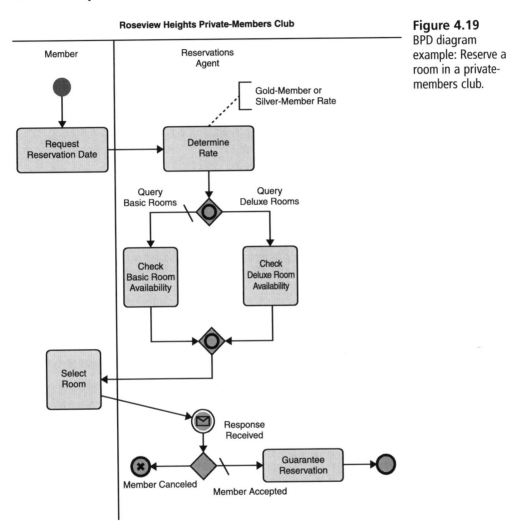

Roseview Heights Private-Members Club

Notes on Figure 4.19:

The diagram describes the process for reserving a room in a private-members club. The process begins when a member requests a reservation for a specified date.

A reservations agent determines the rate and then takes *one or more*[9] of the following actions:

- If the request included a query about basic rooms, the reservations agent checks the availability of basic rooms.
- If the request included a query about deluxe rooms, the reservations agent checks the availability of deluxe rooms.

The slash on the flow marked "Query basic rooms" is a default, indicating this flow is selected if none of the conditions are true.

Next, the member selects a room. When the member's response is received by the reservations agent, one (and only one)[10] of the following actions is taken:

- If the member has cancelled, the reservations process is cancelled.
- If the member has selected one of the available rooms, then the reservations agent guarantees the reservations and the process ends in success.

---

[9]The modeling element in BPD that indicates that one or more flows may be selected is an Inclusive Gateway, shown as a diamond with an "O" in the centre.

[10]The modeling element in BPD that indicates that one and only one flow may be selected is an Exclusive Gateway, shown as a diamond (either empty or with an "X" in the centre).

Symbol Glossary: BPD Flow Objects (with UML Conversion Chart)

Figure 4.20 depicts BPD flow objects. Don't confuse these with the UML control flow (modeled in BPD as a sequence flow). BPD flow objects are events, tasks, or gateways (decisions, Joins, etc.). See following diagrams for more specific forms of these symbols.

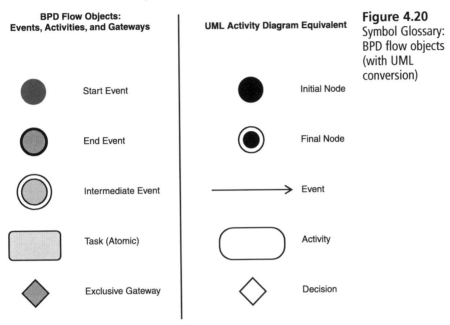

Figure 4.20
Symbol Glossary:
BPD flow objects
(with UML
conversion)

A special symbol may be drawn inside events to give them more meaning. Figure 4.21 shows some of the options available for Start, Intermediate, and End events.

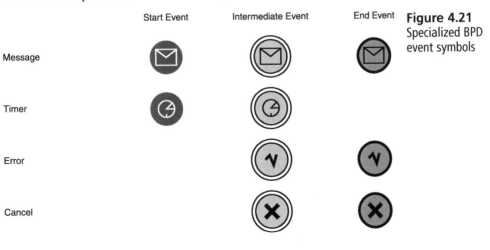

Figure 4.21
Specialized BPD
event symbols

Use compound activities to document complex processes, as shown in Figure 4.22. A compound activity is a large task that consists of smaller tasks, described on a subdiagram.

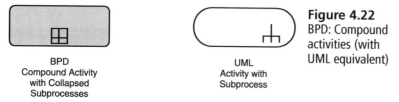

Figure 4.22
BPD: Compound activities (with UML equivalent)

BPD
Compound Activity
with Collapsed
Subprocesses

UML
Activity with
Subprocess

Figure 4.23 depicts BPD connecting objects and their UML equivalents.

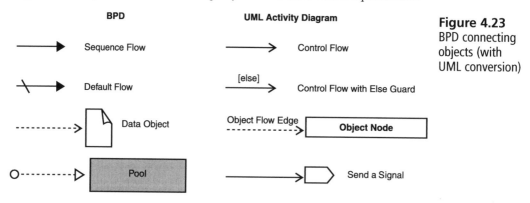

Figure 4.23
BPD connecting objects (with UML conversion)

Notes on Figure 4.23:

- **Sequence flow:** Indicates the direction of time and corresponds to a UML control flow.

- **Default**: When sequence flows emanate from a condition (referred to as a *gateway* in BPD), one of the outgoing flows may be marked as the default, as shown in Figure 4.23. This indicates that the path is taken if none of the other outgoing paths of the decision is taken.

- **Pools:** Used when a process involves independent organizations, as in a B2B process. Each organization is represented as a pool; a pool can be further divided into lanes, each representing a business area within the organization. Use sequence flows between activities in the same pool; use messages between pools. A sequence flow may cross lanes within the same pool but may not cross pools. (For more on pools and lanes, see Figure 4.29.)

See Figure 4.24 for an illustration of how to indicate whether or not a message interrupts an activity when it is received.

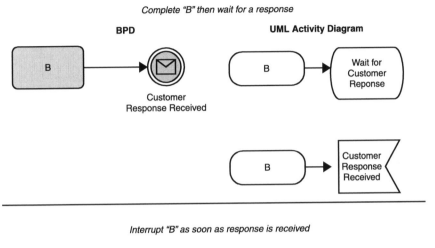

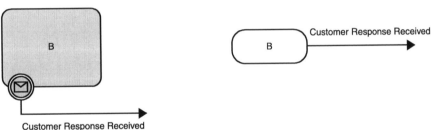

Figure 4.24 Distinguishing between interrupting and non-interrupting events on a BPD (with UML conversion)

Notes on Figure 4.24:

The figure illustrates two ways that the reception of a message can be specified in BPD and their UML equivalents:

- In the top diagram, after B is completed, the process waits until a customer response is received. Two equivalent ways of expressing this in UML are shown, one using an activity symbol (more likely to be understood by stakeholders) and the other using the *accept signal* modeling element.

- In the bottom diagram, as soon as a customer response is received, B is interrupted (even if did not complete).

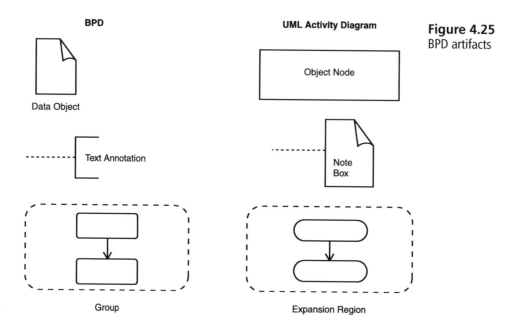

Figure 4.25
BPD artifacts

Notes on Figure 4.25:

Figure 4.25 illustrates BPD artifacts. The Group modeling element is used to group activities without affecting the sequence flow. Its UML equivalent is the expansion region. (UML expansion regions are not covered in this book, as they are seldom used by BAs.)

Figure 4.26 illustrates a BPD Exclusive-Or gateway: Only one of the paths emanating from the decision will be executed.

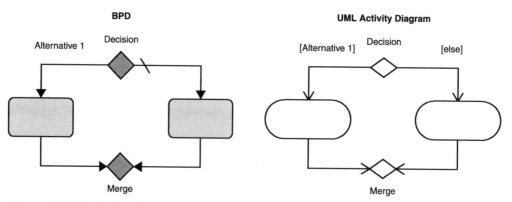

Figure 4.26 Indicating alternative paths in BPD (with UML equivalent)

Figure 4.27 depicts BPD parallel paths:

- After activity A, all of the pathways emanating from the fork are executed, but they may execute in any order.
- All paths must be complete before B may occur.

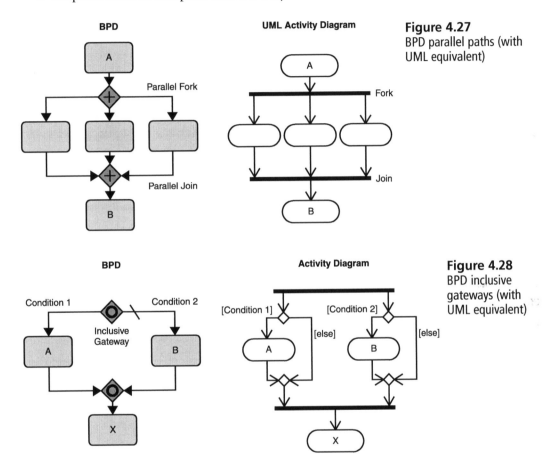

Figure 4.27
BPD parallel paths (with UML equivalent)

Figure 4.28
BPD inclusive gateways (with UML equivalent)

Notes on Figure 4.28:

The diagram on the left illustrates the use of an inclusive gateway on a BPD. Either A or B, or both, may execute (depending on which conditions are true). In the UML, there is no elegant way to indicate an inclusive decision, so a combination of symbols must be used, as shown in the diagram on the right. In the UML construct shown, A or B, or both, may execute, or neither may execute (if neither condition is true).[11]

---

[11]In Figure 4.28, the BPD construct is almost, but not fully, equivalent to the UML diagram on its right. It can be made to be fully equivalent to the UML diagram in the figure by removing the default slash from the B pathway and adding a default path that does not contain any activities.

Communicating with Stakeholders

To model an Inclusive-OR for stakeholders using the UML, do NOT use the translation shown in Figure 4.28. While formally correct, it is confusing. Instead, use a simple decision and add a note to explain that more than one condition may apply.

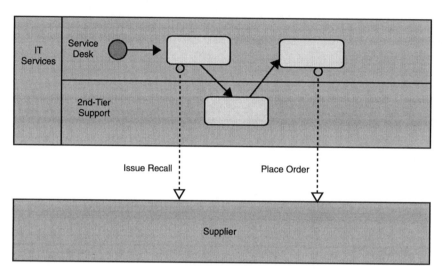

Figure 4.29
BPD pools and lanes

Notes on Figure 4.29:

The diagram illustrates the use of BPD pools and lanes to indicate who does what. Pools and lanes may be drawn horizontally or vertically. Use pools for business areas that operate quite independently of each other and that communicate with each other in limited, well-defined ways (e.g., two businesses involved in a B2B process). A lane is a subpartition within a pool that extends the length of the pool. Use lanes where there is a much greater degree of interaction and dependence between the participants (e.g., two internal employees or departments that collaborate in executing a business process).

Sequence flows may pass between lanes of the same pool. The only flows allowed between pools are message flows; sequence flows may not cross pools.

Business Process Modeling

Table 4.5 Business Process Modeling at a Glance

What?	The abstract representation of a business process. Used as part of business process improvement or as part of business-impact analysis in preparation for an IT project. Resulting documentation includes diagrams, text documentation, and metrics. Focus of diagrams is usually on sequencing rules. Format of diagram depends on standard; see Component Tools row below.
When?	• **Initiation:** To model business processes. • **Discovery:** To model subprocesses and user tasks (interactions with the IT system). • **Construction:** SA uses BA models as input to interface and software design. • **Final V & V:** QA uses BA models as input to integration test design.
Where?	• **BRD:** Business Services and Processes
Why?	• Better than text for depicting complex workflows. • Appropriate for modeling current (As-Is) and new (To-Be) processes. • Visual presentation makes it well-suited for comparing alternatives. • Enables BA to consolidate partial stakeholder views of a process into one end-to-end picture. • Aids identification of bottlenecks and opportunities for improvement. • Enables standardization of processes across the organization. • Visual training aid for new process workers.
What to show stakeholders	Keep diagrams simple.
What to show team members	Use full set of symbols.
Component tools (by standard)	**UML:** Activity diagrams, business use cases, system use cases **Structured Analysis:** System flowchart, block diagram, Functional Decomposition chart, data flow diagrams **BPMN:** Business Process Diagram (BPD) **ANSI:** Flowchart

Business Use Case

Table 4.6 Business Use Cases at a Glance

What?	A business use case is an interaction with a business that provides value to an actor (an entity outside the business). Business use-case analysis involves a number of components: Business use cases to model business services and processes (such as Process Insurance Claim); business use-case diagrams to indicate the participants in each process; business use-case descriptions (referred to in RUP as *business use-case specifications*) to describe the interaction between actors and the business area; and business use-case realizations, representing the internal business process used to implement the functionality. Business use-case descriptions (specifications) are usually documented as a text narrative; the text should be augmented with an activity diagram if the flows connect in complex ways. (Refer to the "Activity Diagram" section in this chapter.) Business use-case realizations are usually expressed as activity diagrams, with one partition for each participant.
When?	• **Initiation:** BA models end-to-end business processes impacted by the project as business use cases, creates business use-case diagrams, business use-case descriptions (specifications), and business use-case realizations. For IT projects, BA uses the business use-case model to derive the system use-case model (user requirements). • **Discovery:** BA uses business use-case realizations to derive precedence rules for system use cases (pre-conditions, triggers). • **Final V & V:** Used as input to integration test design (tests of end-to-end business processes across business functions and IT systems).
Where?	• **BRD/Business Architecture:** Business services and processes
Why?	• For IT projects, business use-case analysis helps ensure that the impact on business processes and roles is taken into consideration when a change is made to an IT system. • For UML shops, business use cases allow the team to employ a consistent approach (use cases) throughout the life cycle. • Business use-case diagrams keep early meetings focused on high-level business impact.
What to show stakeholders	Use business use-case diagrams in early meetings with stakeholders and in documentation to communicate high-level business issues: the business processes impacted by the project and the participants involved with each process. Use business use-case descriptions to describe business façade functionality and business use-case realizations to describe the internal workflow for each impacted process.
What to show team members	Full set of tools and symbols
Standard	Business modeling extension to the UML
Complementary tools	• Use-case analysis, system use case • Business Use-Case Description Template (see the Templates chapter) • Activity diagram
Alternatives	• **Structured Analysis:** DFDs (as alternative to business use-case diagram); block diagram and flowcharts (for diagramming workflow, as alternatives to UML activity diagrams) • **BPMN:** BPDs (as alternatives to UML activity diagrams)

Business Use-Case Diagram Example

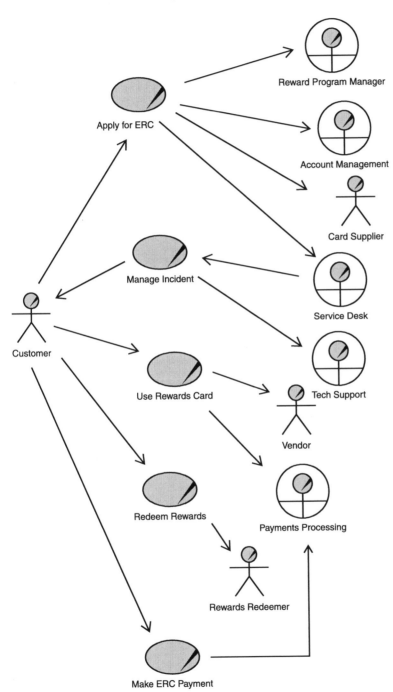

Figure 4.30
Business use-case diagram example: Business processes and actors impacted by new rewards program.

Notes on Figure 4.30:

Figure 4.30 is an example of a business use-case diagram, depicting an overview of the business processes and roles impacted by a project to introduce a new rewards program—an Entertainment Rewards Card (ERC) that earns points towards entertainment events when used for purchases.

Symbol Glossary: Business Use-Case Diagram

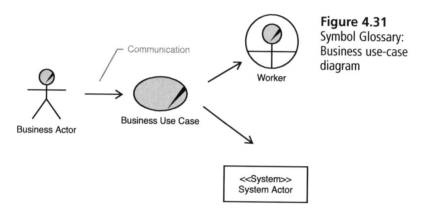

Figure 4.31
Symbol Glossary: Business use-case diagram

Notes on Figure 4.31:

The figure contains the following modeling elements:

- **Business actor:** (Depicted as a stick-figure, with a slash drawn through the head.) An entity external to the business, such as a customer, a supplier, or an external IT system. (See Figure 4.32.)

Figure 4.32
Business actor

- **Communication:** Also referred to in the UML as a *Communication Association.* (Depicted as a solid line between an actor [business actor, worker, etc.] and a business use case, with optional open arrowhead.) Indicates that the actor interacts with the business area over the course of the business use case or works internally to carry it out. If the actor at one end of the communication is the primary actor (initiator) of the business use case, the communication should have an arrowhead away from the primary actor toward the business use case. If the actor is a supporting actor, the arrowhead should point from the business use case to the actor. (See Figure 4.33.)

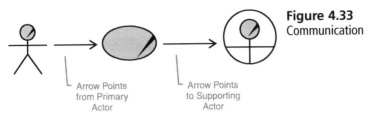

Figure 4.33
Communication

Arrow Points from Primary Actor

Arrow Points to Supporting Actor

■ **Business use case:** (Depicted as an oval with a slash drawn through one end.) An interaction with a business area, business service, or business process. (See Figure 4.34.)

Figure 4.34
Business use case

■ **Worker:** (Depiction is non-standard; shown in Figure 4.35 as a stick figure enclosed in a circular arrow.) Indicates an organizational unit or role within the business area that participates in implementing a business process.

Figure 4.35
Worker

■ **System actor:** (Depiction is non-standard; format shown in Figure 4.36 uses the class symbol, and a user-defined stereotype <<system actor>>.) Indicates an external IT system.

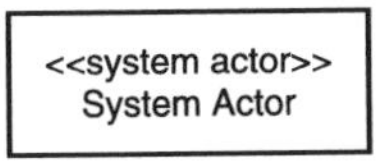

<<system actor>>
System Actor

Figure 4.36
System actor

■ **System-level actor:** (Not shown on symbol glossary; depicted as a stick figure.) A business use-case diagram may also include a system-level actor to represent an actor (human or technology) that interacts with the IT system. (See Figure 4.37.)

Figure 4.37
System-level actor

Cause-and-Effect Diagrams

Table 4.7 Cause-and-Effect Diagrams at a Glance

What?	A diagram that traces an effect back to its root causes. Also known as Ishikawa diagram (for its founder) or *fishbone diagram*. Used by the BA to identify the areas that a process improvement effort should focus on in order to achieve a desired result or avoid an undesirable one. For example, the diagram may be drawn in order to determine what root problems to solve in an upcoming release or what features to include to satisfy a root need of the business or its customers.
When?	• **Initiation and Discovery:** During brainstorming and feedback (review) sessions, the BA uses the diagrams to identify the issues to include within project scope. • **Final V & V:** Used by QA to diagnose root causes of bugs. • **Production:** Used by business and marketing analysts to identify areas to focus on as part of the continual service improvement effort.
Where?	• **BRD:** Business case; BIA (Business Impact Analysis)
Why?	Problems are most effectively dealt with when they are treated at the source.
What to show stakeholders	Full symbol set
What to show team members	Full symbol set
A component of	Root-cause analysis, Six Sigma
Complementary tools	The Five Whys, Pareto analysis

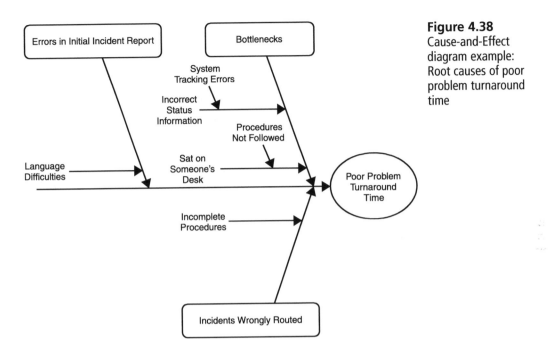

Figure 4.38
Cause-and-Effect diagram example: Root causes of poor problem turnaround time

Notes on Figure 4.38:

The figure is a cause-and-effect diagram drawn by the BA to analyze the root causes of poor problem turnaround time at the Service Desk. Using the diagram as an aid during a brainstorming session, the BA determines that the immediate causes of the problem are incidents being bottlenecked (stuck at a point in the process), incidents being wrongly routed, and errors in the reporting of the original incident. Each of these is followed back to its root causes. For example, two causes are identified for bottlenecks: incorrect status information on incidents and the incident sitting on someone's desk. The root cause of the incident sitting on someone's desk is that procedures are not being followed. The BA might follow cause-and-effect diagramming with Pareto analysis in order to determine which root causes are most worth pursuing in improving a process.

Class Diagrams and Static Model

Table 4.8 Class Diagrams at a Glance

What?	A business-perspective class diagram describes business nouns and concepts and the rules associated with them. It is often referred to as a *Business Entity Diagram* or a *Domain Diagram*. Its main modeling elements are classes and relationships. A class is a category of business object, such as Life Policy, Amendment, and Benefit. The diagram indicates relationships that the solution is required to implement, for example, the requirement that the solution be able to connect a Life Policy to its Amendments and Benefits. The diagram may also indicate the multiplicities (numerical rules) that apply to a relationship—for example, that a Life Policy may have zero or more Amendments. Relationships and multiplicities in business-perspective class diagrams represent business rules that need to be captured, enacted, and tested. The business-perspective class diagram is the key diagram used by the BA to express the static model—the abstract representation of non-time-based business rules related to objects. The business-perspective class diagrams are used by the technical system analyst (software designer) as input in the creation of technical-perspective class diagrams that specify the design of the IT system.
When?	• **Initiation:** BA creates initial class diagrams describing key business concepts and business objects (such as Customer, Supplier, Product Category, and Transaction Type) within the scope of the project, their relationships, and their multiplicities. • **Discovery:** BA adds modeling elements (classes, relationships, multiplicities, etc.) as they are discovered during requirements elicitation. For example, noun phrases appearing in system use-case descriptions (steps within flows, etc.) are modeled as classes if they represent something that the business area requires the IT system to track. The BA documents attributes at this time, if there is risk they will not be handled properly by the developers or to standardize rules associated with them that apply across a number of use cases. • **Construction:** BA models are used by the SA as input to the design of software classes (coding units) and the database. Relationships and multiplicities are enacted. • **Final V & V:** BA models are used as input to the design of test cases. Tests must ensure that each of the relationships and multiplicities is implemented and tested in the software, for example, a multiplicity rule that requires a sale to be able to be credited to more than one salesperson.
Where?	• **Business Architecture:** Domain diagrams (business-perspective entity/class diagrams)—to define enterprise-wide business rules related to categories (classes) of business objects. • **BRD:** IT requirements/static model • **BRD:** User requirements/system use cases/domain (business entity) diagrams (a subsection of the use-case template) to indicate the static modeling elements (business rules) relevant to the use case.
Why?	• During requirements meetings, helps BA understand new business terms introduced by stakeholders. • Helps ensure complete requirements (e.g., missing multiplicities indicate the need to go back to stakeholders). • Helps ensure internal consistency in business requirements documentation by providing a single place to document across-the-board business rules. • Enables future changes to be verified for compliance with existing business rules. • Minimizes errors due to miscommunication with developers: Provides developers with business rules in an unambiguous format that is consistent with the one they use to design the software solution.

(continued)

What to show stakeholders	Full symbol set. Do not show these diagrams to business stakeholders. Translate them into text by creating two sentences for each association and aggregation relationship. For example, each under-writer approves zero or more amendments; each amendment is approved by one and only one underwriter. For more examples, see "Notes on Figure 4.39." Also see the Multiplicity Rules Table in the Static Model section of the BRD Template in the Templates chapter.
What to show team members	Full symbol set
Standard	UML
Complementary tools	**Use cases:** Add class diagrams to use-case documentation to highlight across-the-board business rules that govern a specific use case. See the "Domain (Business Entity) Diagrams" section in the System Use-Case Description Template in the Templates chapter.
Alternatives	ERD , IDEF1[12]

[12]The IDEF standard is not covered in this book.

Class Diagram Example

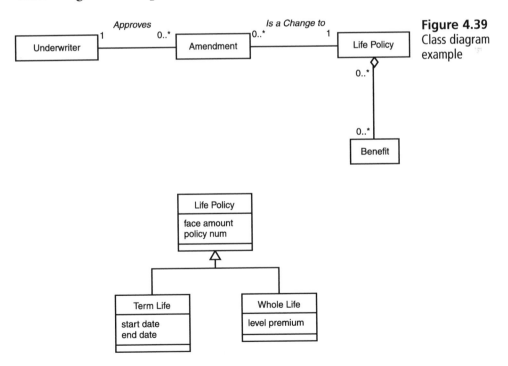

Figure 4.39
Class diagram example

Notes on Figure 4.39:

When communicating with stakeholders, translate class diagrams into text, as shown here for the Life Policy class diagram example.

- Each Underwriter approves zero or more Amendments.
- Each Amendment is approved by one and only one Underwriter.
- Each Amendment is a change to one and only one Life Policy.
- Each Life Policy is changed through zero or more Amendments.
- Each Life Policy has zero or more Benefits.
- Each Benefit may be part of zero or more Life Policies.
- There are two kinds of Life Policies—Term and Whole Life.
  - For all types of Life Policies, the system must track the following information: face amount and policy number.
  - For Term policies only, the system must track start date and end date (in addition to face amount and policy number).
  - For Whole-Life policies, the system must track the level premium (in addition to face amount and policy number).

Symbol Glossary: Class Diagram

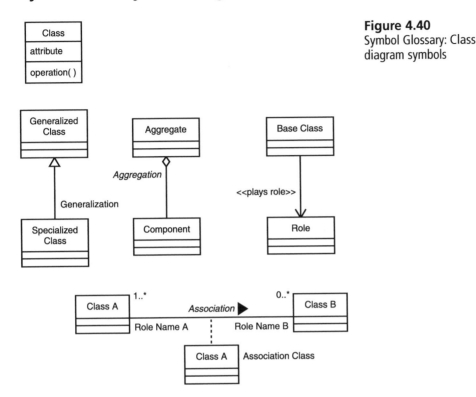

Figure 4.40
Symbol Glossary: Class
diagram symbols

Notes on Figure 4.40:

The figure contains the following modeling elements:

- **Class:** (Depicted as a rectangle with two optional compartments—one for attributes and one for operations.) A class[13] is a category that a group of objects may belong to, such as Employee, Electronic Financial Transaction, or Product. All objects in a class share the same operations and attributes (though the values of the attributes may differ). (See Figure 4.41.)

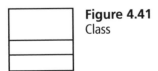

Figure 4.41
Class

---

[13]The formal UML definition is, "Class: A classifier that describes a set of objects that share the same specifications of features, constraints, and semantics."

■ **Attribute**: (Optional; listed in the attributes compartment.) An attribute is a property that the system tracks for each object in the class. Attributes are often stored and displayed as fields. (See Figure 4.42.)

Figure 4.42
Attribute

■ **Operation:** [Optional; listed in the operations compartment, with parentheses () following the name; parameters may be placed inside the parentheses.] An operation is a function that an object can carry out or that is carried out on an object. (See Figure 4.43.)

Figure 4.43
Operation

■ **Generalization**[14]: (Depicted as an arrow with a hollow, closed triangular arrowhead.) Used to indicate subtyping. The relationship points from the specialized class (the subtype) to the generalized class (the larger category)—for example, a generalization that points from the specialized class "Mortgage" to the generalized class "Loan Product." The relationship from specialized class to generalized class is translated to stakeholders as "Is a kind of"—for example, "A Mortgage is a kind of Loan Product." Any objects belonging to a specialized class automatically inherit all attributes, operations, and relationships of its generalized class. Inherited attributes and operations can be overridden, however, by a different definition of them in the specialized class. (This is an example of a property referred to as polymorphism in OO.) This means that the specialized classes are not "stuck" with their inherited definitions; it allows general definitions to be described in the generalized class, with more specific definitions provided in the specialized class. (See Figure 4.44.)

Figure 4.44
Generalization

---

[14]The formal UML definition is, "Generalization: A taxonomic relationship between a more general classifier and a more specific classifier. Each instance of the specific classifier is also an indirect instance of the general classifier. Thus the specific classifier indirectly has features of the more general classifier."

- **Transient role (plays role)**: (Depicted as an arrow with an open arrowhead, labeled <<plays role>>.) An extension to the UML,[15] used to indicate part-time subtypes. In a part-time subtype, an object belongs to the type for some of (but not necessarily throughout) its lifespan.[16] The arrow points from the base class to the role class. The base class contains attributes, operations, and so forth that apply to the object regardless of the role it is playing. The role class contains attributes, operations, and so on that are specific to each role; each time an object of the base class adopts a role, a new set of role attributes is tracked for it. For example, a Participant plays the role of Policy Holder and the role of Life-Insured each time he or she is associated in one of those ways to an Insurance Policy. (See Figure 4.45.)

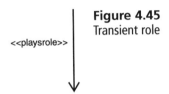

Figure 4.45
Transient role

- **Aggregation:** (Depicted as a line between two classes, with a small hollow diamond at one end.) Denotes a whole-part relationship, for example, between an Order and its Line Items or between an Organization and its Members. The diamond is connected to the aggregate (whole); the other end of the line is connected to the component (part). The UML provides a means for the modeler to indicate that a whole completely owns its part (as is the case, for example, between an Order and its Line Items) by indicating it as a composition (solid diamond). The BA may indicate all whole-part relationships as aggregation (hollow diamond); the distinction between aggregation and composition is typically indicated by the systems analyst, rather than the BA.[17] (See Figure 4.46.)

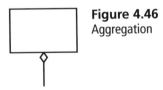

Figure 4.46
Aggregation

---

[15]The modeling element is described in further detail in the book *UML for the IT Business Analyst* (by this author).

[16]Specialization classes cannot be used to model the roles, since they apply to the object throughout its lifespan.

[17]With aggregation, a part may belong to more than one whole at the same time and exists independently of its whole. With composition, a part is contained within the whole; when the whole is destroyed, so are its parts.

▪ **Association[18]:** (Depicted as a solid line; see Figure 4.47.[19]) An association between two classes indicates that the business area needs to be able to track objects of one class against objects of another class. Use a verb phrase to name the association. For example, a Sales Rep is *assigned to* Clients, an Account is *billed to* Customers. Follow the name with a small triangle to indicate the direction in which to read the association.

Figure 4.47
Association

▪ **Role name:** (See Figure 4.48.) (Optional; depicted as a noun-phrase at an end of an association, adjacent to a class.) Names the role that objects of the class it is adjacent to are playing during the association. For example, a customer service rep's role is *Prime Contact* in the association, "User *makes initial report* to customer service rep."

Figure 4.48
Role name

▪ **Multiplicity:** The number of objects that may participate in a relationship, indicated at each end of each relationship (other than generalizations). (See Figure 4.49.) Allowable multiplicities are as follows:

- ▪ 0..1   Zero or one
- ▪ 0..*   Zero or more
- ▪ *   Zero or more (same as 0..*)
- ▪ a..*   a or more; for example, 1..* (one or more), 2..* (2 or more)
- ▪ a..b   a through b; for example, 1..3 (one through 3)
- ▪ a   a and only a; for example, (one and only one)

Figure 4.49
Multiplicity

---

[18]The UML definition is, "Association: A relationship that may occur between instances of classifiers."

[19]An association may be adorned with an arrow at either end (or both) to indicate navigability—the direction in which references may be made. This feature is not widely used in a BA context.

- **Association class:** (Depicted as a class symbol [box] attached to an association by a dashed line.) May be used by a BA as a means of dealing with many-to-many relationships. For example, in Figure 4.50, each account may be co-owned by many customers and each customer may co-own many accounts. The association class "Customer's Account" has been tied to the relationship between customer and account. An occurrence of the association class represents one customer tied to one account and can be used to track attributes specific to the link between the two, such as the date the customer signed up for the account and the individual customer's purchases to date against the account. (See Figure 4.50.)

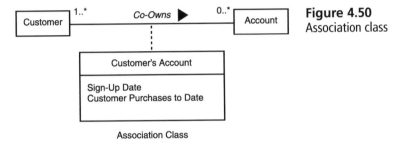

Figure 4.50
Association class

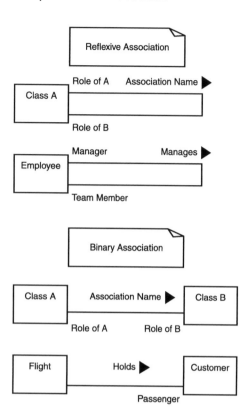

Figure 4.51
Additional Symbol
Glossary and examples:
Class diagram—unary
and binary associations

Notes on Figure 4.51:

An association may be reflexive or binary. A *reflexive* (also referred to as *unary*) association indicates that the system is required to track objects against objects that belong to the
same class. In the reflexive-association example, an employee (acting in the role of manager) manages other employees (acting as team members). Most associations are *binary*,
indicating the requirement to link objects belonging to different classes, such as between
flights and customers, as shown in the binary-association example.

Communication Diagram

Table 4.9 Communication Diagrams at a Glance

What?	A diagram that describes the way objects send messages to each other, using a format that focuses on structure.
When?	• **Initiation:** Used by the BA to analyze high-level interfaces between business areas and systems. • **Construction:** SA uses technical-perspective communication diagrams to design messaging between systems and lower-level software objects. • **Final V & V:** Used as input to integration testing.
Where?	• **BRD:** Scope
Who?	• **BA:** Creates the business-perspective diagram; reviews technical-perspective diagram • **Stakeholders:** Verify the diagram • **Systems Analyst:** Uses technical-perspective communication diagrams[20] to design and illustrate passing of messages between software objects for a given scenario.
Why?	• A convenient way to analyze and document the way business areas and systems are (or are required to be) linked; who talks to whom.
What to show stakeholders	Limited set of symbols included in Figure 4.53 and the accompanying notes.
What to show team members	Limited set is all that is required for most BA work.
Standard	UML
Complementary tools	Static object diagram, class diagram
Alternatives	Sequence diagram, DFD

[20]Steps in the system use case are mapped to messages passed between software objects in the diagrams. Often the software designer (systems analyst) begins by creating a sequence diagram from a textual use-case description, then converts this into a communication diagram, which highlights structural relationships.

Communication Diagram Example

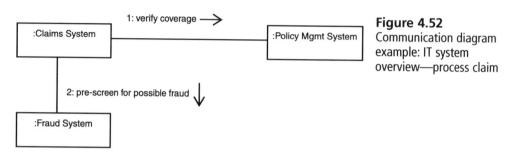

Figure 4.52
Communication diagram example: IT system overview—process claim

Notes on Figure 4.52:

The diagram highlights the patterns of communication (who talks to whom) between IT systems involved in handling claims. (A similar diagram may be drawn from a business perspective, showing communication between business areas.) In the example:

■ The Claims System sends an electronic message to the Policy Management System asking it to verify coverage for the claim.

■ The Claims System Accounts Receivable sends a message to the Fraud System to pre-screen the claim for possible fraud.

Symbol Glossary: Communication Diagram

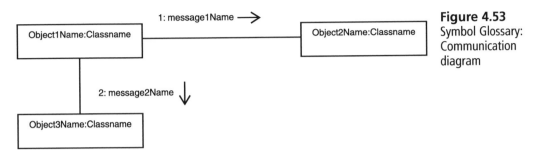

Figure 4.53
Symbol Glossary:
Communication
diagram

Notes on Figure 4.53:

The figure contains the following modeling elements:

- **Object.** An entity (business area, IT system, or component) involved in the interaction. May be named informally by the BA.

    Formal UML naming convention: objectName:ClassName

    objectName is the name of the specific object, and ClassName is the name of the class (category) the object belongs to. One or both names may be provided. For example:
    - primeContact:ServiceAgent   Both object and class are named.
    - primeContact   Only the object is named.
    - :ServiceAgent   Only the class is named.

- **Message.** Indicated as a line between objects, with a message name written adjacent to it. A message represents a request sent from one object to another. The message name is in the following form: sequence number: message name (parameters). UML naming conventions may be relaxed for BA purposes. Sequence numbers indicate the order in which the messages are executed. The message name may be followed by parameters in parentheses. The parameters represent inputs for the message. An arrow following the message name indicates the direction of the communication (pointing from the sender to the receiver of the message).

Data Flow and Context Diagrams

Table 4.10 Data Flow Diagrams at a Glance

What?	Data Flow Diagrams (DFDs) are a set of diagrams that describe the way that data moves through a system. The diagrams depict the breakdown of a system into processes and subprocesses and define the data input and output requirement of those processes.
	There are two perspectives from which DFDs may be drawn: a business perspective, which models the flow of business data in the context of business processes, and a technical perspective, which models the flow of data in the context of IT processes (used to design a software solution). For each perspective, DFDs may be physical or logical. A physical DFD indicates implementation issues, while a logical DFD strips these away. DFDs are used by the BA to model real-world As-Is and To-Be systems. On projects involving an IT solution, logical To-Be DFDs depict the processes the IT system must automate and the informational requirements of those processes. Design and implementation issues are excluded from this model.
	DFDs can be drawn at any level. The highest level, Level 0—also referred to as a Context diagram—describes the data that flows between the system and entities outside of the system, such as customers, users, and IT systems. The Context diagram defines the border between what is in the system and what is outside of it—its scope.
	The next level, Level 1, depicts the main processes of the system and the data that passes between them. Further levels provide successively increasing degrees of detail.
When?	• **Initiation:** BA reviews, creates, or updates (as necessary) business-perspective DFDs. When the project involves an IT solution, BA also reviews, creates, or updates the requirements model Context diagram and Level 1 DFD. The requirements model focuses on aspects of the business model that must be supported by the IT solution. • **Discovery:** BA defines further level DFDs in the requirements model. • **Construction:** SA maps requirements model to logical and physical technical models used to design software units (system, program, and subroutines) and data storage tables. • **Final V & V:** DFDs are used as input to testing of interfaces between processes and systems (integration testing).
Where?	• **BRD:** Scope (Context diagram), Business Services and Processes, IT services
Why?	• More likely than UML to conform to existing documentation on legacy systems. (For the same reason, though, DFDs are not generally recommended when the project involves changes to non-legacy systems, as they are more likely to follow an alternative approach and standard [OO and UML].) • Enables top-down analysis—an effective approach for dealing with complex systems by working progressively downwards to successive levels of detail. • Provides an effective means for analyzing the informational needs of processes. • Can be used to check for completeness. Formal standard violations often point to missing requirements.

(continued)

Table 4.10 Data Flow Diagrams at a Glance

What to show stakeholders	Any of the symbols in Figure 4.54, with liberal use of notes.
What to show team members	Full symbol set
Standard	Structured Analysis (not part of UML standard)
Complementary tools	Functional Decomposition chart, flowchart, ERD
Alternatives	Use-case diagram (UML), communication diagrams (UML)

DFD Example

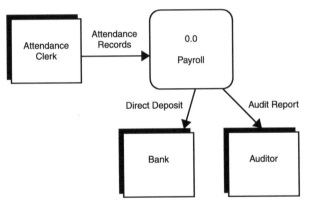

Figure 4.54
Level 0 DFD (context diagram) example: Payroll

Notes on Figure 4.54:

The figure is a context diagram for a Payroll process—a software system to be created as a result of an IT project. This example documents that:

- An Attendance Clerk sends attendance records to Payroll (the system under design).
- Payroll sends direct deposits to the bank and audit reports to the auditor.

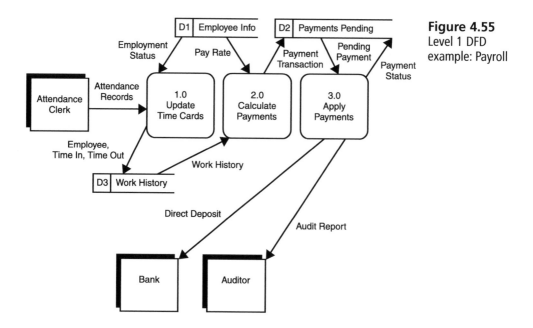

Figure 4.55
Level 1 DFD
example: Payroll

Notes on Figure 4.55:

The figure is a Level 1 DFD for the Payroll process. It identifies the main subprocesses that comprise payroll as well as data stores. A data store is a place to hold data, such as a filing cabinet, a data table, or combination of tables. This example documents that:

- The inputs for the Update Time Cards process are attendance records from the Attendance Clerk, and employment status, pulled from an Employee Info data store; its output is employee information, Time In and Time Out, used to update a Work History data store.

- The inputs for the Calculate Payments process are work history and pay rate; its output is Payment Transaction, stored in Payments Pending.

- The input to Apply Payments is Pending Payment; its output is direct deposit(s)—sent to the bank, an audit report that goes to the auditor, and a (presumably updated) payment status, used to update the Payments Pending data store.

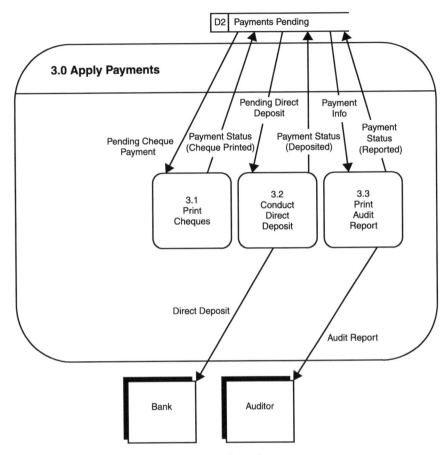

Figure 4.56 Level 2 DFD example: Payroll/Apply Payments

Notes on Figure 4.56:

The figure is a Level 2 DFD that depicts the subprocesses of Process Payments. The subprocesses are numbered hierarchically.

Symbol Glossary: Data Flow Diagram

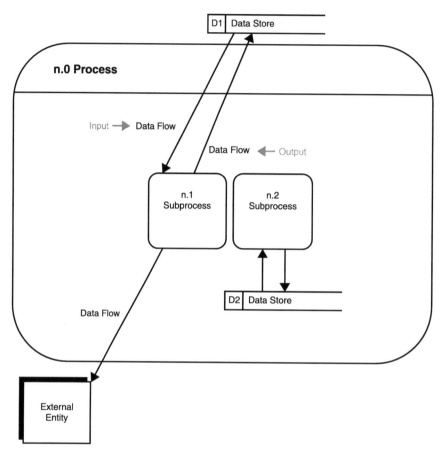

Figure 4.57 Symbol Glossary: Data Flow diagram

Notes on Figure 4.57:

The figure contains the following modeling elements:

- **Process.** A process of any size. If DFD is a business-perspective diagram, this symbol represents a business process. On technical DFDs, a process is a system, subsystem, computer program, or software module (such as a subroutine or function). (See Figure 4.58.)

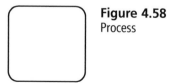

Figure 4.58
Process

- **Data store.** A place where data is stored until it can be used. May be implemented with or without IT; examples include a filing cabinet, a single, partial, or combination of computer data files (tables). (See Figure 4.59.)

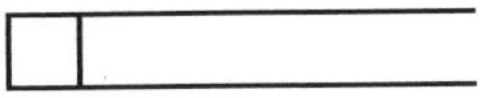

Figure 4.59
Data store

- **Data flow.** A pipeline along which data moves. A "clump" of data—for example, one field, an entire record, a complete file, or a report. May be in any form (paper, electronic, etc.). (See Figure 4.60.)

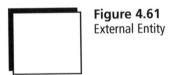

Figure 4.60
Data flow

- **External Entity.** (Also referred to as External Agent). An actor outside the system that interacts with it. Business-perspective examples include Customer and Supplier. Technical-perspective examples include user roles and external IT systems. (See Figure 4.61.)

Figure 4.61
External Entity

Checklist: Inspecting DFDs for errors:

- Every process must have at least one incoming data flow and one outgoing data flow.
- Somewhere within the model, every data store must have at least one incoming data flow and one outgoing data flow.
- A data flow line must either begin or end at a process symbol.
- Every data item that appears on a data flow must originate somewhere and be used somewhere within the model.
- When a process is decomposed on a lower-level DFD, the lower-level diagram must indicate equivalent input and output data flows for the process as those depicted on the higher-level DFD.[21]

---

[21]Equivalent does not mean identical. The higher-level DFD may consolidate a number of data flows into a single data flow. Also, data items that are input in order to be updated are sometimes consolidated into a single "output" data flow from the process to highlight the net effect of the process.

Decision Table/Tree

Table 4.11 Decision Tables (Trees) at a Glance

What?	A decision table or tree documents the way that a system responds to various combinations of input conditions. Used by the BA to describe business rules where the required response depends on a number of factors that must all be considered at the same time, such as the rules for adjudicating a request for a loan.
When?	• **Discovery:** BA uses decision tables or trees to structure interviews and document requirements for complex business rules. • **Construction:** SA uses BA's decision tables or trees as input to software design. • **Final V & V:** Decision tables and trees are used as input to design of test cases; the table is used to construct test scenarios and defines expected test results.
Where?	• Business Rules Repository • **BRD:** Business Services and Processes • **BRD:** IT Services and Processes • If the use-case approach is used, decision tables and trees may be included as an appendix to a use case (business or system), and referred to by a step in the use case, such as a step to adjudicate a loan request.
Why?	• Provides complete, consistent, and easy-to-verify documentation for complex business rules. • Simplifies and structures the interview (see the following section "Interviewing with Decision Tables"). • Ensures all combinations of conditions have been accounted for. • Documents requirements in a form that is highly suitable for testing.
What to show stakeholders	Decision table or tree
What to show team members	Decision table or tree
Standard	N/A
Complementary tools	• (Business and System) Use-Case Template • Boundary-value analysis

Decision Table Example

Cases →	1	2	3	4	5	6	7	8	9	10	11	12
Conditions												
C1: Prior Rejections? (Y,N)	Y	Y	Y	Y	Y	Y	N	N	N	N	N	N
C2: Family History/Genetic Risk Factor (Hi/Lo)	Hi	Hi	Hi	Lo	Lo	Lo	Hi	Hi	Hi	Lo	Lo	Lo
C3: Medical Condition (1–3)	1	2	3	1	2	3	1	2	3	1	2	3
Actions												
A1: Accept						X		X	X	X	X	X
A2: Reject	X	X		X			X					
A3: Refer			X		X							
A4: Apply Standard Rates						X					X	X
A5: Apply High-Risk Rates								X	X	X		

Figure 4.62
Decision table example: Adjudicate application for life insurance

Notes on Figure 4.62:

The figure is a decision table for adjudicating an application for life insurance. Business rules depend on three factors: whether the applicant has had any prior rejections; a risk factor (Hi or Lo) based on family history and genetic profile; and a Medical Condition Code rated from 1–3, where 3 indicates the highest health rating. The table indicates under what set of conditions the application is accepted, rejected, or referred (for further investigation) and what rate schedule applies in each case. For example, column 9 describes a scenario where there were no prior rejections, a high risk factor, and a Medical Condition of 3 (excellent). The response for this scenario is Accept (A1) but apply a high-risk rate (A5).

Interviewing with Decision Tables

Use decision tables to structure the interview whenever many factors affect the outcome. Break the interview down into the following simple steps:

1. **Identify conditions:**

    Q: "What factors affect the outcome?"
    "What questions need to be answered before you can determine what to do?"
    List each factor as a condition in the table.

    For each condition, ask:

    Q: "What different values can this take?"
    "Which of these values impact the outcome?"

2. **Identify actions:**

> Q: "What are all the possible outcomes of this process?"
> "What actions could the business take?"

Document each as an action in the table.

3. **Calculate number of distinct scenarios:**

(No. of scenarios) = (no. of values for condition 1) × (no. of values for condition 2) × (no. of values for condition 3) . . .

Assign a column for each scenario.

For the example, (no. of scenarios) = 2 (for Y/N) × 2 (for Hi/Lo) × 3 (for 1/2/3) = 12

4. **Complete the upper half of the table** so that each column shows a distinct set of values.[22]

5. **Assign actions to scenarios, one column at a time:**

> Q: "For the first scenario (column), when [first row condition] is [value] and [second row condition] is [value] . . . which actions apply?"

Document each required action with an X in the appropriate Action cell.

---

[22]One method is to start by filling in the last row, alternating values. If you run out of values, begin again with the first value. Visually inspect the number of cells [n] it takes until the first set of values ends. Moving one row up, mark the first [n] cells with the first value for the current row; mark the next [n] cells with the second value, and so on, until the row is complete. Repeat for each row, moving up one row at a time.

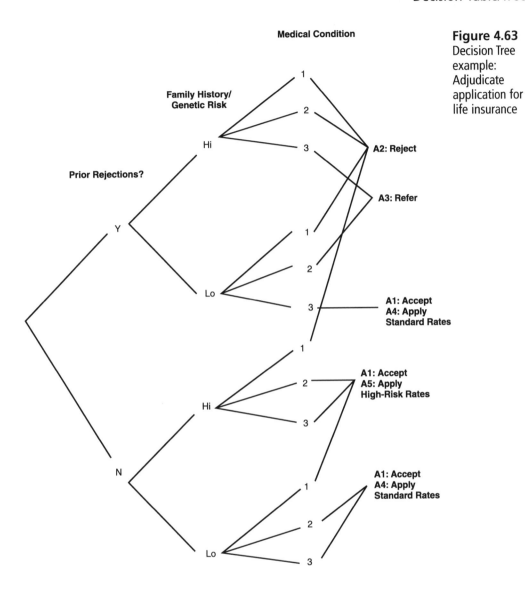

Figure 4.63
Decision Tree
example:
Adjudicate
application for
life insurance

Notes on Figure 4.63:

The figure is a decision tree for adjudicating an application for life insurance. It is equivalent to the decision table example shown in Figure 4.62.

Entity Relationship Diagram (ERD) and Data Model

Table 4.12 Entity Relationship Diagrams at a Glance

What?	A diagram that depicts *entities*—categories of objects—within a system and the relationships between them. The collection of ERDs and related documentation is referred to as the *data model*. ERDs are also a form of static model[23]: the model of the non-time-based rules of a system.
	The BA uses ERDs to express the static model of a business area—its nouns, concepts, and rules. For example, the BA may draw an ERD to describe how Life Policies are related to Amendments and Benefits; the diagram would include rules that dictate the number of Amendments and Benefits tied to a Policy. These latter rules are referred to as cardinality rules. The BA model may also include rules regarding the attributes (properties or fields) of these entities. For example, an attribute of a Life Policy might be face amount.
	The BA's ERDs may be drawn strictly for Enterprise Analysis (to model a real-world business area) or for Requirements Analysis (in order to model the static business requirements for an IT solution). In the latter case, only the modeling elements that must be supported in the solution are included.
When?	• **Initiation:** Creates, reviews, or updates ERDs showing key entities—such as people, products, services, and transactions—tracked by the system (actual business area or IT system) and their relationships to each other.
	• **Discovery:** BA adds entities to the model as new nouns are introduced during requirements elicitation. For example, noun phrases introduced in the user requirements for an IT system are added to the data model if the business area requires the IT system to track them. Attributes and their verification rules are added if there is a risk they will not be handled properly by the solution provider or if there are rules associated with them that apply across a number of requirements documents.
	• **Construction:** The SA uses the BA's model as input to creation of technical ERDs used to design the database. If a third-party solution is contemplated, the BA's ERDs may be used as criteria for the selection of a vendor or service provider. (The solution must support the rules expressed in the model.)
	• **Final V & V:** The BA's ERDs are used as input to test design. Tests should prove that all entities and attributes in the model are tracked and that the cardinality and attribute rules expressed in the model are supported by the solution.
Where?	• In BRD documentation, the diagram appears as part of the static model.
Why?	• On projects resulting in changes to legacy systems, the existing documentation and tools are more likely to use ERDs than UML class diagrams.
	• ERDs are an entrenched best practice due to their wide use in designing tables for RDBMS (Relational Database Management Systems).
	• ERDs help the BA understand and define business concepts and their relationships to each other.
	• ERDs help the BA find missing requirements (for example, missing cardinalities often indicate the need to go back to stakeholders).
	• ERDs help implement internal consistency in business requirements documentation by providing a single place to record across-the-board business rules.
	• Can be used to verify future requirements to ensure they comply with existing business rules.
	• ERDs improve communication with solution providers, lessening the chance of miscommunication; solution providers are given static business requirements in an unambiguous format that is consistent with the one they use to design the software solution.

(continued)

What to show stakeholders	Do not show these diagrams to business stakeholders. Convert diagrams to text for stakeholder review and sign-off. Translate each relationship into two sentences.
	
	• For relationship between A and B:
	    • Each A [relationship name] [cardinality adjacent to B] B.
	    • Each B [reverse the association name] [cardinality adjacent to A] A.
	
	For example, each underwriter approves zero or more amendments; each amendment is approved by one and only one underwriter.
	
	See ERD example and notes in the next section for sample translations.

What to show team members	Full symbol set
Standard	Part of data modeling discipline used in conjunction with structured analysis techniques (not part of UML). A standard notation used for RDBMS.
Alternatives	Class diagram (UML), IDEF1

[23]Another (more recent) approach to static (structural) modeling is based on object-oriented (OO) analysis. It employs class diagrams in place of ERDs.

Entity Relationship Diagram Example

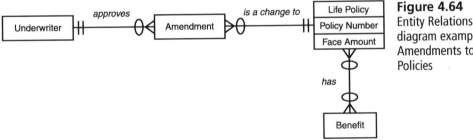

Figure 4.64
Entity Relationship diagram example: Amendments to Policies

Notes on Figure 4.64:

- Each Underwriter approves zero or more Amendments.
- Each Amendment is approved by one and only one Underwriter.
- Each Amendment is a change to one and only one Life Policy.
- Each Life Policy is changed through zero or more Amendments.
- Each Life Policy has zero or more Benefits.
- Each Benefit belongs to zero or more Life Policies.
- For each Life Policy, the system tracks the following attributes (fields):
  - Policy number: Identifies a policy; unique for each Life Policy.
  - Face amount.

Symbol Glossary: Entity Relationship Diagram

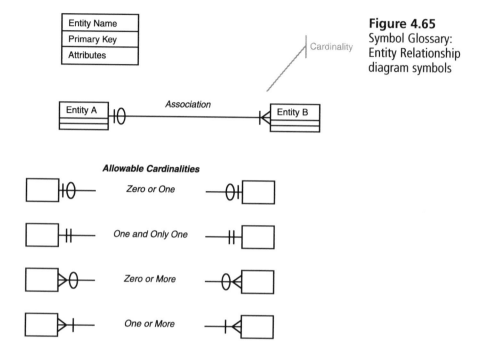

Figure 4.65
Symbol Glossary:
Entity Relationship
diagram symbols

Notes on Figure 4.65:

The figure contains the following modeling elements:

- **Entity:** (Depicted as a rectangle with two optional compartments—one for the primary key [unique identifier] and one for attributes.) An entity[24] is a category that a group of objects may belong to. The BA uses entities to model nouns tracked by the business. In a requirements model, only entities that must be tracked by the IT system are included. Entities are named in the singular; examples include Employee, Supplier, Customer, Product, Electronic Financial Transaction, and Incident.

  A specific instance of an entity, such as Incident 5030, is referred to as an *occurrence* of the entity. All occurrences of an entity share the same attributes (though the values of the attributes may differ).

- **Primary key (optional):** A unique identifier. May be a simple (one attribute) or compound key (more than one attribute).

---

[24]In some usages, the term *entity* refers to a specific instance, or occurrence, and the term *entity class* refers to the category, or type.

- **Attribute (optional):** (Listed in the attributes compartment.) An attribute is a property (field) that the system tracks for each occurrence of the entity.
- **Relationship:** (Depicted as a solid line.) A relationship between two entities indicates that the system needs to be able to link occurrences of one entity against those of the other—for example, Sales Rep to Customer, Account to Customer. Use a verb phrase to name the relationship. For example, a Sales Rep is *assigned to* a Customer.
- **Cardinality:** (Depicted on each end of each relationship.) The number of occurrences that may participate in a relationship. Indicated at each end of each relationship. Allowable cardinalities are shown in the symbol glossary.

The Five Whys

Table 4.13 The Five Whys at a Glance[25]

What?	The Five Whys is a problem-solving technique[25] in which the question "why?" is asked successively until the root cause of a problem is uncovered. As a rule of thumb, it is thought that the question must be asked about five successive times to reach an underlying root cause, though this number is not set in stone. For example, to examine the root causes of problems at a Service Desk (Call Centre): • Why do customers rate the service poorly? Because of poor incident resolution time. • Why is the resolution time poor? Incidents are getting "lost in the system." • Why are incidents getting lost? Poor incident tracking. • Why is the tracking poor? Errors in the automated incident management system. • Why are there errors in the system? Incomplete requirements for new incident types.
When?	• **Initiation:** Used during brainstorming sessions to identify root causes of problems and root needs of stakeholders. Provides input to project scope definition and prioritization of requirements. • **Final V & V:** Used by QA to identify root causes of bugs.
Where?	• **BRD:** Business case, BIA (Business Impact Analysis)
Why?	It is more effective to focus on root causes than symptoms.
What to show stakeholders	Evaluation report. Illustrate with cause-and-effect diagram, if appropriate.
What to show team members	Evaluation report. Illustrate with cause-and-effect diagram, if appropriate.
Standards/ methodologies	Root-cause analysis, Six Sigma
Complementary tools	Pareto analysis, cause-and-effect diagram

[25]The approach was created by Sakichi Toyoda and used at Toyota Corporation; it is now a component of the Six Sigma methodology.

Flowchart

Table 4.14 Flowcharts at a Glance

What?	A diagram that describes the sequencing of activities in a process and (optionally) the participants responsible for each activity and the artifacts used during the process (for example, a flowchart describing the processing of a mortgage application through internal departments and an external credit bureau).
When?	• **Initiation:** BA creates flowcharts to analyze impact of change on end-to-end business processes (as part of process improvement or in order to derive requirements for an IT system). • **Discovery:** BA creates flowcharts to model the user-IT interaction in the user requirements. • **Construction:** Systems analyst (SA) uses BA models as input to interface and software design. • **Final V & V:** BA models are used as input to design; test scenarios must follow the workflow described in BA models.
Where?	• **BRD:** Business Services and Processes • **BRD:** IT Services/User Requirements
Why?	• Well-suited to projects on legacy systems: Existing documentation, tools, and human resources are more likely to use flowcharts than their UML alternative (activity diagram). • A picture is worth a thousand words, especially when process logic is complex. • Picture format is well-suited to consolidating conflicting viewpoints. • Better than text for analyzing cross-functional business processes. • Enables BA to build a complete picture based on partial views supplied by each of the participants in a process. • Recommended as appendix to text for describing user requirements, where flow logic is complex. • Better for BA purposes than the UML alternative, the sequence diagram: more intuitive, captures many scenarios on one diagram.
What to show stakeholders	Use basic symbol set only: Initial Node, Final Node, Control Flow, Activity, Decision, Guard, Fork and Join, and Partitions. Add comments where necessary to clarify issues not covered by basic set.
What to show team members	For other BAs, solution providers, etc., use full symbol set.
Standards	Various, including International Standards Organization (ISO 5807–1985). (Copies of ISO 5807 can be purchased from ANSI's web site at http://webstore.ansi.org/.)
Complementary tools	Functional Decomposition chart, Data Flow diagram
Alternatives	Swimlane workflow diagram, BPD (BPMN standard), sequence diagram (UML), activity diagram (UML)

Flowchart Example and Symbols

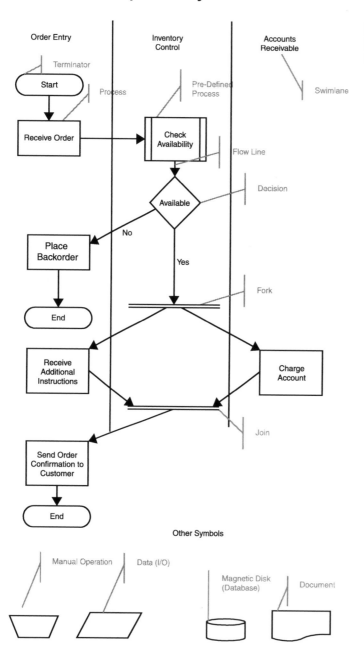

Figure 4.66
Flowchart example:
Process an order

Functional Decomposition Chart

Table 4.15 Functional Decomposition Charts at a Glance

What?	A hierarchical diagram used to decompose functions and processes into progressively lower-level (detailed) procedures. Also known as a *structure chart*. Used by the BA on business process improvement projects to model As-Is and To-Be business functions and processes. Used by the BA on IT projects to model business requirements for processes to be supported by the IT solution.
When?	• **Initiation:** BA reviews, creates, or updates (as necessary) business-perspective functional decomposition charts. When the project involves an IT solution, BA also reviews, creates, or updates high-level decomposition charts for functions and processes to be supported in the IT solution. • **Discovery:** BA defines further levels. • **Construction:** Systems analyst uses BA model as input to technical models used to design software units (system, program, and subroutines). • **Final V & V:** Used to plan incremental testing; *top-down* incremental testing begins with top-level functions on the chart; *bottom-up* incremental testing begins with low-level processes.
Where?	• BA diagrams appear in business process section of the Business Requirements Document; technical diagram appears in software specifications.
Why?	• Enables the analyst to manage complexity by breaking down a complex process into smaller, manageable bits. • Top-down approach encourages analyst to start from the general and work towards the specific. • Used to help define scope by indicating business functions and processes that are in and out of scope.
What to show stakeholders	Full symbol set shown in the next section, Functional Decomposition Chart example and Glossary.
What to show team members	Additional symbols may be added to indicate input, outputs, conditionality, and looping.
Complementary tools	Data flow diagrams (DFD), flowcharts, ERD
Standard	Structured analysis (not UML-compliant)
Alternatives	Class diagram (UML).[26]

[26]OO uses a different approach to managing complexity; rather than the hierarchical approach of functional decomposition, it aims to distribute functionality amongst collaborating objects.

Functional Decomposition Chart Example and Glossary

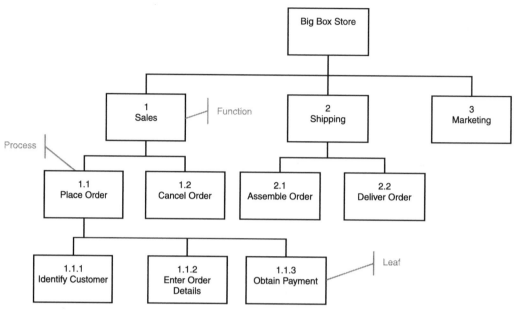

Figure 4.67 Functional Decomposition chart example: Big Box Store

Notes on Figure 4.67:

The figure is an example of a functional decomposition diagram for a Big Box Store. It illustrates the following modeling elements:

- **Function:** A noun that represents a set of logically related activities. Functions in the example are Sales, Shipping, and Marketing. A function cannot be performed. Each function may be decomposed into lower-level functions and processes.

- **Process:** An activity that can be performed. In the example, the Sales function contains the following processes: Place order and Cancel order. A process can be decomposed into lower-level processes. (See "Tip: Naming a Process" in the Tips and Checklists chapter.)

- **Leaf:** Process with no subprocesses.

- **Numbering:** Use a hierarchical numbering system. In the example, the processes below "1 Sales" are "1.1 Place order" and "1.2 Cancel order." Sequencing, however, is *not* indicated by the numbering system or by left-right positioning on the diagram.

FURPS+

Table 4.16 FURPS+ at a Glance

What?	An approach to classifying requirements, developed by Robert Grady[27] at Hewlett-Packard. Each character in the acronym stands for a requirement type: Functionality, Usability, Reliability, Performance, and Supportability. The plus (+) sign stands for other design constraints. (See the notes on "Plus (+)" in the FURPS+ Checklist following this table.)
When?	• **Initiation and Discovery:** FURPS+ categories are used by the BA to structure requirements interviews and documentation. • **Final V & V:** Used by QA to plan non-functional testing.
Where?	• **BRD:** Business and IT non-functional service level requirements (URPS+ classifications.) • **BRD:** User requirements (system use cases); URPS+ requirements specific to a user task (system use case) may be documented with the task (see System Use-Case template).
Why?	• The FURPS+ categories help the BA ensure all types of requirements are considered in the analysis—especially those required by operations.
Complementary tools	See Service Level (Non-Functional) Requirements template for a broader list of non-functional requirement types. See "Define Non-Functional SLRs" in the Meeting Guide for guidelines on eliciting non-functional (URPS+) requirements.

[27]Robert Grady, *Practical Software Metrics for Project Management and Process Improvement* (Prentice Hall PTR, 1992).

FURPS+ Checklist

Use the following checklist, based on FURPS+, as an aid when planning requirements-elicitation events and during structured walkthroughs to verify whether all types of requirements have been covered in the requirements analysis and documentation. The requirements should cover the following FURPS+ categories:

- **Functionality:** Defines what the system must be able to do. Includes features, capabilities, security requirements, and user requirements (documented, for example, as system use cases).

- **Usability:** Requirements related to the user interface, such as user-friendliness, accessibility, look and feel, online help, and visual design guidelines.

- **Reliability**: The ability of the system to perform under specified routine and non-routine conditions for a specified period of time. Includes the following:
  - **MTBF (Mean Time Between Failures)**: Mean time between service failures of the same service.
  - **MTBSI (Mean Time Between System/Service Incidents)**: Mean time between failures (of any service).
  - **MTTR (Mean Time To Repair)**: Mean elapsed time to fix and restore a service from the time an incident occurs.
- **Performance**: Describes how the system must behave with respect to time and resources. Includes the following:
  - Speed
  - Efficiency
  - Availability
  - Accuracy
  - Response time
  - Recovery time
  - Start-up time
  - Resource usage
  - Throughput (transactions per unit time)
- **Supportability**: Requirements related to the ability to monitor and maintain the system. Includes abilities to test, configure, install, and upgrade the system.
- **Plus** (+): Additional constraints on the system, including the following:
  - Design requirements.
  - Implementation requirements: Constraints on the coding and construction of the system. Includes constraints on platforms, coding languages, and standards.
  - Interface requirements: Capability to interact with specified external systems and the nature of those interactions (protocols, formats, and so on).
  - Physical requirements: Physical constraints on the hardware. Includes requirements related to size, temperature control, materials, and so on.
  - Legal, compliance, regulatory, and copyright requirements and constraints.

Object Diagram

Table 4.17 Object Diagrams at a Glance

What?	A diagram that describes how objects are linked together (also referred to as a Static Object diagram). High-level business-perspective diagrams are used by the BA to indicate how business areas and functions are linked to each other. Lower-level diagrams are used to describe links between business objects, such as the link between a Funds Transfer Transaction, and the Withdrawal Account and Deposit Account for the transaction. High-level technical-perspective object diagrams indicate the way that IT systems are linked to each other. The BA may be required to create and update business-perspective diagrams and to review high-level technical diagrams.
When?	• **Initiation:** BA creates, updates, and reviews (as appropriate) high-level object diagrams describing links between business systems and functions. May review technical overview diagrams showing links between IT systems. • **Discovery:** BA creates object diagrams in the static model where appropriate (as an alternative to class diagrams). • **Construction:** BA models are used by the SA as input to the design of software classes (coding units).
Where?	• **BRD:** Static model • **BRD:** System use cases—use an alternative to class diagram subsection to indicate static modeling elements (business rules) relevant to the use case.
Why?	• Recommended diagram, when UML standard is used, for showing system-level overview of how systems and subsystems are linked together. (This is not shown on the use-case diagram, which excludes interactions between actors.) • A clearer visual than the class diagram, when the model needs to refer to two objects belonging to the same class (for example, the two accounts that participate in Funds Transfer).
What to show stakeholders	Text equivalent, for example, "A Funds Transfer debits the Source Account and credits the Destination Account."
What to show team members	Full symbol set
Standard	UML
Complementary tools	Other UML diagrams
Alternatives	Class diagram (UML), communication diagram (UML), context diagram (Level 0 DFD) (structured)

Object Diagram Examples

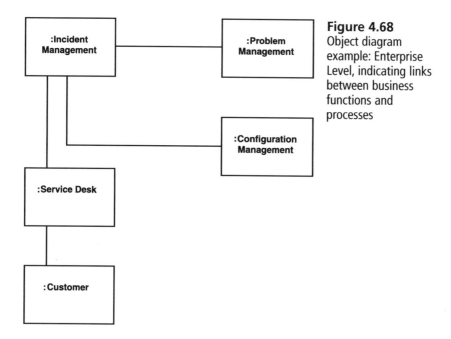

Figure 4.68
Object diagram example: Enterprise Level, indicating links between business functions and processes

Notes on Figure 4.68:

The figure is an example of an object diagram used to describe the links between business areas for a department that manages IT operations. It contains the following elements:

- **Objects:** Incident Management: (responsible for tracking incidents and resolving them as quickly as possible), Problem Management: (responsible for managing known problems and their workarounds), Configuration Management: (responsible for managing items placed under configuration control), and Service Desk: (the business function handling customer calls and the Customer). Note the colon at the end of each name, indicating that the name refers to an object.

- **Links:** Indicated as solid lines. A link indicates that two objects "talk" to each other (by sending messages, requests, information, and so on). The diagram indicates that the Customer has a direct link only to the Service Desk, reflecting the role of Service Desk as primary contact for the customer. In this example, the Service Desk is linked to Incident Management, which then has links to the other business processes.

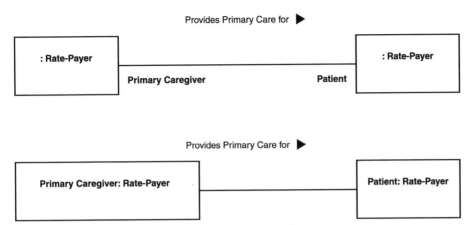

Figure 4.69 Object diagram example: Indicating links between business objects

Notes on Figure 4.69:

Figure 4.69 describes links between business objects in a government-funded insurance company. The two object diagrams in the figure use different modeling elements but are equivalent. Each expresses the business rule that the system must keep track of which primary caregiver provides primary care for which patient, when both the caregiver and patient are Rate Payers.

Symbol Glossary: Object Diagram

Figure 4.70 Symbol Glossary: Object diagram

Notes on Figure 4.70:

The figure contains the following modeling elements:

- **Object:** Indicated as a named rectangle (see Figure 4.71). Name is underlined. Best BA practice: Relax UML naming conventions. Formal UML naming convention is objectName:ClassName, where only one of the two names is required. objectName is the name of the business object (role, organizational unit, customer, etc.) responsible for carrying out the activities listed in its partition. By convention, the first letter in the name is lowercase, the first letter of any subsequent word in the name is uppercase. ClassName is the name of the class (category) the object belongs to. By convention, the first letter of every word in the class name is uppercase. Example of UML-compliant object names are:

  - primeContact:ServiceAgent   Both object and class are named.
  - primeContact   Only the object is named.
  - :ServiceAgent   Only the class is named.

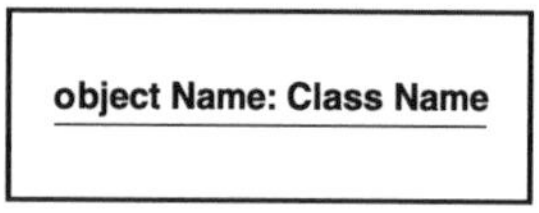

Figure 4.71
Object

- **Link:** Indicated as a line between two objects named using an underlined verb phrase (see Figure 4.72). The link name is optional. A triangle attached to the link name is recommended to indicate the direction in which to read the link.

Figure 4.72
Link

- **Role (optional):** Indicated as a noun phrase at an end of a link, just above or below the line and close to the object (see Figure 4.73). Indicates the role that the object is playing within the relationship.

Figure 4.73
Role

Pareto Analysis (Pareto Diagrams)

Table 4.18 Pareto Analysis at a Glance

What?	An approach used to help make decisions about where to expend effort to obtain the maximum gain. Based on the Pareto Principle, sometimes referred to as the 80/20 rule, stating that 80% of a benefit can be achieved by doing only 20% of the work. Applied to problem management it means that 80% of the occurrences of an undesired effect (e.g., downtime) can probably be traced to 20% of the causes.
When?	• **Initiation:** To identify the most important features and changes for the project. BA uses Pareto analysis to analyze data from incident tracking tools, surveys, etc., to help determine high-priority changes and features. • **Production:** Used by business and marketing analysts to identify areas to focus on as part of continual service improvement effort.
Where?	• **BRD:** Business case; BIA (Business Impact Analysis)
Why?	Technique allows resources to be used most effectively: 20% of the effort yields 80% of the benefit.
What to show stakeholders	Chart and diagram
What to show team members	Chart and diagram
A component of:	Root-cause analysis
Complementary tools	The Five Whys, Cause-and-Effect graph

Pareto Diagram Examples

Table 4.19 Pareto Table: Impact of Proposed Features on Customer Experience

Proposed Feature	Average reported increase in customer experience rating (out of 10)	% increase = [increase]/ [total increase] x 100%	Cumulative increase
Cross-product comparisons	3.4	68%	68%
Complete online specifications	1.05	21%	89%
Same-day response to email questions	.45	9%	98%
FAQs	.1	2%	100%
Total increase	**5.0**		

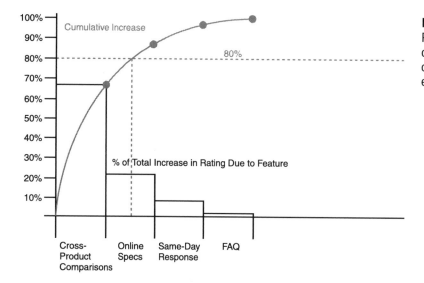

Figure 4.74
Pareto chart: Impact of proposed features on customer experience

Notes on Figure 4.74:

Table 4.19 and Figure 4.74 are examples of Pareto Analysis artifacts created by the BA during the Initiation phase of an IT project to identify the key features to be included in a project to upgrade an existing web store. The list of possible features is a result of brainstorming sessions with target customers. Follow-up surveys were conducted asking target customers to rate the proposed site with and without each feature. The analysis indicates that 80% of the possible total increase in the response can be attained by including two features: cross-product comparisons and by providing detailed product specifications online.

Table 4.20 Pareto Table: Causes of Delayed Responses to Incidents at Service Desk

Cause	Frequency	Cumulative frequency
Incomplete written procedures	68%	68%
Procedures not implemented	21%	89%
Poor communication with customer	9%	98%
System tracking errors	2%	100%

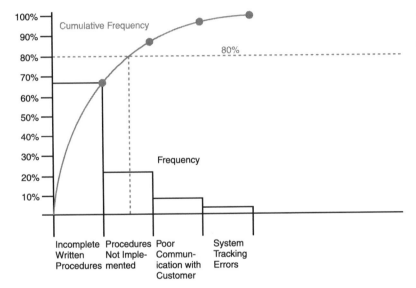

Figure 4.75
Pareto diagram:
Causes of delayed
response to incidents
at Service Desk

Table 4.20 and Figure 4.75 are examples of Pareto analysis artifacts created by a senior BA in a business-process improvement initiative. The purpose of the analysis was to identify the key Service Desk issues that have resulted in most of the delays in responding to incidents reported to the desk. The BA obtained metrics on the root causes of these incidents and found that 80% of the cases were due to incomplete written procedures and to procedures not being implemented in the workplace. Based on the results of the analysis, the BA recommended that efforts to improve the process focus on these two areas.

How to Perform Pareto Analysis

1. Investigate the possible causes of an effect.

2. Define a metric for measuring the desired effect—for example, the number of occurrences of a problem per month. Collect metrics for each cause and express each as a percentage of the total, for example, the percentage of occurrences of the problem that was due to each cause.

3. In the first column, list each cause in decreasing order of percentages, with the most frequent on the top row.

4. In the next column, write the frequency.

5. Calculate the cumulative percentage. This equals the percentages on all rows up to and including the current row. Record this in the next column.

6. Note the first cause (starting from the top) that reaches or exceeds a cumulative percentage of 80%. All causes from this row and up are significant.

7. To draw the diagram, plot the causes along the x-axis. Then create a bar graph with percentages along the y-axis.

9. On the same diagram, plot the cumulative percentages of each cause as a point and connect the points with the best-fitting line.

10. Draw a horizontal line at the 80% mark on the y-axis.

11. Mark the point at which this line crosses the cumulative percentage curve and drop a vertical from this point down to the x-axis.

12. All causes to the left of this point are significant; those to the right are not.

Requirements Attributes Table

Table 4.21 Requirements Attributes Tables at a Glance

What?	A table used to document properties of requirements, such as authorship, priority, and so on.
When?	• **Initiation:** Senior BA selects requirements attributes to use for the project; sets up requirements attributes table. • **Discovery:** Updated by team members as required. • **Construction:** Updated whenever changes occur in requirements attributes, such as changes to status or priority.
Where?	• May be a document (such as a table or spreadsheet) or reside in a requirements management tool.
Why?	• Provides information—such as priority and stability—for making decisions concerning requirements, such as when to schedule implementation. • Central place to look up data about a requirement, such as its author, current version number, etc.
What to show stakeholders	Used as input for status reports.
What to show team members	Make table accessible for viewing by team members.
Standard	(Supports Requirements Management and Communication in *BABOK®* 2)
Complementary tools	Requirements traceability matrix

Requirements Attributes Table Example

Table 4.22 Requirements Attributes Table

Req #	Date Created	Version #	Author	Respon-sible	Status	Verifi-cation Method	Effort	Priority	Stability
FET001	01/01/08	4.2	JNW	SJS	Approved		High	High	High
SUC001	23/05/08	4.9	JNW	DSW	Imple-mented	Structured Walk-through; UAT	Medium	High	Medium
FCR001	13/07/08	5.0	FER	DSW	Proposed	Inspection	Low	High	High

Notes on Table 4.22:

Table 4.22 is an example of a requirements attribute table. It illustrates some of the attributes that might be tracked for a requirement. The attributes selected by the BA in this example include the following:

- **Requirement #:** The unique ID of a requirement. Table may include requirements of any type or level. The example includes a feature (FET001), user requirements (system use case SUC001), and a functional requirement (FCR001), such as a requirement that the system provide a unique tracking number.
- **Responsible:** The person responsible for ensuring the requirement is satisfied.
- **Status:** The current status of the requirement. Your statuses might resemble Proposed, Approved, Implemented (code written and unit tested), Verified (tested or inspected), or Deleted.
- **Verification method:** Inspections, tests, and acceptance test criteria for the requirement.
- **Stability:** The likelihood that the requirement will remain the same over time. Re-evaluate unstable requirements: Lack of stability may undermine the business case for full automation of the requirement.

Requirements Traceability Matrix

Table 4.23 Requirements Traceability Matrices at a Glance

What?	A table used to trace each requirement backwards to the business processes and objectives it supports and forwards to the subsequent artifacts, events, and changed configuration items[28] that result from it.
When?	• **Initiation:** Senior BA determines what will be traced; sets up traceability matrix for the project. • **Discovery:** Updated by team members. • **Construction:** As requirements are designed, coded, and tested, the matrix is updated to tie them to the resulting design specifications, changed tables, test cases, and so on.
Where?	• May be a document (such as a table or spreadsheet) or reside in a requirements management tool or Configuration Management System (CMS).
Why?	• Provides ability to ensure no requirement slips through the cracks by tracing requirements forward to test cases, changed software units, and so on. • Provides ability to analyze upstream and downstream impact of changes. For example, it enables the business impact of an IT change (such as the cancellation of an IT project) to be traced back backwards to business processes, objectives, goals, and customers.
What to show stakeholders	Used as input for status reports.
What to show team members	Make table accessible for viewing by team members.
Standard	(Supports Requirements Management and Communication in *BABOK*® 2)
Complementary tools	Requirements attributes table

[28]A configuration item (CI) is an item that is placed under configuration control. Changes to a CI and its relationship to other CIs are often tracked in a Configuration Management Database (CMDB).

Requirements Traceability Matrix Example

Table 4.24 Requirements Traceability Matrix

Req #	Risk ID	System Use Case/Flow	Business Use Case	Functional Require-ment #	Sub-system	Design Element (Class Name, etc.)	Code, Tables, GUI	Test Case	Iteration
R1	RSK001	SUC3: Review application/ basic flow	BUC1: Apply new card	FCT7: Audit trail	USYS	Class specifica-tions: Review AppCtrl, NewCard Application	Source code: Review AppCtrl, NewCard Application Tables: NewCard Application	T5 T7	A3
R2	RSK005	SUC5: Authorize card/basic flow	BUC1: Apply new card	FCT7: Audit trail	USYS	Class specifica-tions: Authorize CardCtrl	Source code: Authorize CardCtrl	T7	A5
R3	RSK008	SUC1: Submit application/ basic flow	BUC1: Apply new card	FCT7: Audit trail	USYS	Class specifica-tions: Submit AppCtrl, Application	Source code: Review AppCtrl, Application	T5	A1

Notes on Table 4.24:

Table 4.24 is an example of a Requirements Traceability Matrix. It shows examples of the types of artifacts a requirement might be traced to. In the table, each row represents a requirement. The traced requirement may be at any level, such as a system use case, a flow within the use case, or a step within a flow. The first row of the example traces the Review Application system use case basic flow (normal scenario) backwards to the business use case that it supports and forwards to the technical artifacts and test cases that are developed or changed because of it. By reviewing the table, the BA is able to determine the following:

- That the upstream impact of a change to requirement R1 will be on the end-to-end business process for applying for a new card.
- That the downstream impact of a change to R1 will be on the specifications and code for the software classes (units of coding) ReviewAppCtrl and NewCardAppli-cation, the NewCardApplication table, and to the test scripts T5 and T7.
- That a failure of test T5 points to a problem in implementing requirements R1 and/or R3.

Role Map

Table 4.25 Role Maps at a Glance

What?	A diagram used in use-case modeling to document the actors (external systems, user roles, etc.) that interact with the IT system and their relationships to each other, for example, a Role Map that documents the user groups Service-Desk-Agent and Customer and that indicates that a Service-Desk-Agent be able to access all the user tasks (system use cases) that a Customer can access. *Role Map* is not a UML term; the diagram, popularized by Larry Constantine,[29] is a limited form of the UML use-case diagram.
When?	• **Initiation:** BA creates Role Map to describe user roles. • **Discovery:** Updated by BA as new actors are discovered. • **Construction:** Used by network administrator as input in definition of user groups and access privileges.
Where?	• **BRD:** Actors/Role Map
Why?	• Provides a central place to document actors (users, external systems, etc.), helping to ensure consistent treatment in use-case documentation. • Helps define scope. An actor, by definition, is external to the system under development—and hence defines the limits of the system. • Actor relationships (generalization) in Role Maps allow for simpler use-case diagrams in the rest of the model.
What to show stakeholders	Diagrams with accompanying text that explains the relationship between actors in terms that make sense to the stakeholder.
What to show team members	Full symbol set
Standard	While not a standard UML term, the Role Map is a UML-compliant form of the use-case diagram.
Complementary tools	System use cases, Stakeholder and Interests Table, user profile

[29]The Role Map is a diagram used by Constantine. See preprint of *Users, Roles, and Personas* by Larry Constantine, IDSA, Chief Scientist, Constantine & Lockwood, Ltd., p. 9, http://www.foruse.com/articles/rolespersonas.pdf.

Role Map Example and Glossary

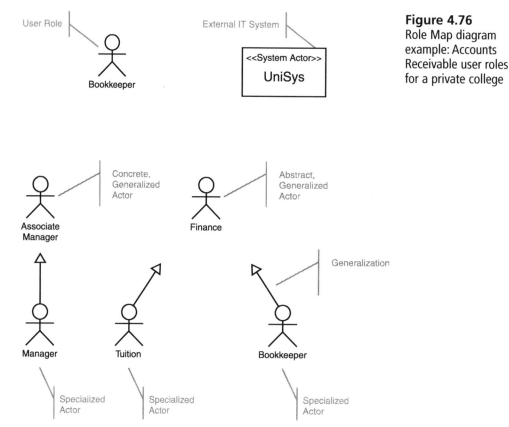

Figure 4.76
Role Map diagram example: Accounts Receivable user roles for a private college

Notes on Figure 4.76:

The figure is a Role Map describing users and external systems that interact with the IT system under development. It contains the following modeling elements:

- **Actor:** An actor is an entity that interacts with the system. An actor may represent a human user role or an external IT system. Recommendation: Use the stick figure for user roles; depict external systems as a rectangle and indicate that it is an IT system by defining and applying a System Actor stereotype. (A stereotype extends the UML definition of a modeling element.) The stereotype is shown on the example as <<System Actor>>.

- **Generalization:** (Depicted as an arrow with a hollow triangular head, pointing from a specialized actor to a generalized actor.) A relationship indicating overlapping roles amongst user groups. The specialized actor is able to access all of the use cases that the generalized actor can; in addition, the specialized actor is able to access additional use cases. Generalization is used to define two kinds of overlapping roles:

  - **One role completely encompasses another:** (Depicted as a generalization relationship between two concrete [real] user groups.) In the example, the Manager is a specialization of Associate Manager. This indicates that the Manager can access all of the use cases that an Associate Manager can and may have additional use cases. Elsewhere in the model, anywhere an Associate Manager communicates with a use case, the Manager is also implicitly indicated.

  - **Two roles partially overlap:** (Depicted as generalization relationships between the concrete [real] actors and an abstract [conceptual] generalized actor.) In the example, Tuition and Bookkeeper are specializations of Finance—an abstract generalized actor. Tuition and Bookkeeper are real user groups. Finance is an abstract concept that represents their overlapping role. The generalization simplifies other use-case diagrams: Anywhere in the model that Finance communicates with a use case, both Tuition and Bookkeeper are inferred.

Root-Cause Analysis

Table 4.26 Root-Cause Analysis at a Glance

What?	An approach to solving problems that focuses on identifying their underlying root causes. The approach can by used by the BA to identify the areas that a business process improvement effort should focus on in order to achieve a desired result or to avoid an undesirable one.
When?	• **Initiation and Discovery:** During brainstorming and feedback (review) sessions, the BA uses the diagrams to identify the issues to include within the project scope. • **Final V & V:** Used by QA to diagnose root causes of bugs. • **Production:** Used by business and marketing analysts to identify areas to focus on as part of continual service improvement effort.
Where?	• **BRD:** Business case, BIA (Business Impact Analysis)
Who?	Problems are most effectively dealt with when they are treated at the source.
Why?	• **Initiation and Discovery:** During brainstorming and feedback (review) sessions, the BA uses the diagrams to identify the issues to include within project scope. • **Final V & V:** Used by QA to diagnose root causes of bugs. • **Production:** Used by business and marketing analysts to identify areas to focus on as part of continual service improvement effort.
What to show stakeholders	See "Component tools," listed in the last row of this table.
What to show team members	Full set
Standard	Six Sigma
Complementary tools	See the following tools: • The Five Whys • Pareto analysis • Cause-and-Effect diagrams

Root-Cause Analysis Work Plan for the BA

1. Conduct brainstorming sessions to identify proposed changes to a business process or IT system: Employ the Five Whys during the brainstorm session to identify root causes of problems.

   For example, if stakeholders identify slow problem resolution time as an issue, then ask, "Why is the problem resolution time too slow?" If the answer is, "Because incidents are getting bottlenecked," then ask, "Why?" Continue until root cause is found, for example, because incident management procedures are not standardized. (The rule of thumb is that it will take five whys to get to the root cause.)

2. Summarize your findings: Draw a Cause-and-Effect graph that traces each effect back to its underlying root causes. Review and verify the Cause-and-Effect graph with stakeholders.

3. Select a metric: Define a metric for measuring the desired or undesired effect, for example, the number of occurrences, customer rating, or number of cancelled transactions. This may be defined as a KPI (Key Performance Indicator) for the project.

4. Collect metrics.

5. Perform Pareto analysis to determine high-priority items to include within project scope, such as features to include in a software enhancement, problems to fix in an upcoming release, or changes to make to a business process.

(See this handbook for notes on each of these tools.)

Sequence Diagram

Table 4.27 Sequence Diagrams at a Glance

What?	A diagram that describes interactions between objects; often used to indicate the sequence in which objects send messages to each other in a scenario of a use case. Each object involved in the scenario is depicted as a *lifeline* (a vertical line) on the diagram. The BA may draw lifelines representing the user and system. These are later expanded by the SA into technical diagrams indicating software objects and messages involved in the scenario.
When?	• **Discovery:** Sequence diagrams of selected use cases created by the BA. Includes messages passed between the user and system. • **Construction:** Systems analyst (SA) uses system use cases and BA sequence diagrams as input to technical sequence diagrams; may be reviewed by the BA. • **Final V & V:** Sequence diagrams used to plan use-case scenario testing.
Where?	• **BRD:** IT Services/System Use Cases (to describe select use-case scenarios).
Why?	• Although not generally recommended for BA use, there are some BA practitioners who prefer this approach to the activity diagram when communicating requirements to the technical team because it can be more easily elaborated into a design model. (However, activity diagrams are always preferable when communicating with business stakeholders.) • The sequence diagram is an excellent tool for the SA to use in developing the BA's use-case descriptions into design specifications. Because they are the next step in the development of a use case, the BA may be asked to review them.
What to show stakeholders	Not for stakeholder use. (Use activity diagrams instead to graphically depict sequencing of steps in a use case.)
What to show team members	Full symbol set
Standard	UML
Complementary tools	Class diagrams
Alternatives/ complements	Communication diagram, activity diagram with partitions; use-case description (see Business and System Use-Case Description Templates in the Templates chapter of this handbook).

Sequence Diagram Example

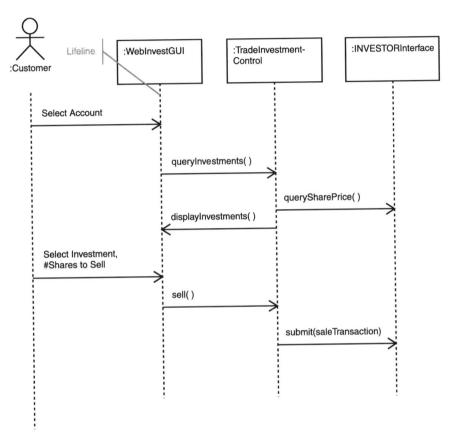

Figure 4.77 Sequence diagram example: Trade investments

Notes on Figure 4.77:

The figure is a design sequence diagram produced from the Basic Flow of the system use case Trade Investments. The diagram indicates the interactions between the user, the user interface, and interfaces to external systems. The original flow had been documented by the BA as follows:

Basic Flow:

1. The user selects an investment account.
2. The system sends a message to the INVESTOR system to query the current share prices of investments for the account.

3. The system displays the current value of account investments.

4. The user indicates the investment and number of shares to sell.

5. The system sends a message to the INVESTOR system to submit the request to sell the requested shares.

In beginning the transition to design, the software designer has introduced three lifelines corresponding to the software objects required to implement the use case. These are WebInvestGUI (to handle the screen), TradeInvestmentControl (to handle the business logic), and INVESTORInterface (to handle communication with the external INVESTOR system). The diagram indicates the following:

1. The customer selects an account.

2. The user interface, WebInvestGUI, sends the message queryInvestments() to TradeInvestmentControl, the software object that handles business logic for the use case.

3. TradeInvestmentControl sends the message querySharePrice() to INVESTORInterface, the software object that interfaces with the external system INVESTOR.

4. TradeInvestmentControl sends the message displayInvestments() back to the WebInvestGUI object.

5. The customer selects the investment and #shares to sell.

6. The WebInvestGUI object sends the message sell() to the TradeInvestmentControl object.

7. The TradeInvestmentControl object sends the message submit(saleTransaction) to the INVESTORInterface object.

The BA reviews the diagram with the designer to ensure it conforms to the system use case. The designer continues by adding other lower-level software objects as required, as well as other sequence diagram elements, such as parameters and timing directives (synchronous vs. asynchronous messaging, and so on).

State-Machine (Harel Statechart) Diagram

Table 4.28 State-Machine (Harel Statechart) Diagrams at a Glance

What?	A diagram that describes the life cycle of an object, focusing on the rules that govern the way its status changes over time. Diagram is known by various names: State-Machine Diagram (UML), statechart, state diagram, and state-transition diagram or table. The BA uses state diagrams to analyze the life cycle of key business objects.[30] Each diagram covers the life cycle of one object and depicts the object's states (statuses), transitions between the states, and the events and activities that cause or result from those transitions.
When?	• **Initiation:** BA uses diagrams to model the states and transitions of key business objects involved in the processes covered by the project, for example, diagrams describing the life cycle of an Investment, Account, or Invoice. Focus is on states and transitions. A senior BA may also work with the PM in developing diagrams describing the life cycle of objects key to project and requirements management, such as RFCs (Requests for Change). • **Discovery:** BA defines activities within states and adds other detail as appropriate. • **Construction:** SA uses BA's models as input to creation of technical state-machine diagrams. • **Final V & V:** BA models are input to test design and to verify test coverage; all states, transitions, and activities in the BA model must be verified by testing.
Where?	• **BRD:** State diagrams
Why?	• Provides an overview of the life cycle of business objects across business processes and use cases. • Helps identify bottlenecks. For example, metrics can be gathered for each state (such as time spent in the state) to determine where an artifact is getting "stuck."
What to show stakeholders	States and transitions. Some internal state activities may be included if named informally using business language. Do not use less-intuitive elements such as send events or parameters.
What to show team members	Full symbol set
Standard	State-machine diagram is UML-compliant
Complementary tools	Class diagrams, system use cases, activity diagrams
Alternatives to UML	IDEF3 object schematic, IDEF3 transition schematic

[30]The UML 2 definition for the model is, "A behavior that specifies the sequence of states that an object or an interaction goes through during its life in response to events, together with its responses and actions."

State-Machine Diagram Example

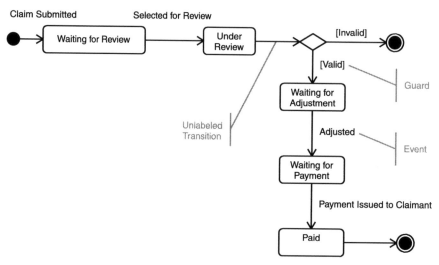

Figure 4.78 State-machine diagram: Life cycle of a claim

Notes on Figure 4.78:

Figure 4.78 illustrates the basic modeling elements of the state-machine diagram; these are the only elements to include in presentations to business stakeholders.

The diagram describes the life cycle of a claim as follows:

- When a claim is submitted to the business area, it is created with the status Waiting for Review.
- When it has been selected for review, its status changes to Under Review.
- Once the activities executed while Under Review have been completed, its status changes according to the following rules:
  - If the claim was deemed (during the review process) to be invalid, no further action is taken.
  - If the claim was deemed to be valid, its status is changed to Waiting for Adjustment.
  - It stays in that state until the claim has been adjusted, at which time its status is changed to Waiting for Payment.
  - It is held in the Waiting for Payment state until a payment has been issued to the claimant, at which time its status is changed to Paid.
  - Once any activities associated with Paid claims are complete, no further actions are taken against the claim.

Symbol Glossary: State-Machine Diagram

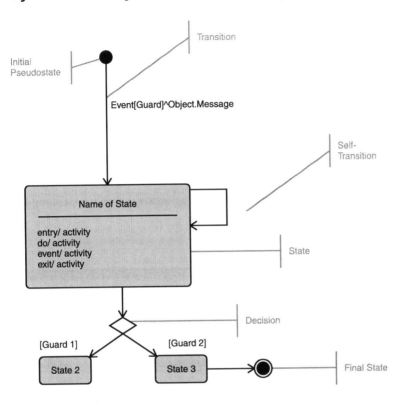

Figure 4.79
Symbol Glossary:
State-machine
diagram

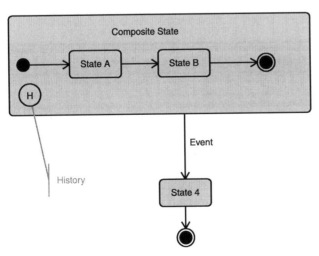

Notes on Figure 4.79:

The figure contains the following modeling elements:

- **Initial pseudostate:** (Depicted as a dot.) Indicates the beginning of the object's life cycle. (See Figure 4.80.)

Figure 4.80
Initial pseudostate

- **Final state:** (Depicted as a bull's-eye.) Indicates the final state of the object (see Figure 4.81). There may be more than one final state on the diagram. Final states may be named. There can be no transitions exiting from a final state, and it may have no internal activities (entry, do, and so on).

Figure 4.81
Final state

- **Transition:** (Depicted as an open-headed arrow.) Indicates a change of state (see Figure 4.82). May be unlabeled, indicating that the transition occurs when any internal activities associated with the previous state have been completed. May be labeled with any combination of the following:
  - **Event:** (Depicted as an unadorned label on a transition.) Indicates the trigger that fires (forces) the transition.
  - **Guard:** (Depicted as a logical expression in square brackets.) The condition must be true for the transition to occur. Unlike an event, a guard does not trigger the transition; it only indicates whether the transition is allowed.
  - **Send event:** (Indicated as ^targetObject.message.) Indicates that when the transition occurs, a message (request) is sent to a target object.

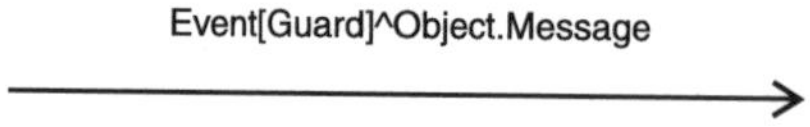

Event[Guard]^Object.Message
⟶

Figure 4.82
Transition

- **Self-transition:** (Depicted as an open-headed arrow that points back to the same state from which it exits.) A transition from and to the same state. Indicates that, under the circumstances described for the transition, an object exits and then re-enters a state. Whenever the transition occurs, the exit/ activities specified for the state are executed as the object leaves the state and any entry/ activities are executed afterwards, as the object re-enters the state. For example, in Figure 4.83, the state "entering order details" is depicted for an order. Whenever a line item is committed, if it has been confirmed (by the customer), then the exit/ activity "add line item to order" is executed, followed by the entry/ activity "display line-item form."

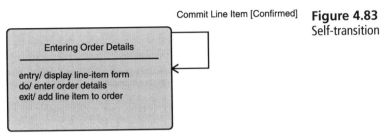

Commit Line Item [Confirmed]

Figure 4.83
Self-transition

- **Choice:** (Depicted as a diamond, with one incoming and two or more outgoing transitions; see Figure 4.84.) Indicates a point at which one of the outgoing transitions may occur, based on the guards attached to the outgoing transitions. Use is optional.[31]

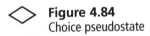

Figure 4.84
Choice pseudostate

- **State:** (Depicted as a rounded rectangle; see Figure 4.85.) Indicates a status that the object can have. Activities or send events may be specified for the state as follows:

    - **entry/ activity:** Indicates that the activity (or send event) occurs whenever the object enters the state ("entry" is a UML keyword).

    - **do/ activity:** Indicates an interruptible activity that occurs while the object is in the state ("do" is a UML keyword).

    - **event/ activity:** Indicates that whenever the specified event occurs while the object is in the state, it triggers the execution of the specified activity (or send event) while the object remains in its state. (Please note that "event" is not a UML keyword; replace it with the name of the event that triggers the response, such as "help.")

    - **exit/ activity:** Indicates that whenever the object leaves the state, the specified activity takes place.

Figure 4.85
State

---

[31]As an alternative, the guarded transitions may be depicted exiting directly from the previous state.

- **Composite state:** Indicates that an object may be in a number of substates (see Figure 4.86). Any transitions from the composite state are inherited by (apply to) the substates. (See "State-Machine Diagram: Advanced Modeling Elements" later in this chapter for more on composite states.)

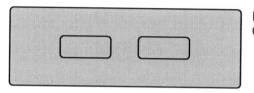

Figure 4.86
Composite state

- **History pseudostate:** (Depicted as a circle with an enclosed "H"; see Figure 4.87.) Optional modeling element that may appear within a composite state. If a transition points to the History icon, this indicates that the object returns to the substate it was in, the last time it was in the composite state. Deep history can also be specified—depicted with an H*—indicating that history goes down a level, that is, to a substate of a substate. (See "State-Machine Diagram: Advanced Modeling Elements" later in this chapter for more on history.)

Figure 4.87
History

- **Fork and Join.** (Depicted as vertical or horizontal lines; not shown in symbol glossary.) Fork and Join are used to indicate parallel transitions (see Figure 4.88). A Fork has one incoming and two or more outgoing transitions. The outgoing transitions of a Fork both occur, but they may be triggered in any order. A Join has two or more incoming transitions and one outgoing transition. All incoming transitions must occur before the outgoing transition of a Join is triggered. (See Figure 4.90 later in this chapter for an example of Fork and Join.)

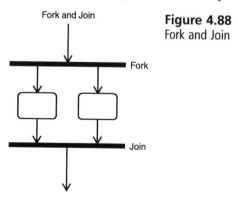

Figure 4.88
Fork and Join

State-Machine Diagram: Advanced Modeling Elements

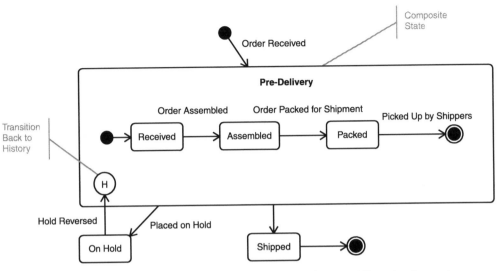

Figure 4.89 Composite Sequential (Disjoint) state-machine diagram: Life cycle of an order

Notes on Figure 4.89:

A composite state is one composed of substates. The diagram is an example of a composite state whereby an object may be in only one substate at a time. This is referred to, in the UML, as a composite *state with sequential (disjoint) substates*. The diagram describes the life cycle of an order as follows:

- When an order is received, it is goes in to a Pre-delivery state.
- Pre-delivery is a composite state that is decomposed into substates.
- The first substate is Received, where the order remains until it has been assembled.
- Once assembled, it remains in the Assembled substate until it has been packed for shipment, when its substate changes to Packed.
- The order status remains Packed until it has been picked up by shippers, at which time its status changes to Shipped.
- Once any activities associated with a Shipped order have been completed, no further action is taken with respect to the object.
- At any time while an order is in Pre-delivery, if the Order has been placed on hold, it moves out of the Pre-delivery composite state and its state changes to On Hold. It remains On Hold until the hold is reversed, at which time it goes back to History, meaning back to the Pre-delivery substate it was in earlier (before the hold was placed).

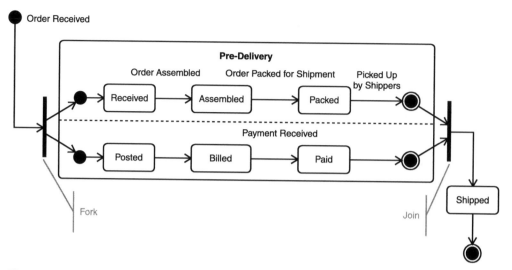

Figure 4.90 Composite Concurrent (Orthogonal) state-machine diagram: Life cycle of an order

Notes on Figure 4.90:

Figure 4.90 is an example of a composite state whereby the object can be in more than one substate at a time. This type of composite is referred to, in the UML, as a *composite state with concurrent (orthogonal) substates.*

The diagram describes the life cycle of an Order. The composite state, Pre-delivery, has two concurrent sets of substates—those in the upper and those in the lower compartment. While the order is in the composite state, Pre-delivery, it may be in a substate in the upper compartment and a substate in the lower compartment at the same time. Further, the order's progress through one compartment does not impact its progress through the other. Once the order has transitioned through to the end of *both*[32] compartments, the order transitions to the single state, Shipped.

---

[32]The requirement that transitions from both compartments be triggered is modeled with a Join, as shown in Figure 4.90.

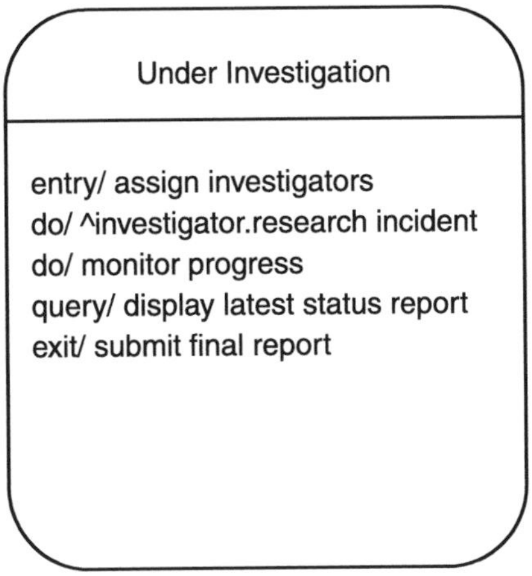

Figure 4.91
Activities of a state:
Incident Under
Investigation

Notes on Figure 4.91:

Figure 4.91 is an example of a state with activities in an Incident Management system. It describes the activities that take place while an Incident is in the Under Investigation state. It indicates the following:

- As an Incident enters into the state, the activity Assign Investigators is triggered.
- Once in the state, a message, Research Incident, is sent to an investigator. (This is an example of a send event.)
- While in this state, the activity Monitor Progress occurs.
- If, while in this state, a query event occurs, the activity Display Latest Status Report occurs.
- Whenever the Incident exits this state (regardless of the reason/event that causes this to happen), the activity Submit Final Report is triggered.

Structured Walkthroughs

Table 4.29 Structured Walkthroughs at a Glance

What?	A structured walkthrough is a meeting held to review artifacts produced at any stage of a project. The BA facilitates structured walkthroughs of requirements artifacts and may participate in walkthroughs of design artifacts.
When?	• **Initiation:** Review To-Be business process models, such as end-to-end business process workflows and high-level IT requirements produced during this phase, such as system use-case diagrams and Role Maps. • **Discovery:** Review BA artifacts, such as S(L)Rs, detailed user requirements (system use cases), and static business model (ERDs or class diagram). • **Construction:** In each iteration, review design models to verify compliance with requirements. For example, verify that sequence diagrams and GUI screens comply with system use cases.
Where?	• Plans for structured walkthroughs should appear in Requirements Work Plan.
Why?	• Uncover errors early when they are relatively easy to fix.
What to show stakeholders	Distribute changed artifacts and meeting agenda before the meeting.
What to show team members	Distribute changed artifacts and meeting agenda before the meeting.
Standard	N/A
Refer to:	Please see "Review Meeting (Structured Walkthrough and Gate Review)" in the Meeting Guide for lists of questions, input documents, etc.

System Use Cases (and Diagrams)

Table 4.30 System Use Cases at a Glance

What?	• A way that the software will be used by an actor. (An actor is an external entity that uses the IT system under discussion.) • A user task: The task must be complete from the user's point of view[33] and yield a result of value to the user. (The term user, in this context, refers to any entity that uses the system and may be human or an external IT system; it is equivalent to the term actor.) May be of any size[34] but typically represents a unit of work accomplished in one IT session by a single initiating (primary) actor. Consists of sequences of interactions between an initiating (primary) actor and an IT system, covering normal and alternative pathways for carrying out the task. May also contain interactions that the IT system initiates with other (secondary) actors. A related term, *scenario*, refers to a specific sequence of actions that illustrates behaviors.[35] A scenario may be used to illustrate one way the actor-system interaction may play out over the course of a system use case. The use-case approach is user-centric: BAs take their cue from users in defining what their tasks are; the system use-case description focuses on the user's experience of the interaction. System use-case analysis involves a number of components[36]: • System use-case modeling element. • System use-case diagram, indicating which actors are associated with which system use cases.[37] • System use-case brief—a short paragraph describing the use case, mentioning only significant activities and failures.[38] • System use-case description (referred to in RUP as *system use-case specification*), describing the various ways that the interaction may play out. Best practice is to use a text narrative that describes a normal interaction (often called a Basic or Normal Flow) as well as alternative pathways through the use case, such as optional flows, errors, and cancellations. If the pathways connect to each other in complex ways, the text should be augmented with an activity diagram. • System use-case realization (for which the BA is not responsible) that represents the technical implementation of the interaction.
When?	• **Initiation:** BA identifies the system use cases required to support the new or changed business use cases (end-to-end business processes) impacted by the project. BA creates system use-case diagrams and system use-case briefs. • **Discovery:** BA develops system use-case descriptions; works with PM to assign system use-case flows to iterations. • **Construction:** In each iteration, BA completes system use-case descriptions for assigned system use-case flows and oversees their implementation and testing. The software designer uses system use cases as input to the design of interfaces and software units, for example, creating sequence diagrams for use-case scenarios as part of the design of software classes and their operations. • **Final V & V:** System use cases are input to design of user acceptance tests.
Where?	• **BRD:** IT Services/User requirements

(continued)

Why?	• State-of-the-art approach to eliciting and documenting user requirements. • User-centric: results in software more likely to match user's expectations. • Narrative style is easy to verify with stakeholders. • Documentation style lends itself well to test design. • Well-suited to objectives of iterative-incremental development: Each iteration implements a subset of system use-case flows, adding an increment of value from the point of view of stakeholders.
What to show stakeholders	System use-case diagrams using basic symbol set; do not show include or extend relationships.
What to show team members	Full symbol set
Standard	The term *system use case* is not part of the UML. The UML refers only to *use case* and defines it as an interaction with a system. Extensions to the UML distinguish between interactions with an IT system (system use case) and interactions with a business (business use cases).[39]
Complementary tools	Business use cases, activity diagrams, class diagrams, sequence diagrams
Alternatives	User requirements using other formats.

[33]Refer to *Applying Use Cases: A Practical Guide, 2ⁿᵈ Edition* by Geri Schneider and Jason Winters (Addison-Wesley Professional, 2001), p. 14: "A use case should be a complete task from a user's point of view."

[34]Refer to *UML Distilled: Applying the Standard Object Modeling Language* by Martin Fowler (Addison-Wesley, 1997), p. 43: "A use case may be small or large." Cockburn also discusses different sizes of use cases. In practice, system use cases, unless otherwise qualified, are sized so that they occur in a single session. These correspond to Cockburn's "sea-level" use cases. Higher-level system use cases may also be defined, as a container for end-to-end interactions. Lower-level system use cases that encompass a subset of the interactions in a session may be modeled using *included use cases.*

[35]Refer to UML 2.0 Infrastructure Specification, OMG, 2004, p. 16.

[36]Not all components are used on every project or in every methodology that employs use-case analysis.

[37]A system use-case diagram may also indicate relationships between use cases and relationships between actors.

[38]For more on use-case briefs, see *Writing Effective Use Cases* by Alistair Cockburn (Addison-Wesley Professional, 2000), pp. 37–38.

[39]In practice, the term *use case* is often used to denote an interaction with an IT system. To avoid confusion, this handbook uses the term *system use case* to denote an interaction with an IT system and *use case* to denote an interaction with any system.

Don't be dogmatic with stakeholders about use-case terminology. The value of the use-case approach lies not in its terminology (which is not particularly elegant or intuitive) but in how it breaks up and documents requirements from the user's perspective.

Key System Use-Case Terms

Actor

A role that a user or any other system plays when interacting with the system under consideration. It is a type of entity that interacts, but which is itself external to the subject. Actors may represent human users, external hardware, or other subjects. An actor does not necessarily represent a specific physical entity. For instance, a single physical entity may play the role of several different actors and, conversely, a given actor may be played by multiple physical entities. [UML 2]

Use case

The specification of a sequence of actions, including variants, that a system (or other entity) can perform, interacting with actors of the system. [UML 2]

Rule of Thumb: A system use case represents a unit of work that one actor performs during a single session with the IT system.

System Use-Case Diagram Example

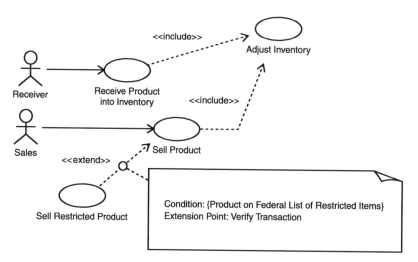

Figure 4.92
System use-case diagram: Receive and sell products

Notes on Figure 4.92:

Figure 4.92 is an example of a system use-case diagram showing some of the use cases required to support the selling and receiving of products. It describes the following requirements:

- Receiver and Sales are user roles, modeled as actors (stick figures).
- A Receiver triggers the system use case, Receive Product into Inventory. (For example, the Receiver might select the option to receive from a menu or toolbar.)
- The system use-case description for Receive Product into Inventory includes a reference to a separate (included) use-case, Adjust Inventory.
- Sales triggers the system use case Sell Product. Its description also includes a reference to Adjust Inventory.
- Adjust Inventory is an example of an included use case. It contains common steps and flows included in (inserted into) other use cases.
- The workflow for Sell Product changes if the product is on a federal list of restricted items. The changes occur at a location within Sell Product, labeled Verify Transaction. This location is referred to as an *extension point*.
- Changes to the flow are documented in the extending use case Sell Restricted Product.
- Sell Restricted Product contains only the steps and flows that are inserted into the Sell Product use case when the condition attached to the extend relationship is true. In this example, the product must be on a federal list of restricted items for the extension to be triggered.

Symbol Glossary: System Use-Case Diagram

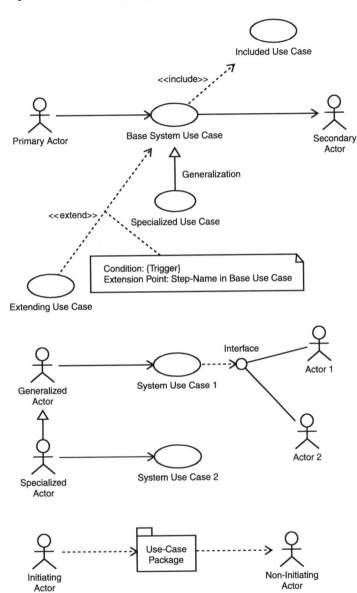

Figure 4.93
Symbol Glossary:
System use-case
diagram

Notes on Figure 4.93:

The figure contains the following modeling elements:

- **Primary actor:** (Depicted as a stick figure with an arrow pointing from actor to use case.)[40] The primary actor is the user role or external system that triggers (initiates) the use case. (See Figure 4.94.)The line (or arrow) between an actor and a use case is referred to as a communication association.

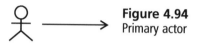

Figure 4.94
Primary actor

- **Secondary actor:** (Depicted as a stick figure with an arrow pointing from use case to actor; see Figure 4.95.) The system initiates the interaction with the actor.

Figure 4.95
Secondary actor

- **System use case:** (Depicted as an oval; see Figure 4.96.) A complete user task. A task may be any size, but the rule of thumb is a goal attained by one initiating user in one IT session.

Figure 4.96
System use case

- **Include:** (Depicted as a dashed line with an arrow pointing from the base [including] system use case to the included use case. The line is labeled with the stereotype notation <<include>>; see Figure 4.97.) Use when two or more system use cases share a set of steps and/or flows. Remove the common flows from the original use cases. Place the common steps in an included use case. Refer to the included wherever the common steps have been extracted from the original use cases.

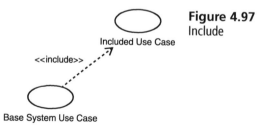

Figure 4.97
Include

Included Use Case

<<include>>

Base System Use Case

---

[40]UML practitioners vary on whether or not they use arrows between actors and use cases. If your standards do not allow arrows, specify within the system use-case documentation whether the actor is acting as a primary or secondary actor and/or add a note on the diagram.

■ **Extend:** (Depicted as a dashed line with an arrow pointing from the extending use case to the base use case. The line is labeled with the stereotype notation <<extend>>. A note may be added as shown, indicating a triggering condition and extension points; see Figure 4.98.)

Use an extending use case to add alternate flows to a use case without altering the original use case. The added flows must all be triggered by the same condition. The base use case is the original use case. The extending use case contains the added flows. The extension points are the locations within the base use case where the flows are triggered. The condition is the condition that triggers the flows in the extending use case. The condition is evaluated once—the first time an extension point is reached in the base use case. If the condition was found to be true at that point, it triggers the extending use case at all subsequent extension points.

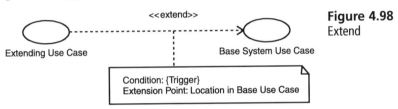

Figure 4.98
Extend

■ **Generalization between actors:** (Depicted as a triangular-headed arrow pointing from a specialized actor to a generalized actor; see Figure 4.99.) A *generalized actor* is an actor with subtypes, referred to as *specialized actors*, for example, the generalized actor, Finance, with two subtypes (specialized actors), Accounts Receivable and Accounts Payable. A specialized actor inherits all the communication associations that its generalized actor has to use cases. The specialized actor may have additional associations to use cases (not shared by the generalized actor). In the symbol glossary, Specialized Actor has an inherited association to Use Case 1 and an explicit one to Use Case 2.

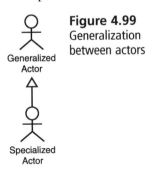

Figure 4.99
Generalization
between actors

- **Generalization between use cases:** (Depicted as a triangular-headed arrow pointing from a *specialized use case* to a generalized use case; see Figure 4.100.) This feature is not widely used, but has some advocates.[41] A *generalized use case* is a use case with subtypes, referred to as *specialized use cases,* for example, the generalized use case, Pay Bill, with two subtypes, Pay Bill Using ATM and Pay Bill Using Web. The generalized use case may be used to capture common workflow patterns, while the specialized use case may override these with workflows specific to the (specialized) use case.

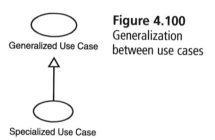

Figure 4.100
Generalization
between use cases

- **Interface:** (Depicted as a circle; see Figure 4.101.) A set of operations that actors that conform to the interface must support. Add interfaces to models in order to make it easier to interchange actors (for example, external IT systems).[42]

○   **Figure 4.101**
Interface

- **Use-case package:** (Depicted as a folder; see Figure 4.102.) Indicates a set of use-case modeling elements. Use-case packages are used in order to organize system use cases, for example, by the business use case that they support. You may also create an overview of the actors that participate in each set of use cases by drawing high-level use-case diagrams, depicting actors connected to use-case packages with a dependency (dashed arrow) as shown at the bottom of Figure 4.93. A dependency pointing from an actor to the package indicates that the actor initiates use cases in the package. An arrow pointing in the other direction indicates that the system initiates the interaction.

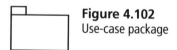

Figure 4.102
Use-case package

---

[41]Refer to *Applying Use Cases: A Practical Guide* by Schneider and Winters, p. 58 and to *UML for the IT Business Analyst* by Howard Podeswa (Thomson Course Technology, 2005), pp. 141–144.

[42]An *interface* in this context is essentially a generalized actor class, with operations but no methods.

Use-Case Analysis

Table 4.31 Use-Case Analysis at a Glance

What?	A use of the system; a type of interaction between an actor and the system under discussion that yields a result of value to the initiating actor. The system may be of any type (business or IT). (See the sections "Business Use Case" and "System Use Cases" in this chapter for notes specific to use cases for business and IT systems, respectively.) A related term, *scenario*, refers to a specific sequence of actions that illustrates behaviors.[43] A scenario may be used to illustrate one way the actor-system interaction may play out over the course of a use case. The main points of the approach are to maintain a user perspective—both in the segmentation or activities into meaningful user goals and in the description of a user's interaction with the system over the course of each task. The use-case approach impacts terminology, diagramming standards, and requirements-elicitation and documentation styles. Use-case analysis involves a number of components[44]: • Use-case modeling element. • Use-case diagram, indicating which actors are associated with which use cases.[45] • Use-case brief—a short paragraph describing the use case, mentioning only significant activities and failures.[46] • Use-case description (referred to in RUP as a use-case specification), describing the various ways that the interaction may play out. • Use-case realization that represents the implementation of the interaction, including activities internal to the system. The BA uses the use-case approach over the course of a project to model business processes and IT user requirements. If the project is being developed incrementally (over a number of iterations), the BA also works with the PM to assign use cases (or flows within them) to iterations of the project.
When?	• **Initiation:** BA identifies end-to-end business processes and services and models them as business use cases. BA identifies system use cases required to support each business use case. Selected system use cases or flows may be implemented, (e.g., proof of concepts for high-risk technology). • **Discovery:** BA elaborates system use cases. Selected system use cases or flows may be implemented. BA works with PM to assign system use-case flows to iterations. • **Construction:** Remaining system use cases are elaborated and implemented incrementally.
Where?	• **BRD:** Business Services and Processes (business use cases) • **BRD:** IT Services/User requirements (system use cases)
Why?	• Enables a consistent approach across the life cycle. The same approach is used to model business and IT service requirements; the same terminology, documentation formats and tools can be used for both. • Consumer-centric: results in process requirements more likely to match the expectations of the consumer of the service. • Narrative style is easy to verify with stakeholders. • Documentation style lends itself well to test design. • Well-suited to objectives of iterative-incremental development: Each iteration implements a subset of use-case scenarios, adding an increment of value from the point of view of stakeholders.

(continued)

What to show stakeholders	See business use cases and system use cases for details.
What to show team members	See business use cases and system use cases for details.
Standard	UML
Refer to:	Business use cases, system use cases, Role Map

[43]Refer to UML 2.0 Infrastructure Specification, OMG, 2004, p. 16.

[44]Not all components are used on every project or in every methodology that employs use-case analysis.

[45]A system use-case diagram may also indicate relationships between use cases and relationships between actors.

[46]For more on use-case briefs, see *Writing Effective Use Cases* by Alistair Cockburn, pp. 37–38.

Key Points about Use Cases

- Both business and system use cases are interactions with an entity that achieve a goal for the initiator.

- In *all* (business and system) use cases, only the interaction is described. Design details ("the how") are not included as part of the use-case proper. (These are included, however, in a *use-case realization*.)

- The *entity* that the actor interacts with may vary:

  - In a business use case, the entity is the real-world business.

  - In a system use case, the entity is the IT system under discussion.

Use-Case Goal Levels

The *goal level* of a use case may vary:

- In a high-level ("kite-level"[47]) use case, a large goal is achieved through an end-to-end process.

- In a low-level ("sea-level") use case, a smaller goal is achieved through a single interaction.

---

[47]The terms *kite-level* and *sea-level* were introduced by Alistair Cockburn in *Writing Effective Use Cases*. Cockburn's "below sea-level" use cases have not been included in this discussion. (The "below sea-level" designation, if used, applies to included use cases.)

Both business and system use cases may be low- and high-level. As a rule of thumb, when the level is not specified:

- A business use case is high-level and represents an end-to-end business process.
- A system use case is low-level and represents one initiating user in one session on an IT system.

These levels are summarized in Table 4.32, where **bolded** definitions represent the common usage of the term when the level is not specified.

Table 4.32 Overview of Use-Case Levels and Types

Level	Business Use Case	System Use Case
High-level	**End-to-end business process. Focuses on real world environment, not IT systems.** **Other terms: business service, end-to-end business process**	End-to-end IT process. May be cross-functional (many user roles) and cross a number of IT systems.
Low-level	Small business process; a useful unit of work that a business actor or worker may perform, typically as part of an end-to-end process. Other terms: business activity	**Unit of work accomplished in one IT session by a single initiating (primary) actor.** **Other terms: user task, user goal, IT service**

Use-Case Analysis for Different Objectives

To improve an existing business process supported by IT services, see Figure 4.103.

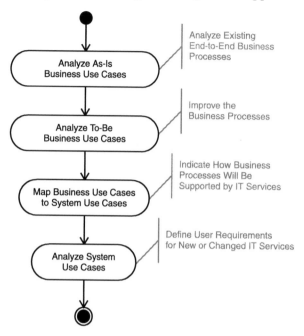

Figure 4.103
Improve existing business process supported by IT

To add a new business service with an IT component, see Figure 4.104.

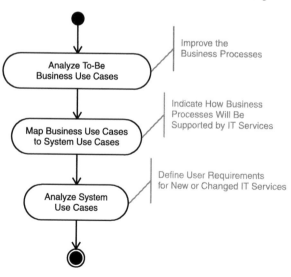

Figure 4.104
Add new business service with IT component

To make a small change to IT services, see Figure 4.105.

Figure 4.105
Minor change to IT Services

To improve an existing business service with no IT component, see Figure 4.106.

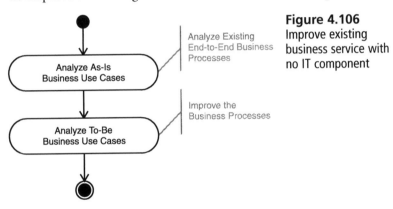

Figure 4.106
Improve existing business service with no IT component

To add a new, outsourced IT service, see Figure 4.107.

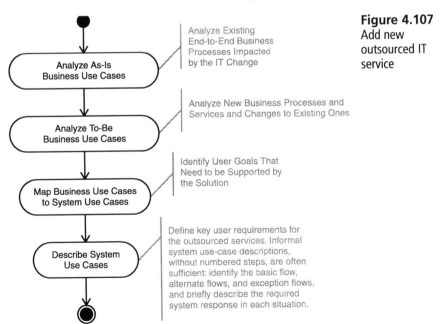

Figure 4.107
Add new outsourced IT service

To outsource IT services currently provided in-house where little documentation exists, see Figure 4.108.

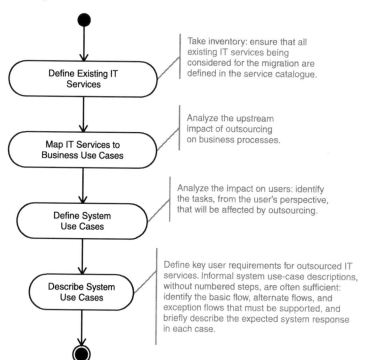

Figure 4.108
Outsource IT services currently provided in-house, where little documentation exists

Interviewing Users about Use Cases:
1. Discuss one scenario at a time.
2. Begin with the basic flow.
3. Whenever the stakeholder says "if," note it for future reference but veer the discussion back to the basic flow

Use-Case Writing Guidelines

The following guidelines (adapted from Alistair Cockburn) apply to both business and system use-case descriptions. Terminology should be adjusted accordingly. When documenting a system use case, refer to the user and the system. When documenting a business use case, refer to the consumer of the business service,[48] and the business they are interacting with.

1. Tell a story: Write sentences that describe the unfolding narrative of the user's (or customer's) interaction with the system (or business).

2. Use a simple subject-verb-object sentence structure. User (customer) does . . . . System (business) does . . . .

3. Use a consistent tense (present or future tense).

4. Each step should contain one testable, traceable requirement.

5. Keep the number of steps in a flow small (maximum 9 to 25 steps).

6. Avoid the word "if." Use alternate and exception flows instead.

7. Handle validations by writing, in the basic flow, "The system (business) validates (or verifies) that . . . ." Describe what happens when the validation fails in the alternate or exception flows.

8. Merge data fields and use the merged data name in the use case. For example, merge the fields Name, Address, Phone Number into the merged field Contact Information. Describe merged fields elsewhere (such as in the data dictionary or the static model).

9. Describe only the workflow for the interaction; do not include design directives. (These should be documented elsewhere and linked to the use case.) For example, do not refer to drop-down boxes or radio buttons, as these indicate specific design solutions.

10. Document the timing of each step in a clear and consistent manner. For example
    - One step follows the other:
        - User provides contact information.
        - System validates user input.
    - A group of steps can be triggered in any sequence:
        - Steps 20 through 30 can happen in any order.
    - Optional steps:
        - Describe optional steps in the Alternate Flow section.

---

[48] A business use-case realization (which describes internal workflow) refers to internal workers as well as external business actors.

11. Establish a standard for documenting repetitive steps, for example:

   1. User selects payee.

   2. System displays accounts and balances.

   3. User selects account and provides payment amount.

   4. System validates that funds are available.

   (User repeats steps 1 through 4 until indicating end of session.)

12. Standardize triggers to external systems, for example, for a synchronous message to an external system:

   ▪ The System queries the share value from ValuTrade and waits for a response.

   For a non-synchronous message:

   ▪ The System submits the Trade to ValuTrade and does not wait for a response.

13. Number (or label) the requirements.

14. Avoid the word "it." "It" is ambiguous. For example, in the step "The system verifies it," what exactly is to be verified?

Mapping from Business to System Use Case:
   ▪ Determine which activities within the business use cases will be IT-assisted.
   ▪ Group activities into units of work that represent a goal or task that one user would accomplish in a single IT session.
   ▪ Model each task as a system use case.

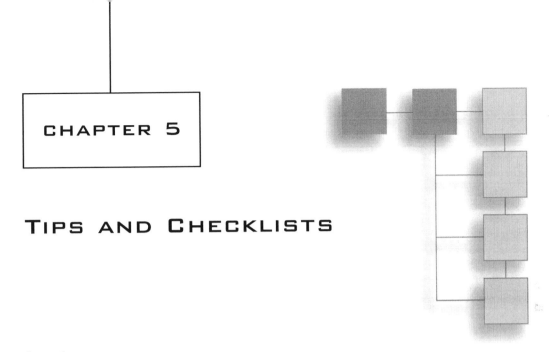

CHAPTER 5

Tips and Checklists

This chapter contains tips and checklists useful to the BA in carrying out his or her duties over the course of a project.

Checklist: Requirements Investigation Methods

- Brainstorming sessions
- Focus groups: All participants perform the same role
- Cross-functional groups: All business functions involved in an end-to-end process
- Job shadowing
- One-on-one interviews
- Research of existing artifacts
- Prototyping
- Wiki (A tool that can be used to allow stakeholders and team members to collaboratively contribute to the requirements)
- Surveys

Tip: What to Do When Key Participants Can't or Don't Show

- Substitute the participant: Ask if there are representatives available to act on behalf of those missing from the meeting.
- Redefine the scope and goals of the meeting so that they are attainable with only those present.

- Investigate whether missing stakeholders can participate remotely through Web meetings, teleconferencing, and so on.

- Hold meeting as planned: Follow up after with missing stakeholders.

- Consider an alternative investigation method. (For a list of alternatives, refer to the "Checklist: Requirements Investigation Methods" section in this chapter.)

- Consider escalating to sponsors if non-participation is an ongoing problem.

Checklists: Change Advisory Board

The Change Advisory Board (CAB) meets regularly to evaluate and prioritize changes. The BA should be included in the CAB, or advise the CAB, in order to ensure that stakeholder needs are properly communicated to solution providers.

The CAB is most commonly chaired by the Change Manager, includes representatives of business stakeholders and solution providers as required, and will likely include the Problem Manager, Service Level Manager, and Customer Relations staff, at least as part-time participants. The composition of the CAB is not static, but will vary greatly based on the changes being considered. (For more on the Change Manager, Problem Manager, and other participants listed here, refer to the subsection "Contribution to Meeting by Role and Stakeholder Type" of the section "Planning for the Meeting" in the Meeting Guide chapter.)

Emergency changes may be dealt with by a smaller body, referred to as the ECAB (Emergency Change Advisory Board). The Change Management process should indicate under what circumstances a change is to be handled by the ECAB and provide guidance regarding its composition and procedures.

Checklist of Potential CAB Members

Use the following ITIL checklist when deciding who to include in the CAB[1]:

- Customers
- Customer Relations staff
- User Managers
- User group representatives
- Application developers
- System administrators
- Application maintenance
- SMEs

---

[1]Foundations of IT Service Management Based on ITIL V3, p. 233, and ITIL V3 Core Book: Service Transition, OMG, 2007, p. 58.

- Test Management representatives
- IT Service Continuity Management (ITSCM) representatives
- Security Management representatives
- Capacity Management representatives
- Service Desk representatives
- Other services and operations staff
- Logistics staff for changes that require changes to (or are a result of a change to) facilities or office services
- Contractors and third parties for outsourced solutions
- Problem Manager
- Service Level Manager
- Other parties specific to the change (marketing, legal, etc.)

CAB: Standard Items for Review

ITIL V3 recommends the following as standard items for review by the CAB[2]:

- Unauthorized changes detected through Configuration Management
- Review of changes made without reference to the CAB (such as those applied by incident management and problem management)
- RFCs to be reviewed by CAB members
- Ongoing, outstanding, and closed changes
- Assessment of implemented changes
- Scheduling of changes
- Change Management process
- Any changes, made or proposed, to the Change Management process
- Review of business costs and benefits of the Change Management process

Tip: ITIL Seven Rs of Change Management

Use the Seven Rs[3] of Change Management when assessing a change:

- **Raised**: Who submitted the change?
- **Reason**: What is the reason for a change?

---

[2]Foundations of IT Service Management Based on ITIL V3, p. 234 and ITIL V3 Core Book: Service Transition, OMG, 2007 p. 59.

[3]Foundations of IT Service Management Based on ITIL V3, p. 236.

- **Return**: What is the result of the change?
- **Risk**: What are the risks associated with the change (positive and negative)?
- **Resources**: What resources does it require?
- **Responsible**: Who is responsible for the change (requirements analysis, construction, testing, and transition into production)?
- **Relationship**: What relationships does this change have with other changes?

Tips: Five Keys to Requirements Management[4]

The following tips apply to projects using iterative-incremental and waterfall approaches. For agile projects, the following modifications to the tips apply: Less emphasis is placed on written documentation, and the requirements (if they exist) often are not baselined and may be changed at any time without undergoing a Change Management process, as long as they are not being implemented.

1. **Write the requirements down**: Use templates to ensure consistent requirements documentation and to institutionalize best practices.
2. **Use requirements attributes**: (See "Requirements Attributes Table" in the BA Toolkit chapter for examples of attributes.)
3. **Use traceability matrices**: Map requirements to other artifacts and configuration items so that the upstream and downstream impact can be determined.
4. **Practice requirements management**: Establish a strategy and plan for managing requirements.
5. **Baseline the requirements (non-agile projects)**: Take copies of the requirements, such as the Vision Document and user requirements (system use cases) at specific points in time so that it is easy to determine whether a requirement is new or was previously introduced.

Tips: Planning Iterations

- Keep the schedule of an iteration fixed.
- Manage the scope of the iteration to meet that schedule.
- Rule of thumb for number of iterations on a RUP project: six to eight iterations.
- Rule of thumb for iteration length: two to six weeks long.
- Early iterations are more likely to be requirements and architecture focused, while later iterations will be more focused on scope completion.

---

[4]Thanks to Chris Reynolds for these tips.

Tips: SMART Requirements

Requirements must be as follows:

- SMART[5]
  - **S**: Specific
  - **M**: Measurable (verifiable)
  - **A**: Achievable/Appropriate
  - **R**: Realistic/Relevant
  - **T**: Timely/Time-bound
- Unambiguous
- Complete
- Correct
- Consistent

Checklist: Features

The features are the key elements that stakeholders need to see in the solution. A feature may be a high-level or important functional requirement, or a non-functional requirement, such as performance. Use the following checklist to review your list of features:

- Not too many features (25–99)
- Design issues have been excluded
- Features are mapped to business and IT services (or use cases)
- High-level and key functional requirements included
- Key performance requirements addressed
- Key usability requirements addressed
- Key robustness requirements addressed
- Key fault-tolerance requirements addressed
- Key volume and scalability requirements addressed

Tip: Naming a Process

Following are tips and a list of suggested names to use when identifying processes on DFDs, activity diagrams, functional decomposition charts, and so on:

- The name should consist of a verb phrase followed by a noun phrase, for example, *validate insurance coverage.*
- Use a verb phrase with a single verb, such as *adjudicate.*

---

[5]Foundations of IT Service Management Based on ITIL V3, p. 81.

- Avoid weak verbs, like *process* (unless the process is so broad that there is no better name for it).

- The verb phrase should highlight the goal of the process, rather than the method used to carry it out. For example, *determine* is better than *calculate* or *look up*.

- The name should end with a noun phrase that relates to the object that the verb is acting on, for example, determine *tax bracket*.

Suggested verbs for process names:

- acquire
- add
- adjudicate
- assess
- calculate
- cancel
- change
- check
- conduct
- control
- create
- delete

- determine
- identify
- maintain
- manage
- merge
- modify
- obtain
- plan
- query
- record
- receive
- request

- remove
- report
- reject
- review
- roll back
- select
- specify
- submit
- update
- validate
- verify

Tips: How to Spot the Static Modeling Elements from the System Use-Case Model

1. **Look for nouns:** These are often classes or attributes, for example, *Responsibility Center*.

2. **Look for verbs:** These often indicate an association. For example, The user *assigns* a Client to a Responsibility Center.

3. **Look for actors:** If the business tracks them, they are classes, for example, *Supplier*.

4. **Look for interactions between an actor and a system use case:** If the business tracks (saves) the interaction, these may indicate associations, for example, the interaction indicated by a communicates association between a *Customer Service Representative* actor and the system use case (*log a complaint*).

5. **Look for alternate flow triggers:** These may indicate multiplicity rules. For example, the alternate flow trigger "Ticket already issued for booking" (if treated as an error) indicates that each booking may have a maximum of one ticket issued against it.

Tips: Determining How Much Static Modeling to Do

1. Don't do the static model just in order to produce more documentation; do it where there is a value in doing it.

2. For most projects, you'll need to model the main business classes, relationships, and multiplicities.

3. Model attributes if there are rules related to them that are at risk of being missed in the solution.

4. The broader the rule is applied, the more important it is to model it. For example, if a verification rule about an attribute applies only to one use case, do not include it in the static model; if it applies across many use cases, then include it.

Tips: Managing Risk

Characterize and evaluate each risk's impact, likelihood, level, type, and risk-management strategy. Tips for determining risk levels based on likelihood and impact and for managing risks are provided in the following subsections. For a Risk Analysis Table Template, please refer to the Templates chapter of this handbook.

Tip: Risk Assessment Matrix

At the beginning of the project, and periodically as the project progresses, the BA supports the PM in analyzing risk. (See the "Analyze Risk" section of the Meeting Guide chapter for more on the BA contribution to risk analysis.)

There are a number of schemes for evaluating risk. A risk assessment matrix is often used. For example, Table 5.1 assigns a risk level based on its impact on the business and its likelihood of occurrence.

Table 5.1 Sample Risk Assessment Matrix[6]

Impact	High	High	Low	Low
Likelihood	High	Low	High	Low
Level	1	2	3	4

[6]Foundations of IT Service Management Based on ITIL V3, p. 235.

Checklist: Risk Types

The BA supports the PM in identification and analysis of risks related to the elicitation, analysis, and documentation of requirements. Project, product, and process risks related to the requirements include the following:

- **Time (Project risk)**: Risk that there will not be enough time to complete the requirements.
- **New techniques (Requirements/Process risk)**: Examples include a first-time adoption of the use-case approach, iterative development, or new standards, such as the UML.
- **New IT Service offering (Product risk)**: With first-time offerings in the marketplace, users and stakeholders may not really know what they want until they begin to use it.
- **Access to stakeholders and users**: Risk that stakeholders may not be available as needed for requirements elicitation and feedback.
- **Validation (Requirements/Process risk[7])**: Risk that requirements documentation will not represent the expectations of the customer.
- **Verification (Requirements/Process risk)**: Risk that the requirements documentation will not be able to be used effectively by solution providers and testers.
- **Requirements management (Requirements/Process risk)**: Risk of problems and difficulties managing requirements, such as a geographically diverse project team and user population or new requirements-management tools.

Checklist: ITIL Risk Types

ITIL recognizes the following risk types related to a change.[8]

- **Contract risk**: Risk that problems with a service provider will make it impossible for the organization to fulfill its contractual obligations with its customers.
- **Design risk**: Risk that the design will achieve undesirable results, such as poor performance.
- **Operational risk**: Risk of operational problems resulting from the change—either in business or IT operations.
- **Market risk**: Risk that the change will not meet the demands of the market, for example, because of an increase in supply or a decrease in demand for the impacted services.

---

[7]This and other risks indicated as Requirements/Process risks may be thought of as either requirements or process risks (or requirements-process risks) because they deal with the risks associated with the process used to gather, verify, document, and manage requirements.

[8]Foundations of IT Service Management Based on ITIL V3, p. 66.

Checklist: Other Risks the BA Should Be Aware Of

- **Technological risk**: New technology issues that could affect the project.
- **Skills risk**: Risk of not getting staff with the required expertise for the project.
- **Cancellation risk**: Business implications if the project is cancelled.
- **Quality risk**: Risk to the quality of product
- **Security risk**: Vulnerability to an attack resulting in danger or loss.

Risk-Management Strategies

Each risk should have an associated plan for managing it. Your plan should consider the following strategies:

- **Avoid**: Prevent the risk from happening. Possible avoidance plans include changing the scope and replanning the project.
- **Transfer**: Transfer the responsibility for dealing with the risk to another entity.
- **Accept**: Accept the risk.
- **Mitigate**: Take action to reduce the impact. Mitigation plans may be proactive or retroactive—such a contingency plan ("Plan B").

Tips: Quality Assurance (QA)

Tip: Testing Throughout the Life Cycle with the Service V-Model

Use Figure 5.1, the Service V-model,[9] to plan quality assurance (QA) activities throughout the life cycle. On iterative projects (agile approaches, RUP, etc.), the model depicts one iteration within the life cycle; on waterfall projects, it depicts the complete life cycle. In test-driven development (TDD), an iterative approach, test cases covering an iteration's requirements should be written before coding begins, as they form the basis for initial coding.

The Service V-model provides guidance on the validation and verification of deliverables. To *validate* a deliverable of an activity means to check whether the output of the activity properly reflects the input to the activity; to *verify* the output of an activity is to check whether it can be effectively used by its intended users as input to subsequent activities.

Development of a service proceeds down the activities listed on the left side of the "V," beginning with a definition of requirements and ending with the design and construction of the service—or the component of the service scheduled for that iteration.

---

[9]ITIL V3 Core Book: Service Transition, p. 92.

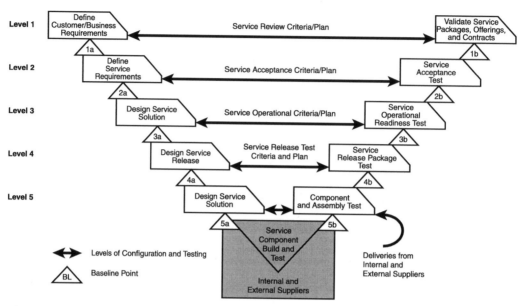

Figure 5.1 Service V-model

At each step:

- The output of the activity is validated against the input provided by previous activities, listed above the step.

- The output of the activity is verified by those who require it as input to the steps below it.

- The output is verified by those involved in the corresponding testing activity listed across it, on the right-hand side of the V.

The BA is most involved in the validation and verification of the requirements. For example, in Level 2, the BA should ensure that Service Requirements produced by the activity are validated against the high-level Customer and Business Requirements from the level above (Level 1), that the Service Requirements are verified by the designers to confirm that they are of a sufficient quality to be used effectively as input to the activity on the level below (Level 3, Design Service Solution), and that the Service Requirements are verified across the level (Level 2) by those responsible for planning and managing the Service Acceptance Test (to ensure the requirements are testable).

Once the system has been built (at the bottom of the V), the initiative continues with testing activities up the right-hand side. Each testing step along the right involves those responsible for the corresponding activity on the left-hand side. For example, in Level 2, customers who have signed off on the Service Requirements also sign off on the Service Acceptance Test with the involvement of the BA—the role responsible for preparing those requirements.

Checklist: Test Types

Use the checklist in Table 5.2 when reviewing test plans to ensure that all types of tests have been considered.[10] Each type of test determines whether or not the solution is acceptable from the perspective of the stakeholders identified in the last column.

Table 5.2 Test Checklist by Type

Test Type	Also Known As	Description	Perspective
Service Specification testing	"Fit for purpose" testing, functional testing, black-box testing	Verifies whether the solution does what the client expects it to do.	☐ Suppliers (external or internal organization that provide solution) ☐ Users ☐ Client
Service Level testing	Non-functional tests, system tests	Verifies whether the solution meets specified service levels.	☐ Service Level Managers ☐ Operation managers ☐ Client
Service Guarantee testing	"Fit for use" testing, non-functional tests, system tests	Verifies availability, capacity, continuity, and security.	☐ Client
Usability testing	User-friendliness	Verifies user-friendliness and compliance with accessibility requirements.	☐ End users ☐ Managers

(continued)

---

[10]Foundations of IT Service Management Based on ITIL V3, p. 260.

Test Type	Also Known As	Description	Perspective
Contract and Regulation testing		Tests supplier compliance with contracts, standards, and regulations.	☐ Suppliers
Service Management testing		Verifies that standards and best practices on service management are being followed.	☐ Suppliers
Operational testing	Non-functional tests, system tests	Verifies that the system meets operational requirements (includes stress tests, load tests, and security tests).	☐ System ☐ Services
Regression testing		Verifies that aspects of the system that were supposed to remain unchanged still function as before, by repeating earlier tests and comparing results.	☐ System ☐ Services ☐ Client
Production Verification testing	Production Validation Testing (PVT)	Testing done in the production environment to verify the satisfactory operation of the implemented solution.[11]	☐ System ☐ Services ☐ Client

[11]Definition formulated by Chris Reynolds.

Tips: Structured Testing Guidelines

Use the following guidelines when developing and evaluating the QA plan:

1. There are two schools of thought with respect to the role of testing. In test-driven development, where tests are used to accurately confirm expected behaviour, a tester's goal is to verify that requirements are implemented correctly. In traditional testing,[12] where tests are used to raise the quality or reliability of the product, a tester's objective is to locate errors.

---

[12]Refer to a classic text in this area, *The Art of Software Testing* by Glenford Myers (John Wiley, 1979), p. 5.

2. Focus on locating the maximum number of errors in the available time.
   - Except for minor changes, it is practically impossible to do enough testing to guarantee a 100% error-detection rate.[13] Efforts, therefore, should focus on a test plan that maximizes errors found with the available time and resources.

3. Clearly define the expected results of each test so that test results are easy to analyze.

4. The more removed the test designer is from the developers and the project team, the better.
   - An outsider is likely to take a more critical approach than an insider and is less likely to be operating under the same mistaken assumptions as they do.

5. A complete functional test plan for a user task (system use case) covers:
   - The basic workflow for performing the task.
   - All alternate flows.
   - All exception flows (workflows leading to failure).
   - Combinations of flows.
   - Rarely occurring scenarios.

6. Save test plans, test cases, and test results.
   - You can reuse them during regression testing.

Checklist: Selecting Solution Providers

Use the following ITIL checklist in selecting IT solution providers.[14]

- Demonstrated competencies with respect to:
  - Staff
  - Use of technology
  - Innovation
  - Experience
  - Certification
- Track record:
  - Quality
  - Financial value
  - Dedication

---

[13]Myers, *The Art of Software Testing*, pp. 8-10.

[14]This checklist is presented in Foundations of IT Service Management Based on ITIL V3, p. 49.

- Relationship dynamics:
  - Vision and strategy of provider fits with those of the organization
- Quality of solutions:
  - Solutions meet or exceed expectations
- Overall capabilities:
  - Financial stability
  - Resources
  - Management systems
  - Scope and range of services

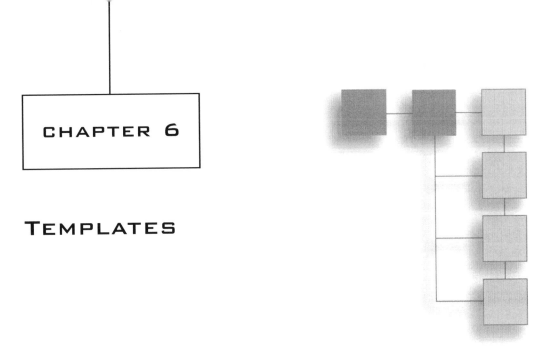

CHAPTER 6

TEMPLATES

This chapter contains templates for artifacts that the BA is responsible for or contributes to. As described in the Business Requirements Document (BRD) template that follows, the manner in which BA documentation is compiled into larger, aggregate documents is non-standard in the industry. This chapter provides a suggested template for a comprehensive BRD, an alternative configuration into a number of documents, each with its own focus, and separate templates for each of the individual types of requirements documentation so that these may be easily reconfigured as required for the project.

The BRD template supports ITIL guidelines and is methodology-neutral, using generic headings wherever possible, with suggestions about what artifacts to include in each section based on the approach used in the project.

Business Requirements Document (BRD) Template

At present, there is no universally accepted standard in the industry for the contents of a BRD, with practices varying widely based on what the subject of the document—the "business requirements"—actually refer to. In the following template (and throughout this book), a *business* is a private or public organization (such as a government department); a *requirement* is a capability that a solution must provide or a condition that it must meet; and a *business requirement* is any requirement made on behalf of the business (i.e., one that originates from the business side), whether the target of the requirement is the business area or the IT system. (In other usages, for example, the term may refer only to high-level business objectives and requirements.) The Business Requirements Document, as described in the template included in this handbook, consolidates all of the requirements stemming from the business and conforms, in principle, to the concept of the Requirements Package referred to by the *BABOK*®. (The *BABOK*® does not use the term BRD.)

Ideally, the BRD is an electronic assembly of smaller components placed under version control. The level of detail that is viewable in the BRD should be adjustable as appropriate for its intended readers. Separate housing of the subdocuments should allow them to be assembled into various other packages and views, as appropriate.

An example of an alternative configuration for the documentation follows the BRD template.

Business Requirements Document

Project No. _____
Priority _____
Target date: _____

Approved by:

_____   _____
Name, Department   Date

_____   _____
Name, Department   Date

_____   _____
Name, Department   Date

Prepared by: _____   **Date:** _____

                                                     Version no.:

The template is generic with respect to methodology while providing guidance on tailoring it to specific approaches, such as use-case analysis, structured analysis, UML, and BPMN.

BRD Table of Contents

Version Control
> Revision History
> RACI Chart

External References

Glossary

Executive Summary
> Overview
> Background
> Objectives
> Requirements
> Proposed Strategy

Product/Solution Scope
> Included in Scope
> Excluded from Scope
> Constraints

Business Case

Business Services and Processes
> Impact of Proposed Changes on Business Services and Processes
> Business Service and Process Overview Diagrams
> Business Process Workflow Requirements
> Business Service Level (Non-Functional) Requirements

Actors
> Workers
> Business Actors
> Other Systems
> Role Map

Business Rules

State Diagrams

IT Requirements

    User Requirements

        User Task Overview Diagram

        User Task Descriptions

    IT Service Level (Non-Functional) Requirements

    System State Requirements

        Testing State

        Disabled State

    Static Model

        Static Model: Diagrams

        Multiplicity Rules Table

        Entity Documentation

Test Plan

    Quality Assurance Responsibilities

    QA Standards and Guidelines

    Review and Audit Plan

    Quality Records

    Tools, Techniques, and Methodologies

    Testing Activities

        Preparatory Activities

        White-Box Testing

        "Fit for Purpose" Testing

        Non-Functional Testing

        User-Acceptance Testing

Deployment Plan

    Training

    Conversion

    Scheduling of Jobs

    Rollout

End-User Procedures

Post-Implementation Follow-Up

Other Issues

Sign-Off

Version Control

(Track revisions made to this document in Table 6.1.)

RACI Chart

The RACI chart in this subsection of the BRD describes the roles played by team members and stakeholders in the production of the artifact. RACI is an acronym for Responsible, Accountable, Consulted, and Informed, representing the ways that a stakeholder may be involved with a process or an artifact. The following codes are used in Table 6.2. Note that an additional Supports classification has been added to further clarify roles associated with this document:

*	Authorize	Has ultimate signing authority for any changes to the document.
R	Responsible	Responsible for creating this document.
A	Accountable	Accountable for accuracy of this document (for example, the project manager).
S	Supports	Provides supporting services in the production of this document.
C	Consulted	Provides input.
I	Informed	Must be informed of any changes.

External References

(In Table 6.3, list all other documents referenced in this document.)

Glossary

(List all terms, acronyms, and abbreviations used in this document, and provide definitions or links to entries in the project Glossary.)

Executive Summary

(This is a one-page summary of the document, divided into the following subsections.)

Overview

(This subsection of Executive Summary is a one-paragraph introduction that explains the nature of the project.)

Background

(This subsection of Executive Summary provides details leading up to the project that explain why the project is being considered. Discuss the following where appropriate: marketplace drivers, business drivers, and technology and other drivers.)

Table 6.1 Revision History

Version #	Date	Authorization	Responsibility (Author)	Description

Table 6.2 RACI Chart for This Document

Name	Position	*	R	A	S	C	I

Table 6.3 External References

Document	Location	Publisher	Author

Objectives

(This subsection of Executive Summary details the business objectives addressed by the project.)

Requirements

(This subsection of Executive Summary is a brief summary of the requirements addressed in this document.)

Proposed Strategy

(This subsection of Executive Summary recommends a strategy for proceeding based on alternatives.)

Product/Solution Scope

(Following is a brief description of what is to be included and excluded from the product or solution, divided into the following subsections.)

Included in Scope

(This subsection of Product/Solution Scope is a brief description of the business area and services covered by the product or solution.)

Excluded from Scope

(This subsection of Product/Solution Scope briefly describes business areas and services not covered by the product or solution.)

Constraints

(This subsection of Product/Solution Scope lists predefined requirements and conditions.)

Business Case

(Describe the business rationale for this project and document Critical Success Factors [CSFs]. This section may contain estimates on cost/benefit, Return on Investment [ROI], payback [length of time for the project to pay for itself], market-share benefits, and so on. Quantify each cost or benefit so that business objectives may be measured after implementation.)

Business Services and Processes

(Complete this section if the project involves changes to the workflow of business services and processes. Include all impacted business services and processes, regardless of whether or not they have an IT component.)

Impact of Proposed Changes on Business Services and Processes

(Summarize the impact of changes on the business area in Table 6.4 by identifying the business services and end-to-end processes impacted by the project. If your project employs business use-case modeling, model each end-to-end process as a business use case. If your project is using Structured Analysis, model each as a high-level process.)

Business Service and Process Overview Diagrams

This subsection of Business Services and Processes provides an overview of the business processes impacted by the project. Include diagrams that depict new or changed business services and processes and link them to the actors that initiate them or participate in carrying them out. Include all impacted business services—regardless of whether they have an IT component or not.

Table 6.4 Impact of Proposed Changes on Business Services and Processes

Business Service or Process	[N]ew/ [C]hanged	Desired Functionality	Current Functionality (If a Change)	Stakeholders/ Systems	Priority

If your project is using the business use-case modeling approach, include business use-case diagrams here, indicating business service and end-to-end business processes as business use cases.

If your project is using Structured Analysis, include business-perspective Data Flow Diagrams (DFDs), indicating business services and end-to-end business processes as well as External Entities (actors); model process input and output requirements using data flows.

Business Process Workflow Requirements

This subsection describes the workflow for each business service and process impacted by the project. If necessary, describe existing (As-Is) workflow as well as the new (To-Be) workflow. Workflow diagrams (swimlane workflow diagrams, activity diagrams, BPDs, etc.) are the preferred documentation for cross-functional processes because of the way they visually convey the responsibilities of each participant. (See the BA Toolkit chapter of this book for details on each diagram type.) Diagrams may be augmented with, or substituted by, text, typically using a template included as part of the methodology used on the project.

If your project is using the business use-case modeling approach with UML, document the interaction with the business area textually (for example, using the Business Use-Case Description Template provided in this chapter) and augment with an activity diagram if the flows connect in complex ways. Document the internal workflow used to carry out the process graphically, using activity diagrams with partitions.

If your project employs the business use-case realization modeling element (a UML business modeling extension included, for example, in IBM RUP), distinguish between a business service and the internal processes used to carry it out as follows:

- *Model the business service as a* business use case. *Describe the interaction between the business area and its users (customers) in a business use-case description (referred to in RUP as a business use-case* specification*) using text augmented if necessary with activity diagrams; do not include activities internal to the business.*
- *Model the internal process as a* business use-case realization. *Describe the internal workflow in a business use-case realization description (referred to in RUP as a* specification*) using activity diagrams with partitions.*

If your project is using the BPMN standard, include BPDs. Other diagram types that may by used in this subsection include Block diagrams, flowcharts, and Swimlane Workflow diagrams.

Business Service Level (Non-Functional) Requirements

(This subsection of Business Services and Processes describes Business Service Level Requirements. Service Level Requirements define across-the-board requirements for services and focus on non-functional requirements. For subsections, please refer to the Service Level Requirements Template.

Actors

(This section describes entities that interact with the business area and IT system.)

Workers

(In this subsection of Actors, list and describe stakeholders who act within the business in carrying out business use cases; see Table 6.5.)

Table 6.5 Workers

Department/ Position	General Impact of Project

Business Actors

(In this subsection of Actors, list and describe external parties, such as customers and partners, who interact with the business; see Table 6.6.)

Table 6.6 Business Actors

Business Actor	General Impact of Project

Other Systems

(In this subsection of Actors, list external computer systems potentially impacted by this project. Include any system that will be linked to the proposed system; see Table 6.7.)

Table 6.7 External Systems

System	General Impact of Project

Role Map

(This subsection of Actors provides a centralized easy-to-reference visual summary of actors, depicting the users and external systems that interact with the IT system and their relationships to each other. See "Role Map" in the BA Toolkit chapter of this book for a UML-compliant glossary of symbols and example of a Role Map [limited for the use-case diagram]. If using Structured Analysis, provide a limited version of a DFD depicting only External Entities.)

Business Rules

(List business rules or provide references or links to external business rules documentation. Your business rules may resemble the following example.)

Whenever inventory falls below a trigger level, an automatic order is placed with the supplier.

State Diagrams

(Describe the events that trigger changes of state for key business objects. If your project uses the UML standard, include UML State-Machine diagrams here. See "State-Machine Diagram" in the BA Toolkit chapter for more on state diagrams.)

IT Requirements

(This section of the BRD describes requirements originating from the business that the product or solution must fulfill.)

User Requirements

(This subsection of IT Requirements describes requirements for automated processes from a user perspective. If the use-case approach is being employed, model each user task as a system use case. If Structured Analysis is used, model each user task as a Process; place the task in context by defining it as a subprocess of the end-to-end business process it supports.)

User Task Overview Diagram

This subsection of User Requirements provides a graphical overview of user tasks and the user roles that are associated with each task. Each user task represents a piece of meaningful work that a user accomplishes with the assistance of an IT system and is typically completed in a single interaction. If the use-case approach is being employed, model user tasks as system use cases and include system use-case diagrams depicting the actors that interact with each system use case and the dependencies between use cases. See "System Use Cases" in the BA Toolkit chapter of this handbook for a glossary of symbols and example of a system use-case diagram. If Structured Analysis is being used, include Data Flow Diagrams (DFDs) modeling user tasks as IT processes, and indicating the external entities (actors) that interact with them. Indicate the data that is input and output from each process on data flows. See "Data Flow Diagram" in the BA Toolkit chapter of this handbook for a glossary of symbols and examples of DFDs.

User Task Descriptions

In this subsection of User Requirements, describe each user task by documenting the required interaction between the user and the IT system, but without specifying the design.

(For example, do not include screen design or programming specifications.) If the steps of the interaction connect to each other in complex ways, augment the text with work-flow diagrams, such as flowcharts, activity diagrams, and Business Process Diagrams (BPDs), keeping in mind that the focus of these diagrams is specifically the interaction between the user and the system for this user task and not the entire business process[1] (which might include manual steps, interactions with third parties, etc.)

Develop descriptions incrementally. For example, during Initiation, provide only short descriptions. During Discovery, complete the description for each medium- to high-risk user task. Describe low-risk user tasks informally.

If the use-case approach is being employed, include system use-case descriptions (referred to in RUP as use-case specifications) here. For a suggested template, see the System Use-Case Description Template in this chapter.

If Structured Analysis is being used, consider IPO documentation for each process: The acronym refers to the three sections of the documentation: Input, Output, and Process logic. Process logic describing the user-IT interaction may be documented using text such as pseudo-code (a structured writing style using programming-like constructs) or graph-ically, using a workflow diagram.

IT Service Level (Non-Functional) Requirements

(This subsection of IT Requirements describes IT Service Level Requirements. Service Level Requirements define how well the service must perform, rather than the nature of the interaction and workflow. Service Level Requirements are sometimes referred to by other terms, such as "quality attributes" and "non-functional requirements." For a suggested template, see the Service Level [Non-Functional] Requirements Template provided in this chapter.)

System State Requirements

(This subsection of IT Requirements describes how the IT system's behaviour changes when in different states. Describe the features that will be available and those that will be disabled in each state. Please note the distinction between this subsection of IT Requirements and the prior BRD section, State Diagrams. System State Requirements [this subsection] refer to the states of the IT system [Disabled, etc.] and the features that are active or inactive when it is in different states, whereas the prior section was concerned with the life cycle and states of business objects central to the project, such as a Regis-tration Application, an Order, and so on.)

---

[1]Despite the term "Business" in "Business Process Diagram," BPDs are useful for documenting any workflow—even where the focus is not on the whole business process, but on the interaction with the IT system, as is the case here—because of their wealth of modeling elements (such as inclusive ORs) for handling a variety of situations.

Testing State

(This subsection of System State Requirements describes what the user may and may not do while the system is in the test state.)

Disabled State

(This subsection of System State Requirements describes what is to happen when the system, or part of a system or IT service, is down. Clearly define what the user will and will not be able to do and Vital Business Functions [VBFs] that must remain operational.)

Static Model

(The static model describes the non-timed based business requirements for the IT system. It includes definitions of business entities [business concepts and object types] and related across-the-board business rules that must be supported by the IT system, such as the rule that each policy may be owned by one or more customers.)

Static Model: Diagrams

(In this subsection of Static Model, include static-modeling diagrams depicting business entities and associated business rules and data requirements. If using the UML standard, include class diagrams here; see "Class Diagrams" in the BA Toolkit chapter of this book for details. If using the data-modeling approach, include Entity Relationship Diagrams (ERDs); see "Entity Relationship Diagram" in the BA Toolkit chapter of this book.)

Multiplicity Rules Table

(Include this subsection of Static Model when presenting to business stakeholders, who are likely to be unfamiliar with static modeling diagrams. Include textual descriptions of the business rules expressed in the static model, converting each entity relationship [association] in the model to two business rules [one for each direction].

Table 6.8 is a template for a Multiplicity Rules Table that expresses business rules regarding multiplicity—the number of business objects that may be related to each other—in textual form. Note that the data-modeling term cardinality *and the UML term* multiplicity *are equivalent, that a data- modeling relationship and UML association are equivalent, and that the terms* entity, class, *and* entity class, *as used in a BA context, are roughly equivalent.[2])*

Your documentation may resemble the example shown in Table 6.9.

---

[2]The term *cardinality* is used in data modeling and in the UML. The term *multiplicity* is a UML term. *Entity* is the data modeling term for the UML term *entity class.* Not all classes in the UML are entity classes, but these are the primary classes of interest to the BA.

Table 6.8 Multiplicity Rules Table

Each . . . (Name the entity class at one end of the association.)	(Use a verb phrase to name the association between the entity classes at either end.)	At least . . . (Document the minimum multiplicity at the other end of the association.)	(Document the maximum multiplicity at the other end of the association.)	(Name the entity class at the other end of the association. Use plural form if maximum multiplicity is more than 1.)

Table 6.9 Multiplicity Rules Example

Each . . .	(Name the association)	At least . . .	(Document the maximum multiplicity at the other end of the association.)	(Name the entity class at the other end of the association.)
Policy	Is owned by	1	Or more	Policy Holders
Policy Holder	Owns	1	And only 1	Policy

Entity Documentation

(In this subsection of Static Model, include text documentation to support entities [classes] that appear in the static model diagrams. Not every entity needs to be fully documented by the BA; do a risk analysis to determine where full documentation would most benefit the project.)

Entity Name: *(Name the entity [class]. Use a singular noun phrase, such as Customer.)*

Alias: *(List any other names by which the entity is known within the business domain.)*

Description: *(Provide a short description of the entity.)*

Example: *(Provide an example of an instance [individual object] of this entity.)*

Primary Key: *(List the attribute[s] used to uniquely identify an instance of this class.)*

Attributes: *(Document attributes [data fields]. See Table 6.10.)*

Volume: *(Document the maximum number of objects of this type that the system must be able to handle.)*

Rate of Growth: *(Document the rate at which the number of objects of this type is expected to increase.)*

(Table 6.10 is a template for documenting attribute properties, such as the method used to derive an attribute's value [if applicable], its data type, and default display format [e.g., MM DD/YY for a date]. In the Dependency column, document any dependencies the attribute may have on other attributes or conditions. For example, dependencies for the attributes of an Invoice might include that a due date must be on or after an invoice date and that the product code on the invoice must match that used in the inventory system.)

Entity (class): (Name of entity or entity class)

Table 6.10 Attributes Table

Attribute	Derived?	Derivation	Type (Numeric, Date, etc.)	Format	Length	Range	Dependency

Test Plan

(These requirements are often described in a separate test plan. If they are not addressed elsewhere, describe them here in the BRD. Your test plan should address the steps required to verify whether the solution is "fit for purpose" [does what it is supposed to do] and "fit for use" [works well under specified conditions].)

Quality Assurance Responsibilities

(In this subsection of Test Plan, identify the responsibilities of the quality assurance personnel and specify who those responsibilities will be assigned to.)

QA Standards and Guidelines

(In this subsection of Test Plan, identify the QA standards and guidelines that will be used on the project and indicate how compliance with these standards and guidelines will be determined.)

Review and Audit Plan

(This subsection of Test Plan establishes the reviews and audits that will be performed on the project, their schedule, and their goal.)

Quality Records

(This subsection of Test Plan describes the quality records that will be maintained for the project.)

Tools, Techniques, and Methodologies

(This subsection of Test Plan describes the specific tools, techniques, and methodologies that will be used for quality assurance.)

Testing Activities

(This subsection of Test Plan should address the following testing activities.)

Preparatory Activities

This subsection of Testing Activities describes activities that must be completed prior to executing (running) tests. The BA supports QA in preparing for "fit for purpose" testing (also known as functional or black-box tests) based on the requirements. BA support may include the design of test cases, test scenarios, and test scripts, and the tracing of tests backward to requirements (such as use-case flows) and forward (from requirements to tests) to ensure complete test coverage of the requirements. Decision tables may be used to identify test scenarios when system actions depend on a number of factors. See "Decision Table/Tree" in the BA Toolkit chapter of this book for more on decision tables.

White-Box Testing

(This subsection of Testing Activities describes white-box testing activities that occur once software changes have been made. White-box testing is conducted by the technical team in order to verify whether programs, fields, and calculations function as specified. The BA or technical team specifies the required white-box testing coverage. The lowest coverage is statement coverage [each statement in the code has been executed at least once during testing]. The highest required coverage is, generally, multiple-condition coverage

[every combination of conditions in every decision has been executed at least once]. Technical tests are usually done at the unit level first [testing of the module that was changed]. These are followed by technical integration tests that test the integration of the changed units into progressively larger subsystems and systems.)

"Fit for Purpose" (Black-Box) Testing

(This subsection of Testing Activities describes "fit for purpose" [functional] testing, also known as black-box testing. The BA or dedicated QA staff administers or supervises "fit for purpose" tests, executed to check compliance of the solution with the requirements. Tests should check that all formulae are calculated properly, and that each flow [basic and alternate flows] for each user task [system use case] is tested. Describe principles and techniques to be used, such as structured testing guidelines and boundary-value analysis. Verify requirements coverage by tracing test cases backward to requirements [such as system use cases and flows]. Use decision tables to verify that all required combinations of test scenarios were tested. Use boundary-value analysis to verify the quality of test data.)

Non-Functional Testing

(In this subsection of Testing Activities, describe system tests executed to check compliance of the solution with Service Level Requirements, such as response-time requirements. Tests should verify that the integrity of the system and data remain intact. For more information on test types, see "Checklist: Test Types" in the Tips and Checklists chapter of this handbook.)

For example, your test plan might include the following tests:

- Service specification testing (also known as functional or black-box testing)
- Service level testing
- Service guarantee testing (tests whether guarantees are met regarding availability, capacity, continuity, etc.)
- Usability testing
- Contract and regulation testing
- Service management testing
- Operational testing
- Regression testing
- Load testing
- Stress testing
- Reliability testing
- Security testing

User-Acceptance Testing

(This subsection of Testing Activities describes User-Acceptance Testing procedures.)

Deployment Plan

(The deployment plan is often described in a separate document. If it is not addressed elsewhere, describe it here in the BRD. In this section of the BRD, describe steps required for deploying the product or service into production.)

Training

(In this subsection of Deployment Plan, specify who is responsible for training, who is to be trained, and how training will be done.)

Conversion

(In this subsection of Deployment Plan, specify steps required to convert to the new system. Your plan should describe existing data that must be converted, programs to be promoted to new releases, the granting of user privileges, and so on.)

Scheduling of Jobs

(In this subsection of Deployment Plan, advise IT operations of any changes to the job schedule, often known as the application or system "run book." Indicate jobs to be added to the production run and their frequency, reports to be printed, and jobs and reports that are to be discontinued or changed.)

Rollout

(In this subsection of Deployment plan, describe procedures for rolling out the solution to the production environment and to end users. The plan should include preparations for production-verification testing [also known as production-validation testing], an important and all-too-often neglected part of the life cycle and one that the BA should be instrumental in. The rollout plan should also ensure that all affected users are advised when the project is promoted.)

End-User Procedures

(Document user procedures for the affected user roles. Distribute to end users and provide hands-on user training.)

Post-Implementation Follow-Up

(Follow up within a reasonable time frame after implementation to ensure that the project is running successfully and that its objectives have been met. Determine whether any further enhancements or changes are needed to ensure success of the solution.)

Other Issues

(Use this section for any other issues not covered elsewhere in the BRD.)

Sign-Off

(In this section of the BRD, stakeholders, solution providers, and others confirm their acceptance of the document.)

Alternative Requirements Packaging

Following is an alternative for packaging the requirements into separate documents, with a focus on the contribution made by the BA.

- Document 1: Customer Wants and Needs
  Referred to by various names, such as Market Requirements Document and Business Requirements. Documents high-level business objectives and requirements. Often prepared by a product manager after consultation with customers. Contains:
  - Summary: High-level overview of client request, scope and need
  - Stakeholders and Interests
  - Wants and Needs (customer objectives)
  - Business Drivers
  - Business Strategies
  - Regulations and Standards
  - Assumptions
  - Issues
  - Risks
  - Constraints
- Document 2: Customer Business Requirements Document
  Documents business services and business service levels that the business must be able to provide to its customers. Contains:
  - Business Scope and Objectives
  - Acceptance Criteria

- Metrics
- Business Service (Level) Requirements: Includes non-functional business service level requirements, list of new or changed business services and descriptions of the business façade (business use-case descriptions [known in RUP as business use-case specifications])—the required interactions between actors and the business area for each service. (Some practitioners include internal cross-functional business process descriptions [business use-case realizations]; in the configuration shown here, these are housed in the business architecture.)

- Document 3: Business Architecture
  Defines enterprise-wide requirements. The BA contribution to the document includes:
  - Domain Diagrams (business-perspective entity/class diagrams): Define enterprise-wide business rules related to categories (classes) of business objects.
  - Business Process Overview Diagrams (business use-case diagrams): Define the participation of actors in business services and processes.
  - Business Process Cross-Functional Workflow (business use-case realizations): Define the internal workflow for implementing the business process. Usually expressed graphically, using swimlane workflow diagrams, BPDs, activity diagrams, and so forth.

- Document 4: Software Requirements Specification (SRS)/Product Specifications Document
  Defines the requirements that must be satisfied by the IT organization. May include requirements resulting from the business as well as technical specifications. The BA contribution includes:
  - Acceptance Criteria
  - Non-Functional IT Service Level Requirements
  - User Profile: Defines and describes user groups (actors) that will access the IT system. Includes Role Map.
  - Functional Requirements (user requirements/system use-case diagrams/system use-case documentation)

Business Use-Case Description Template

The following is a suggested template to be used in creating a business use-case description (referred to in RUP as a *business use-case specification*). Please note that there are many different styles in use for this template; the template that follows contains an extensive list of sections to be taken into consideration—though not necessarily completed—when describing a use case.

1. **Business Use-Case Name:** *(The business use-case name as it appears on business use-case diagrams. Name the goal of the primary actor for this use case.)*

   Level: *(Specify the level of business service or process described by the business use case. For example: high-level = end-to-end business process; mid-level = mid-level business process with subprocesses; low-level = business process with no smaller subprocesses. If the level is unspecified, a high-level [end-to-end] business process is assumed.)*

   Type: *(Base use case/extending/included/generalized/specialized)*

   1.1 **Business Context**

   1.1.1 **Brief Description**

   (Briefly describe the use case in approximately one paragraph.)

   1.1.2 **Business Goals and Benefits**

   (Briefly describe the business rationale for the use case.)

   1.1.3 **Business Area**

   (Name the business area being modeled, for example, Incident Management.)

   1.2 **Actors**

   1.2.1 **Primary Business Actor**

   (Identify the entity [or entities] outside the business area that may initiate the business use case.)

   1.2.2 **Other Actors**

   (Identify other actors directly involved in achieving the use-case goal. You may classify other actors as shown below.)

   1.2.2.1 Secondary Business Actors (Table 6.11)

   (List entities, such as Supplier, that lie outside the business area but participate in the process once the use case has been triggered.)

   1.2.2.2 Workers (Table 6.12)

   (List internal workers—such as Customer Service Representatives—who execute steps in the business process once the use case has been triggered.)

Table 6.11 Secondary Business Actors

Secondary Business Actor	Responsibility

Table 6.12 Workers

Worker	Responsibility

1.2.3 Off-Stage Stakeholders[3] (Table 6.13)

(Identify non-participating stakeholders who have interests in this use case.)

Table 6.13 Off-Stage Stakeholders

Off-Stage Stakeholder	Interest

1.3 Triggers

(Describe the event or condition that kick-starts the use case, such as "Application Received." If the trigger is time-driven, describe the temporal condition, such as end-of-month.)

1.4 Pre-Conditions

(List conditions that must be true before the use case begins. However, if the condition forces the use case to start, do not list it here; rather, list it as a trigger.)

---

[3]The term is used by Alistair Cockburn in *Writing Effective Use Cases* (Addison-Wesley Professional, 2000).

1.5 Post-Conditions

(Post-conditions are guaranteed outcomes of the use case. Any post-condition is guaranteed to be true after the use case ends. The subsections of post-conditions distinguish between outcomes that are guaranteed only when the use case ends successfully and outcomes that are guaranteed in all cases.)

1.5.1 Post-Conditions on Success

(Describe outcomes that are guaranteed for every interaction that ends in success, that is, where the goal of the use case is achieved. Post-conditions on Success are additional to any guarantees listed in Guaranteed Post-Conditions.)

1.5.2 Guaranteed Post-Conditions

(Describe outcomes that are guaranteed for every interaction—regardless of whether the use case ends in success or failure.)

1.6 Extension Points

(An extension point is a feature of a use case that identifies a point where the behaviour of a use case can be augmented with elements of another [extending] use case.[4] The extension takes place at one or more specific extension points defined in the extended base use case.[5] In this subsection of the template, name and describe points at which other [extending] use cases may extend this use case.[6] [Alternatively, you may define extension points graphically, in the lower half of the oval symbol used for the base use case.[7]] Your extension-point declaration may resemble the following. In the example, the extension point, "Preferred Customer," refers to any points within the range of steps 2.5 through 2.9 in this use case. The implication is that while a scenario is executing steps 2.5 through 2.9, if the condition attached to an extension that uses this point becomes true, the extending use case is activated.)

1.6.1 Preferred Customer: Steps 2.5-2.9

---

[4]Unified Modeling Language Superstructure, V2.1.2, OMG, 2007, p. 591.

[5]Unified Modeling Language Superstructure, V2.1.2, OMG, 2007, p. 589.

[6]The UML states that extension points are a feature of the base use case and are defined within it, an approach consistent with that used in the template. However, some contend that Jacobson's view—that the extended use case should have no knowledge of whether or not it is extended—argues for the extension points to be declared elsewhere. Also, note that just because an extension point is declared for a base use case does not mean it will necessarily be used by all extending use cases. The extension points that are used by a particular extending use case may be indicated in a note attached to the extend relationship.

[7]Unified Modeling Language Superstructure, V2.1.2, OMG, 2007, p. 591.

1.7 Local View Business Use-Case Diagram

(A Local View use-case diagram indicates the use case in question and all its direct relationships. Include a business use-case diagram showing this business use case, all of its relationships [includes, extends, and generalizes] with other business use cases and its associations with actors.

The priority and status of the use case should be tracked elsewhere, ideally, in a requirements or project-management tool, such as ReqPro or MS Project. If it is not, add sections here for priority and status.)

2. Flow of Events

Basic Flow

2.1 Insert Basic Flow Steps, starting from 2.1, following with 2.2, 2.3, and so on.

Alternate Flows[8]

Xa Alternate Flow Name

(The flow name should describe the condition that triggers the alternate flow. In the Cockburn numbering system used here, "X" is the step number where the interruption occurs. For example, the first alternate flow that diverges from step 2.5 is named 2.5a; the second is named 2.5b, etc. Describe the flow's steps in paragraph or point form. The last step in the flow should either direct the reader to a step in another flow [Basic or Alternate], or, if the use case ends at that point, should identify whether the use case ends in success or failure. Guaranteed Post-Conditions apply regardless of how the use case ends; Post-Conditions on Success are guaranteed only when the use case ends in success.)

Your alternate flow header might resemble the following example, triggered at step 2.5 in the basic flow.

2.5a Product Not Available

3. Special Requirements

(List any special requirements or constraints that apply specifically to this use case.)

3.1 Business Service Level (Non-Functional) Requirements

(List requirements from the business area that do not pertain directly to work-flow. List only those that are particular to this use case; list across-the-board non-functional requirements in the Business Service Level [Non-Functional] Requirements [external to this use case]. Sample subsections follow. For a more complete list of subsections, refer to the Service Level Requirements Template in this chapter.)

3.1.1 Business Usability Requirements

3.1.2 Business Reliability Requirements

---

[8]The term *alternate flow* is used because of its popularity; however, the correct term would be *alternative flow*.

3.1.3 Business Performance Requirements

3.1.4 Business Supportability Requirements

3.1.5 Business Security Requirements

3.1.6 Legal and Regulatory Requirements

3.2 Constraints

(List technological, architectural, and other constraints on the use case.)

4. Activity Diagram

(If the flows in this business use case connect to each other in complex ways, include an activity diagram showing workflow for this use case or for select parts of the use case.)

5. Process Artifacts

(Initially, include description/prototypes/sample layouts of artifacts used as input to or created by the business use case to help the reader visualize the interaction, but not to constrain the design. Later, provide links to design artifacts.)

6. Domain (Business Entity) Diagrams

(Include class diagrams depicting business entity classes, relationships, and multiplicities of all objects participating in this use case.)

7. Open Issues

(List any assumptions, notes, and questions that need to be verified with stakeholders. Make sure all of these items have been addressed and removed from this section before final sign-off.)

8. Information Items

(Include a link or reference to documentation describing rules for data items that relate to this use case. Documentation of this sort is often found in a data dictionary.)

9. Prompts and Messages

(Any prompts or messages should only be referenced in the use-case flows. The details of the prompt or message should be included here or in a message catalogue.)

10. Business Rules

(This section of the use-case documentation should provide links or references to the specific business rules that are active during the use case. An example of a business rule for an airline package is, "Airplane weight must never exceed the maximum allowed for its aircraft type." Organizations often keep such rules in an automated business rules engine or manually in a binder.)

11. Related Artifacts

(Include references to other artifacts such as decision tables, complex algorithms, and so on.)

System Use-Case Description Template

The following is a suggested template to be used in creating a system use-case description (referred to in RUP as a use-case specification). Please note that there are many different styles in use for this template (RUP, Cockburn, Bittner/Spence, and so forth). The template that follows contains an extensive list of sections to be taken into consideration when describing a use case; however, not all sections need to be completed.

1. **System Use-Case Name:** *(The system use-case name as it appears on system use-case diagrams. Name the goal of the primary actor for this use case.)*

   Level: *(Specify the level of IT service described by the system use case. For example, kite-level = end-to-end IT service, and sea-level = goal obtained by one actor in one IT session.[9] [A use case that represents a sub-goal is characterized below by type, as an included use case.] If the level is unspecified, a sea-level [single session] use case is assumed.)*

   Type: *(Base use case/extending/generalized/specialized/included.)*

   1.1 Business Context

   1.1.1 Brief Description

   (Briefly describe the use case in approximately one paragraph.)

   1.1.2 Business Goals and Benefits

   (Briefly describe the business goals addressed by the use case.)

   1.1.3 Business Area

   (Name the business area that will require the use case, for example, Incident Management.)

   1.1.4 System under Design (SuD)

   (Identify the IT system or systems [if known] that will implement the requirements for the project. The SuD may consist of a collection of IT components, such as software applications, databases, and supporting systems.)

   1.2 Actors

   1.2.1 Primary Actor

   (Identify the users or systems that initiate the use case.)

   1.2.2 Secondary Actors

   (List the users or systems that receive messages from the use case. Include users who receive reports or online messages.)

---

[9]These levels were introduced by Alistair Cockburn.

1.2.3 Off-Stage Stakeholders

(Identify non-participating stakeholders who have interests in this use case; see Table 6.14.)

Table 6.14 Off-Stage Stakeholders

Stakeholder	Interest

1.3 Triggers

(Describe the event or condition that "kick-starts" the use case, such as "Call received by call center" or "Inventory low." If the trigger is time-driven, describe the temporal condition, such as end-of-month.)

1.4 Pre-Conditions

(List conditions that must be true before the use case begins. However, if the condition forces the use case to start, do not list it here; rather, list it as a trigger.)

1.5 Post-Conditions

(Post-conditions are guaranteed outcomes of the use case. Any post-condition is guaranteed to be true after the use case ends. The subsections of post-conditions distinguish between outcomes that are guaranteed only when the use case ends successfully and outcomes that are guaranteed in all cases.)

1.5.1 Post-Conditions on Success

(Describe outcomes that are guaranteed for every interaction that ends in success, that is, where the goal of the use case is achieved. Post-Conditions on Success are additional to any guarantees listed in Guaranteed Post-Conditions.)

1.5.2 Guaranteed Post-Conditions

(Describe outcomes that are guaranteed for every interaction—regardless of whether the use case ends in success or failure.)

1.6 Extension Points

(An extension point is a feature of a use case that identifies a point where the behaviour of a use case can be augmented with elements of another [extending] use case.[10] The extension takes place at one or more specific extension points

---

[10]Unified Modeling Language Superstructure, V2.1.2, OMG, 2007, p. 591.

defined in the extended [base] use case.[11] *In this subsection of the template, name and describe points at which other [extending] use cases may extend this use case.*[12] *[Alternatively, you may define extension points graphically, in the lower half of the oval symbol used for the base use case.*[13]*] Your extension-point declaration may resemble the following. In the example, the extension point, "Preferred Customer," refers to any points within the range of steps 2.5 through 2.9 in this use case. The implication is that while a scenario is executing steps 2.5 through 2.9, if the condition attached to an extension that uses this point becomes true, the extending use case is activated.)*

1.6.1 Preferred Customer: 2.5-2.9

1.7 Local View System Use-Case Diagram

(A Local View use-case diagram indicates the use case in question and all its direct relationships. Include a system use-case diagram showing this system use case, all of its relationships [includes, extends, and generalizes] with other system use cases, and its associations with actors.

The priority and status of the use case should be tracked elsewhere, ideally, in a requirements or project-management tool, such as ReqPro or MS Project. If it is not, add sections here for priority and status.)

2. Flow of Events

Basic Flow

2.1 Insert Basic Flow Steps

Alternate Flows[14]

Xa Alternate Flow Name

(The flow name should describe the condition that triggers the alternate flow. In the Cockburn numbering system used here, "X" is the step number where the interruption occurs. For example, the first alternate flow that diverges from step

---

[11]Unified Modeling Language Superstructure, V2.1.2, OMG, 2007, p. 589.

[12](The following footnote on extension points is repeated here for convenience.) The UML states that extension points are a feature of the base use case and are defined within it, an approach consistent with that used in the template. However, some contend that Jacobsen's view—that the extended use case should have no knowledge of whether or not it is extended—argues for the extension points to be declared elsewhere. Also, note that just because an extension point is declared for a use case does not mean it will necessarily be used by all extending use cases. The extension points that are used by a particular extending use case may be indicated in a Note attached to the extend relationship.

[13]Unified Modeling Language Superstructure, V2.1.2, OMG, 2007, p. 591.

[14]The term *alternate flow* is used because of its popularity; however, the correct term would be *alternative flow.*

2.5 is named 2.5a; the second is named 2.5b, etc. Describe the flow's steps in para-graph or point form. The last step in the flow should either direct the reader to a step in another flow [Basic or Alternate] or, if the use case ends at that point, should identify whether the use case ends in success or failure. Guaranteed Post-Conditions apply regardless of how the use case ends; Post-Conditions on Success are guaranteed only when the use case ends in success.)

Your alternate flow header might resemble the following example, triggered at step 2.5 in the basic flow.

2.5a Product Not Available

3. Special Requirements

(List any special requirements or constraints that apply specifically to this use case.)

3.1 IT Service Level (Non-Functional) Requirements

(List requirements that the product or solution must satisfy or that do not pertain directly to workflow. List only those that are particular to this use case. List across-the-board non-functional requirements in the IT Service Level [Non-Functional] Requirements. Sample subsections follow. For a more complete list of Service Level Requirements, refer to the Service Level Requirements Template in this chapter.)

3.1.1 Usability Requirements

3.1.2 Reliability Requirements

3.1.3 Performance Requirements

3.1.4 Supportability Requirements

3.1.5 Security Requirements

3.1.6 Legal and Regulatory Requirements

3.2 Constraints

(List technological, architectural, and other constraints on the use case.)

4. Activity Diagram

(If the flows in the system use case connect to each other in complex ways, include an activity diagram of the steps and flows.)

5. User Interface

(Initially, include descriptions, storyboards, or prototypes of screens as appropriate, in order to help the reader visualize the interface, but not to constrain the design. Once a UI has been designed, trace the link between the interface and this document using a traceability table or by providing a link to the UI from this section of the use-case doc-ument.)

6. **Domain (Business Entity) Diagrams**

   (Include class diagrams depicting business classes, relationships, and multiplicities of all objects participating in this use case.)

7. **Open Issues**

   (List any assumptions, notes, and questions that need to be verified with stakeholders. Make sure all of these items have been addressed and removed from this section before final sign-off.)

8. **Information Items**

   (Include a link or reference to documentation describing rules for data items that relate to this use case. Documentation of this sort is often found in a data dictionary.)

9. **Prompts and Messages**

   (Any prompts or messages should only be referenced in the use-case flows. The details of the prompt or message should be included here or in a message catalogue.)

10. **Business Rules**

    (This section of the use-case documentation should provide links or references to the specific business rules that are active during the use case. An example of a business rule for an airline package is, "Airplane weight must never exceed the maximum allowed for its aircraft type." Organizations often keep such rules in an automated business rules engine or manually in a binder.)

11. **Related Artifacts**

    (Include references to other artifacts such as decision tables, complex algorithms, and so on.)

Service Level (Non-Functional) Requirements Template

The following is a suggested template for documenting Service Level (Non-Functional) Requirements (SLR).

Service Level Type

(This section of the Service Level Requirements specifies whether the Service Level Requirements relate to business or IT services.)

Overview

Objective

(This section of the Service Level Requirements describes the purpose of the document. Your description may resemble the text provided below.)

The purpose of the SLR is to document system-wide non-functional IT Service Level Requirements. Non-functional requirements are those not directly related to what the system can do; they correspond to the URPS+ categories (Usability, Reliability, Performance, Supportability, plus other constraints) of FURPS+. This document supplements the functional requirements (system use cases). Service Level Requirements specific to a user task (system use case) are documented in the user requirements (system use-case descriptions); across-the-board requirements are documented here to avoid duplication. Requirements listed in this document form the basis of Service Level Agreements (SLAs) with customers and must be supported, where applicable, by Underpinning Contracts (UCs) with vendors.

Scope

(In this section of the Service Level Requirements, describe the scope of this document: the business area, dependencies of this document on other documentation, and items that are explicitly in and out of scope.)

Glossary

(In this section of the Service Level Requirements, list all terms, acronyms, and abbreviations used in this document, with explicit definitions or links to entries in the project glossary.)

System-Wide Capabilities

(This section of the Service Level Requirements describes system-wide capabilities, such as auditing and logging requirements that apply across system use cases.[15])

Auditing and Reporting Requirements

(This subsection of System-Wide Capabilities describes the types of records, reports, and so on required by auditors. Your requirements might resemble the following example.)

A record of each change to an account must be created and retained for five years.

Activity Logging Requirements

(This subsection of System-Wide Capabilities describes the activity records required to support IT or business services and the length of time that the records must be kept. Your requirements might resemble the following example.)

The system must keep an activity log of all site visits for a period of five years.

---

[15]These are classified as functional requirements in the FURPS+ system. They are included here because they apply across user tasks (system use cases).

Licensing Requirements

(This subsection of System-Wide Capabilities describes requirements related to the installing, tracking, and monitoring of licenses.)

Security Requirements

(This subsection of System-Wide Capabilities describes security requirements related to access to data, privacy restrictions, homeland security, and so on.)

Dependencies and Rules of Precedence

(This subsection of System-Wide Capabilities describes dependencies and precedence rules regarding the performing of services and processes, the movement of work items, approvals, and so on. Include any timing dependencies between internal processes and those performed by external systems.)

Concurrency Requirements

(This subsection of System-Wide Capabilities describes the number of users that must be able to be engaged in the same operation at the same time.)

Usability Requirements

(This section of the Service Level Requirements describes the requirements that relate to the user interface.)

User-Friendliness

(This subsection of Usability Requirements documents requirements related to the ease with which users are able to access and use the service. Your requirements might resemble the following example.)

An end-user, given a goal but no precise directions, must be able to achieve a 90% success rate completing transactions.

User Interface Standards and Guidelines

(This subsection of Usability Requirements lists standards and guidelines that constrain the design of the user interface.)

Accessibility Requirements

(This subsection of Usability Requirements documents accessibility requirements for users with special needs, such as those with disabilities.)

Reliability Requirements

(This section of the Service Level Requirements describes the level of fault-tolerance required by the system.)

Accuracy Requirements

(This subsection of Reliability Requirements describes the degree of correctness required for metrics generated by the services covered in this project. Your requirements might resemble the following example.)

The system must be able to automatically detect 90% of faults.

Precision Requirements

(This subsection of Reliability Requirements describes the level of exactitude required. Your requirements might resemble the following example.)

All taxes must be calculated and recorded to the nearest cent.

Availability Requirements

(This subsection of Reliability Requirements describes the system's ability to perform its required function at a stated instant or over a stated period of time.[16] Your requirements might include the following metrics.)

- **MTBF (Mean Time Between Failures)**: Mean time between an occurrence of a service failure and a failure of the same service.
- **MTBSI (Mean Time Between System/Service Incidents)**: Mean time between the occurrence of a system or service failure and the occurrence of the next failure.
- **MTRS (Mean Time to Restore Service)**: Mean elapsed time to fix and restore a service, from the time an incident occurs until it is available to the customer.
- **MTTR (Mean Time to Repair)**: Mean time to repair a Configuration Item or IT service after a failure, measured from when the CI or IT service fails until it is repaired (not including the time required to recover or restore).
- **Detection/recording**: Time between occurrence of an incident and its detection.

Redundancy

(This subsection of Reliability Requirements describes extra assets required to support reliability and sustainability requirements. It includes the following subtypes.[17])

---

[16]Evans and Macfarlane, "A Dictionary of IT Service Management Terms, Acronyms, and Abbreviations," itSMF®, p. 9.

[17]These subtypes are defined by ITIL.

- *Active redundancy*: This type of redundancy supports continuous operation of non-interruptible services. List redundant assets that must operate simultaneously and always be ready to replace their counterparts. Specify whether each redundancy is diverse *(requires different types of assets to provide the same service in order spread the risk)* or homogenous *(redundant assets of the same type).*
- *Passive redundancy*: This type of redundancy supports reliability requirements for services that may be interrupted. List redundant assets that will be kept offline (on standby) until required. Specify whether each redundancy is diverse *or* homogenous (as defined under the preceding bullet).

Error-Handling

(This subsection of Reliability Requirements describes the types of errors the system should be able to handle and the ways the system should respond to these errors. Your requirements might resemble the following examples.)

System Faults:

When a component of any IT service in this project is temporarily unavailable, the user must be able to continue to use the service using a workaround solution until the problem is corrected.

Undesirable Actions:

The system must allow the customer to roll back transactions before they have been committed.

Error Avoidance:

The system must prevent incorrect data from being entered by the user (for example, by using drop-down selection boxes containing only valid options and locking up invalid areas of the keyboard).

Performance Requirements

(This section of the Service Level Requirements describes requirements related to speed.)

Stress Requirements

(This subsection of Performance Requirements describes the degree of simultaneous activity that the system must be able to support. For example, "The system must be able to support 2,000 users accessing financial records simultaneously.")

Turnaround-Time Requirements

(This subsection of Performance Requirements describes the maximum allowable wait time from service request until delivery.)

Response-Time Requirements

(This subsection of Performance Requirements describes the maximum allowable time that a user must wait for a response after submitting input.)

Throughput Requirements

(This subsection of Performance Requirements describes the volume of transactions or information per unit of time that the system must be able to process. The required volume of data transfer per unit time is referred to as bandwidth. *)*

Startup and Shutdown Requirements

(This subsection of Performance Requirements describes constraints on startup and shutdown procedures.)

Supportability Requirements

(This section of the Service Level Requirements describes requirements related to the ability to monitor and maintain the system.)

Scalability

(This subsection of Supportability Requirements describes the system's ability to be enlarged, for example, by increasing throughput or maximum number of simultaneous users.)

Expected Changes

(This subsection of Supportability Requirements describes expected changes in services, such as those due to regulations or changing market conditions, and how these how these changes are to be accommodated.)

Maintainability Requirements

(This subsection of Supportability Requirements describes the acceptable degree of effort required to change a process, for example, in order to clear bottlenecks, maximize efficiencies, or correct deficiencies.)

Configurability

(This subsection of Supportability Requirements describes the required ability to adjust the assembly of the product or solution, such as by adding or removing components.)

Localizability

(This subsection of Supportability Requirements describes the ability of the product or solution to be geared toward local conditions and requirements, such as the requirement to support different languages and tax systems.)

Installability

(This subsection of Supportability Requirements describes requirements related to system installation and the ease with which it can be done.)

Compatibility Requirements

(This subsection of Supportability Requirements describes components that the system under design must be compatible with, such as drivers, operating systems, and so on.)

Testing Requirements

(This section of the Service Level Requirements describes the level of testing required for services and components and the requirements for setting up and conducting these tests.)

Training Requirements

(In this section of the Service Level Requirements, describe the level of training required and state which organizations will be required to develop and deliver training programs.)

Capacity Requirements

(This section of the Service Level Requirements describes maximum amounts that the product or solution must be able to support, for example, maximum number of accounts, customers, etc.)

Backup/Recovery Requirements

(This section of the Service Level Requirements describes the backup and recovery facilities required, including the components to be restored in case of failure. Include Service Continuity requirements describing contingency plans and Vital Business Functions [VBFs] that must be kept on life support in case of full or partial service failure.)

Other Constraints

(This section of the Service Level Requirements describes other constraints on the product or solution, such as design constraints.)

Design Constraints

(This subsection of Other Constraints describes constraints on the design of the product or solution.)

Implementation Constraints

(This subsection of Other Constraints describes constraints on the construction of a product or solution, such as the constraint that a specific programming language must be used.)

Interface Constraints

(This subsection of Other Constraints describes protocols, formats, and so on that must be followed when interfacing with external organizations or systems.)

Physical Constraints

(This subsection of Other Constraints describes physical constraints on the product or solution, such as hardware restrictions related to size, temperature control, and materials.)

Legal and Regulatory Requirements

(This section of the Service Level Requirements describes legal and regulatory requirements, existing or pending legislation, governing bodies, and standards that constrain the system.)

Risk Analysis Table Template

The BA supports the PM in risk analysis. For a discussion of the BA role in risk analysis and for guidelines to the BA in facilitating Risk Analysis meetings, see "Meeting Objective: Analyze Risk " in the Meeting Guide chapter of this handbook. For tips on assigning risk types, risk level, and risk management strategies, see " Tips: Managing Risk" in the Tips and Checklists chapter. Examples of risk statuses are as follows: New, Accepted, Transferred, Assigned to an Iteration, and Mitigated.

Table 6.15 may be used for documenting and analyzing risks.

Test Script Template

Table 6.16 may be used for documenting test scripts.

Table 6.15 Risk Analysis Table Template

Risk ID	Risk Type	Description	Consequence (Short Term)	Business Impact (Long Term)	Likelihood	Impact	Level	Status	Risk Management Strategy

Table 6.16 Test Script Template

Test # _____   Project # _____

System: _____   Test environment: _____

Test type (e.g., regression/ requirements-based, etc.): _____

Test objective: _____

System use case: _____   Flow: _____

Priority: _____   Next step in case of failure: _____

Planned start date: _____   Planned end date: _____

Actual start date: _____   Actual end date: _____

times to repeat: _____

Preconditions: _____

Requirement	Action	Expected Result	Actual	Pass/Fail	Bug#

Pass/fail: _____   Severity of failure: _____

Solution: _____

Comments: _____

Sign-off: _____

Vision Document Template[18]

Following is a suggested template for creating a Vision Document describing the background, rationale, and vision for the project.

Positioning

(This section of the Vision Document summarizes the business case for the project.)

Problem Statement

(In this subsection of Positioning, describe the problem and its impact on stakeholders. Avoid language that implies a specific solution to the problem. Use the following syntax in Table 6.17 as a guide to formulating the problem statement.)

Table 6.17 Problem Statement

The problem of	*(Describe the problem.)*
Affects	*(List the stakeholders affected by the problem.)*
The impact of which is	*(Describe the impact of the problem.)*
A successful solution would	*(List some key benefits of a successful solution.)*

Key Stakeholder and User Needs

(This section of the Vision Document summarizes the key needs addressed by the project, as perceived by stakeholders, providing background and justification for the project. Include only a summary here; provide a more detailed analysis in the following section.)

Stakeholders and Interests[19]

(List stakeholders that suffer from the problem, will be affected by the solution, or whose needs constrain the solution, for example, by imposing regulatory restrictions. Assign a stakeholder type to each stakeholder to clarify how the stakeholder is tied to the service or product. Stakeholder types might include the following: Customer, User, Developer, and Regulatory Body. Assign a stakeholder role to describe how the stakeholder will interact with the project. Stakeholder roles might include Executive Sponsor, Visionary, Ambassador User, and Advisor User. Describe each stakeholder's main responsibilities with respect

---

[18]Adapted from *Use Case Modeling* by Kurt Bittner and Ian Spence (Addison-Wesley Professional, 2002).

[19]DSDM: Dynamic System Development Method.

to the project. These might include Monitor Progress, Usability Testing, and Approve Funding. Finally, summarize each stakeholder's interest in the project by describing the need or opportunity addressed by the project from the stakeholder's perspective.)

Table 6.18 may be used as a template for documenting stakeholders and their involvement.

Table 6.18 Stakeholder Interests

Stakeholder	Brief Description	Stakeholder Type	Stakeholder Role	Responsibilities	Interest

Service/Product Overview

(Provide a high-level description of capabilities of the proposed service or product.)

Assumptions

(List any assumptions that, if changed, would alter the vision.)

Dependencies

(Describe any dependencies the service or product has on other services, products, or components or on the target environment.)

Capabilities

(This section describes the capabilities required of the solution. It is divided into the following subsections.)

Features

(List the high-level capabilities, services, or qualities required of the solution. Include a maximum of 25 to 99. Later, map features to business and IT services. Provide a description that does not constrain the design; see Table 6.19.)

Table 6.19 Features

Feature	Description	Priority

Business Service Briefs

(List the end-to-end business services or processes impacted by the project. If your project employs the use-case approach, model end-to-end business services/processes as business use cases; see Table 6.20.)

Table 6.20 Overview of Business Services

Business Service ID	Business Service (Name)	New?	Business Service Brief (Summary of Desired Functionality)	Current Functionality (If a Change)	Priority	Trigger	Inputs/ Outputs	Stakeholders

Constraints

(Specify any predetermined constraints on the solution.)

Service Level (Non-Functional) Requirements

(List requirements that describe the level of service required under stated conditions. Include usability, availability, and performance requirements. See the Service Level [Non-Functional] Requirements Template in this chapter for a complete list of subsections.)

Requirements Work Plan Template

(The Requirements Work Plan document helps plan for gathering and managing requirements. Individual components of this document may be housed separately and brought together in this document.)

Purpose

(This section of the Requirements Work Plan describes the purpose of this document. Your description may resemble the following example.)

The purpose of this document is to describe the plan for discovering, analyzing, and managing requirements and risks related to those requirements.

Document Overview

(This section of the Requirements Work Plan describes the content of this document.)

Organization

(This section of the Requirements Work Plan describes how requirements-related responsibilities and roles are organized.)

Organizational Structure

(This subsection of Organization describes the organizational structure for the project.)

Requirements Roles and Responsibilities

(This subsection of Organization describes how requirements management responsibilities are distributed on the team.)

Requirements Schedule

(This subsection of Organization identifies the start and end dates for requirements activities and maps them to phases and iterations; see Table 6.21.)

Requirements Resourcing

(This subsection of Organization describes assets and resources that will be used to create, maintain, and manage requirements.)

Budget

(This subsection of Organization describes the budget for requirements management.)

Table 6.21 Requirements Schedule

Phase	Iteration	Activity	Start Date	Stop Date	Effort Estimate

Tools, Techniques, and Methodologies

(This subsection of Organization describes the specific tools, techniques, and methodologies that will be used to assist with requirements management.)

Requirements Repository

(This section of the Requirements Work Plan describes the plan for housing requirements.)

Requirements Artifacts

(This subsection of Requirements Repository describes the requirements artifacts that will be part of the project.)

Requirements Types

(This subsection of Requirements Repository describes the types of requirements that will be collected for the project. For examples of requirements types, see "FURPS+" in the BA Toolkit chapter of this handbook and the headings of the SLR template included in this chapter.)

Requirements Attributes

(This subsection of Requirements Repository describes the requirements attributes that will be used for requirements management. See "Requirements Attributes Table" BA Toolkit chapter of this book for examples of requirements attributes.)

Requirements Traceability

(This subsection of Requirements Repository describes the requirements traceability strategy for the project. See "Requirements Traceability Matrix" in the BA Toolkit chapter of this book for an example of this matrix.)

Risk Management Plan

(This section of the Requirements Work Plan describes the plan for managing risks.)

As noted in the "Analyze Risk" section of the Meeting Guide chapter, risk is often defined to mean an uncertain outcome—a positive opportunity or a negative threat. In practice, risk usually connotes a negative threat. The *BABOK*® lists risk analysis under the BA Knowledge Area Enterprise Analysis. The project manager (PM) is the primary role responsible for risk analysis, often delegating the responsibility for discovering, analyzing, and managing risk to the BA, who plays a supporting role. For a discussion of the BA role in risk analysis and for guidelines to the BA in facilitating risk-analysis meetings, see "Meeting Objective: Analyze Risk" in the Meeting Guide chapter of this handbook.

Purpose

(Describe the purpose of the Risk Management Plan.)

Risk Management Strategy

(This subsection of Risk Management Plan describes the approach to be used to identify, analyze, and prioritize risks. It also describes how the status of the risks and how their management strategies will be monitored. For tips on assessing and managing risk, see "Tip: Risk Assessment Matrix" and other risk-related tips and checklists in the Tips and Checklists chapter of this book.)

Responsibility and Accountability

(This subsection of the Risk Management Plan describes how risk management responsibilities are distributed amongst the roles in the project team.)

Risk List

(This subsection of the Risk Management Plan contains the list of risks for the project. See the Risk Analysis Table Template in this chapter for a suggested layout for listing risks.)

Requirements Acceptance Plan

(This section of the Requirements Work Plan describes the plan for acceptance and sign-off of the requirements.)

Purpose

(This subsection of the Requirements Acceptance Plan describes the purpose of the Requirements Acceptance Plan.)

Requirements Acceptance Responsibilities

(This subsection of the Requirements Acceptance Plan describes the responsibilities of the stakeholders/customers and the development team in the acceptance and sign-off of the requirements and identifies the resources that will be required.)

Requirements Acceptance Criteria

(This subsection of the Requirements Acceptance Plan describes the objective criteria that will be used to determine the acceptability of the deliverable requirements artifacts from the project.)

Requirements Acceptance Schedule

(This subsection of the Requirements Acceptance Plan describes the timeline for requirements review and sign-offs.)

Requirements Management Metrics Plan

(This section of the Requirements Work Plan describes the plan for managing metrics related to the requirements.)

Purpose

(This subsection of the Requirements Management Metrics Plan describes its purpose.)

The purpose of the Requirements Management Metrics Plan is to document the approach used to monitor metrics for the requirements analysis and management process.

Requirements Management Goals

(This subsection of the Requirements Management Metrics describes the overall goals for collecting metrics.)

Requirements Management KPIs

(This subsection of Requirements Management Goals documents Key Performance Indicators [KPIs]—metrics used to evaluate the success of the process. Table 6.22 is a template for documenting KPIs.)

Table 6.22 KPI Table

KPI:	*(Name of the KPI.)*
Description:	*(What is being measured, and how is the metric calculated?)*
Goals:	*(Why is the data being collected?)*
Analysis Approach:	*(How will the data be analyzed and used?)*
Responsibilities:	*(Who will collect the data, who will analyze the data, and who will act on the analysis?)*

Examples of KPIs for requirements analysis and management are as follows:

- Descending percentage of non-implemented (lost) requirements
- Descending percentage of untested requirements put into production
- Descending percentage of unapproved requirements
- Client satisfaction percentage

Client Product Acceptance Plan Template

(The BA contributes to and reviews the plan for acceptance of changes to the software. This plan may form part of a larger document, such as the Project Plan.)

Purpose

(Describe the purpose of this section.)

The purpose of this document is to describe the procedures for acceptance of the changes resulting from this project.

Acceptance Responsibilities

(This section describes the responsibilities of the stakeholders/customers and the development team in the acceptance of new or revised software and identifies the human resources that will be required.)

Change Acceptance Criteria

(This section describes the objective criteria that will be used to determine the acceptability of the deliverables of the project.)

Change Acceptance Schedule

(This section describes the timeline for acceptance activities.)

Acceptance Environment

(This section describes the requirements regarding the environment in which the product acceptance will be carried out, such as hardware, software, documentation, test data, special equipment, etc.)

Product Acceptance Tools, Techniques, and Methodologies

(This section describes the specific tools, techniques, and methodologies that will be used for product acceptance. For example, the procedures used in User-Acceptance Testing are documented here.)

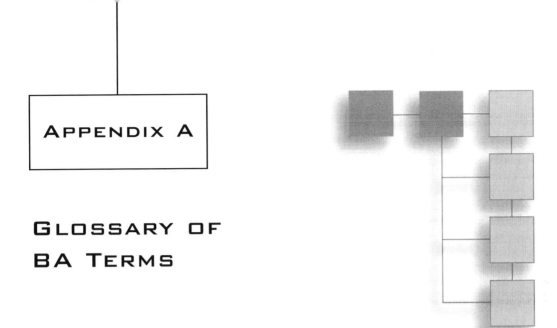

APPENDIX A

GLOSSARY OF BA TERMS

Following is a glossary of terms used within business analysis. Where applicable, the glossary contains definitions from common standards and guidelines (identified in parentheses in the second column of the glossary, under "What They Say"). For terms specific to ITIL and *BABOK®*, please refer also to the Standards and Guidelines chapter of this book. For more information on ITIL terms and concepts, refer to the ITIL V3 Glossary (available for free download at www.get-best-practice.co.uk/glossaries.aspx), *Foundations of IT Service Management: Based on ITIL V3* (edited by Jan Van Bon , Van Haren, 2007), and to the Office of Government Commerce ITIL® core books (Continual Service Improvement, Service Design, Service Operation, Service Strategy, and Service Transition) for more detailed explanations. ITIL core books are available from The Stationery Office at www.tsoshop.co.uk.

For more detailed information about *BABOK®* terms and concepts, download the current version of the *BABOK®* from the International Institute of Business Analysis (IIBA™) web site at www.theiiba.org.

Term	What They Say (Standard or Guideline)	What It Means to the BA
Accessibility		*Accessibility* requirements describe the ease with which an application, product, or IT Service can be used by a person with special needs. Accessibility requirements are a component of the non-functional requirements documented by the BA and packaged in documents such as the Software Requirements Specifications (SRS), Statement of Requirement (SOR), Service Level Requirements (SLR), and Business Requirements Document (BRD).
Action	"An action is the fundamental unit of behavior specification."[1] "An action represents a single step within an activity, that is, one that is not further decomposed within the activity."[2] (UML)	An *action* is an elementary step in a process. One or more actions can be assembled to form an activity. (See *activity*.) The BA uses actions to model elementary steps within a business process (such as the action "Approve change") and steps involved in user tasks (such as the action "Display account information"). The BA includes actions on activity diagrams and state-machine (statechart) diagrams.
Activity	"An activity represents a behavior that is composed of individual elements that are actions."[3] (UML)	An *activity* is a task. It may be of any size and complexity: a simple task, consisting of only one step, or a complex task, consisting of a set of indivisible steps (actions). The BA uses activities to model and document complex steps within a business process (e.g., "Determine Rating") or within a user task (e.g., "The system verifies the transaction"). The BA includes activities on activity diagrams and state-machine (statechart) diagrams.

Glossary of BA Terms (continued)

Term	What They Say (Standard or Guideline)	What It Means to the BA
Activity diagram	"A diagram that depicts behavior using a control and data-flow model."[4] (UML)	An *activity diagram* is a diagram that describes the sequencing of activities. The BA uses activity diagrams to model business processes and user-IT interactions. Activity diagrams (or other workflow diagrams) are recommended for describing the internal workflow of business processes (business use-case realizations) and, as an adjunct to text, in describing user-IT interactions (system use cases) when the flows connect in complex ways. Activity diagrams created by the BA form part of the requirements package; activity diagrams for business processes may reside within the business architecture. (See *activity*.)
Actor	"An actor specifies a role played by a user or any other system that interacts with the subject."[5] (UML)	An *actor* is a type of user or an external system that interacts with the system under discussion. The BA uses actors to model user groups and external systems. They are depicted on Role Maps and use-case diagrams. (See *Role Map, use-case diagram*).
Aggregation	"A special form of association that specifies a whole-part relationship between the aggregate (whole) and a component part."[6] (UML)	*Aggregation* is the relationship between a whole and its parts. Aggregations are depicted on class diagrams The BA uses aggregation to model whole-part relationships between objects tracked by the business. For example, an Invoice is an aggregation of Line Items; an Organization is an aggregation of Members. The use of aggregation by the BA is a matter of some dispute; the Association modeling element may be used by the BA as an alternative to aggregation.[7] (See *Association, Class Diagram*.)

Glossary of BA Terms (continued)

Term	What They Say (Standard or Guideline)	What It Means to the BA
Agile	**Manifesto for Agile Software Development[8]:** We are uncovering better ways of developing software by doing it and helping others do it. Through this work we have come to value: • Individuals and interactions over processes and tools • Working software over comprehensive documentation • Customer collaboration over contract negotiation • Responding to change over following a plan That is, while there is value in the items on the right, we value the items on the left more. **Principles behind the Agile Manifesto (excerpt)[9]:** • Our highest priority is to satisfy the customer through early and continuous delivery of valuable software. • Welcome changing requirements, even late in development. • Deliver working software frequently, from a couple of weeks to a couple of months, with a preference to the shorter timescale. • Working software is the primary measure of progress • At regular intervals, the team reflects on how to become more effective, then tunes and adjusts its behavior accordingly.	The term *agile* refers to an approach (rather than a specific methodology) for developing software systems. Agile approaches are characterized by an ability to change direction quickly, iterative-incremental development with frequent deliveries of working code, a preference for face-to-face meetings with customers over formal documentation, and continual assessment and retooling of the development process. (For information on the agile community, visit www.agilealliance.com.)

Term	What They Say (Standard or Guideline)	What It Means to the BA
Analysis	"The. . .primary purpose [of analysis] is to formulate a model of the problem domain that is independent of implementation considerations. Analysis focuses on what to do; design focuses on how to do it."[10] (UML)	The purpose of *analysis* is to create an abstract representation of the business area under discussion. The representation should be valid regardless of the technology used. In waterfall approaches to software development, analysis occurs in the early part of a project; with agile and other iterative approaches, it may occur throughout the life cycle. The BA is the primary role responsible for analysis.
Architecture	"The structure of a System or IT Service, including the Relationships of Components to each other and to the environment they are in. Architecture also includes the Standards and Guidelines that guide the design and evolution of the System."[11] (ITIL Service Design)	The *architecture* is the repository for across-the-board knowledge about a system, including its structure, standards, templates, and process models. The term architecture may be applied to any type of system or part thereof, such as a business, an IT system, or a service. The BA contributes business process models and static (structural) models to the architecture.
Association	"A relationship that may occur between instances of classifiers."[12] (UML)	An *association* in a business model indicates that the business tracks objects against each other, for example, Invoices against the Customers they are billed to. Association is a UML term that is equivalent (from a BA perspective) to the term *relationship* as it is used in the context of Entity Relationship Diagrams (ERDs).[13] The BA uses associations and their related cardinalities (multiplicities) to model business rules (such as the number of Sales Reps that may be credited to a Sale) and define the relationships between business concepts (such as that between a Policy and a Benefit).

Term	What They Say (Standard or Guideline)	What It Means to the BA
Attribute	"A structural feature of a classifier that characterizes instances of the classifier. An attribute relates an instance of a classifier to a value or values through a named relation-ship."[14] (UML)	An *attribute* is a piece of informa-tion about something. For example, the attribute Price represents a piece of information about a Product. The term is similar to the term *field*. The BA models the attributes of sub-jects (entity classes or types) tracked by the business in the static model (data model or structural OO model). The BA may include attributes on Entity Relationship Diagrams (ERDs) and class diagrams. (See *entity class*.)
	"A piece of information about a Configuration Item. Examples are name, location, Version number, and Cost. Attributes of CIs are recorded in the Configuration Management Database (CMDB)."[15] (ITIL Service Transition)	Within ITIL, the term *attribute* is used to refer, specifically, to a piece of information about a Configuration Item (CI)—an item tracked by Configuration Management. (Examples of CIs include requirements documents, models, software and hardware components, and suppliers.) Attributes of CIs are recorded in the Configuration Management Database (CMDB).
Audit	"Formal inspection and verification to check whether a Standard or set of Guidelines is being followed, that Records are accurate, or that Efficiency and Effectiveness targets are being met. An Audit may be carried out by internal or external groups."[16] (ITIL)	An *audit* is a formal inspection to verify compliance with required standards, guidelines, procedures, and/or outcomes. The BA contributes to the Auditing Plan, which estab-lishes the reviews and audits that will be performed on the project, their schedule, and their goal; the BA documents Auditing Requirements, describing the types of records, reports, and so on required by auditors. Auditing requirements are a compo-nent of the non-functional require-ments documented by the BA and packaged in documents such as the Statement of Requirement (SOR), SLR, and BRD.

Term	What They Say (Standard or Guideline)	What It Means to the BA
Availability	"Ability of a Configuration Item or IT Service to perform its agreed Function when required. Availability is determined by Reliability, Maintainability, Serviceability, Performance, and Security. Availability is usually calculated as a percentage. This calculation is often based on Agreed Service Time and Downtime. It is Best Practice to calculate Availability using measurements of the Business output of the IT Service."[17] (ITIL Service Design)	*Availability* is the fraction (percentage) of time that a service or system is available, relative to the agreed-upon time. Availability requirements are a component of the non-functional requirements documented by the BA and packaged in documents such as the SRS, Statement of Requirement (SOR), SLR, and BRD.
Base use case	"An extend relationship. . .from the use case providing the extension to the base *use case*."[18] ". . . behavior defined in the including use case is included in the behavior of the *base use case*."[19] (UML)	When a use case has a relationship (*extend* or *include*) with another use case, the *base use case* is the one whose behaviour is being modified and that the actor interacts directly with. With respect to an extension, the base use case is the one being extended; in the case of an inclusion, the base use case is the one that includes (contains a reference to) the included use case. Base use cases are modeled by the BA on use-case diagrams. (See *extending use case, included use case*.)
Baseline	"A Benchmark used as a reference point. For example, an ITSM Baseline can be used as a starting point to measure the effect of a Service Improvement Plan; a Performance Baseline can be used to measure changes in Performance over the lifetime of an IT Service; a Configuration Management Baseline can be used to enable the IT Infrastructure to be restored to a known Configuration if a Change or Release fails."[20] (ITIL CSI)	To *baseline* something is to tag it so that changes may be evaluated against it later. (A baseline is a benchmark, but a benchmark is not necessarily a baseline; to be a baseline, the benchmark must be used as a reference point.) Any BA requirements artifacts and models may be baselined at agreed-upon points in a project. Baselining is a very important element of the "V" Model approach described in ITIL Service Transition.[21] The model specifies baseline points between levels in the development process. In a mature ITIL organization, the BA is likely to be involved in signing off on baseline approvals at Level 1 (Define Customer/Business

Glossary of BA Terms (continued)

Term	What They Say (Standard or Guideline)	What It Means to the BA
(Baseline)		Requirements), Level 2 (Define Service Requirements), and may be involved in Level 3 (Design Service Solution). (See "Testing Throughout the Life Cycle with the Service V-Model" in the Tips and Checklists chapter of this book.)
Benchmark	"The recorded state of something at a specific point in time. A Benchmark can be created for a Configuration, a Process, or any other set of data. For example, a benchmark can be used in Continual Service Improvement, to establish the current state for managing improvements; Capacity Management, to document performance characteristics during normal operations.[22] (ITIL CSI)	A *benchmark* is a record of something at a given moment in time.
Black-box test	"[In black-box testing] test data are derived solely from the specifications (i.e., without taking advantage of knowledge of the internal structure of the program)."[23]	A *black-box test* is a test that can be designed without knowledge of the inner workings of the system. Also referred to as data-driven, input/output-driven, and requirements-based testing. The BA supports the planning, execution, and analysis of black-box tests.
Block diagram		A *block diagram* provides a high-level view of a business process, indicating steps, inputs, and outputs but not decisions. The BA uses block diagrams to describe the main steps and information flows for business processes.
Brainstorming	"A group method of problem solving, used in product concept generation. It is sometimes thought to be an open, free-wheeling idea session, but more correctly is a specific procedure developed by Alex Osborn, with precise rules of session conduct. Now it has many modifications in format of use, each variation with its own name."[24]	*Brainstorming* is a technique used to stimulate creative approaches to problem-solving. Key features are that all ideas are considered and that none are challenged. The BA may be asked to facilitate or participate in brainstorming sessions, for example, in the early stages of requirements analysis.

Term	What They Say (Standard or Guideline)	What It Means to the BA
Business	"An overall corporate entity or Organization formed of a number of Business Units. In the context of ITSM, the term Business includes public sector and not-for-profit organizations, as well as companies. An IT Service Provider provides IT Services to a Customer within a Business. The IT Service Provider may be part of the same Business as its Customer (Internal Service Provider), or part of another."[25] (ITIL)	A *business* is an organization; it may be private or public (such as a government ministry or department). Customers for IT services reside within a business. If IT services are provided internally, the IT service provider and customer reside within the same business. The BA represents the needs of the business to the solution provider and translates technical issues from the solution provider into business terms.
Business actor	"A business actor is any person, system or thing that interacts with the business or organization."[26] (Business modeling extension to UML)	A *business actor* is an entity, outside the business area, that interacts with the business, for example, a customer or supplier. The BA includes business actors in the business use-case model and depicts them on business use-case diagrams.
Business analysis	"Business analysis is the set of tasks and techniques used to work as a liaison among stakeholders in order to understand the structure, policies, and operations of an organization, and recommend solutions that enable the organization to achieve its goals."[27] (*BABOK*®)	*Business analysis* is the discipline concerned with analyzing a business area, its structure, its processes, and its problems, and with representing business needs to solution providers. Business analysis is usually practiced within the context of a project, where the practitioner acts as an intermediary between interested parties, consolidating the views of business stakeholders and communicating their needs to a solution provider. Projects involving business analysis may or may not contemplate an IT solution.
Business Analysis Body of Knowledge (BABOK)®	"The *BABOK*® is intended to describe and define business analysis as a discipline, rather than define the responsibilities of a person with the job title of business analyst (which may vary significantly between organizations)."[28] (*BABOK*®)	The *Business Analysis Body of Knowledge*®, or *BABOK*®, defines core knowledge areas and best practices in the business analysis discipline. The *BABOK*® is owned by the International Institute of Business Analysis (IIBA). (See *International Institute of Business Analysis*.)

Term	What They Say (Standard or Guideline)	What It Means to the BA
Business Analysis Planning and Monitoring (BAP & M)	"Business Analysis Planning and Monitoring describes how to determine which activities are necessary to perform in order to complete a business analysis effort. It covers identification of stakeholders, selection of business analysis techniques, the process we will use to manage our requirements, and how we assess the progress of the work in order to make necessary changes in work effort."[29] (*BABOK®*)	*Business Analysis Planning and Monitoring* (BAP & M) is a *BABOK®* Knowledge Area (KA). BAP & M is typically carried out by senior business analysts, working with and supporting the project manager. BAP & M responsibilities include the selection of the right techniques and templates for a project. (See *BABOK®*, *Knowledge Area*. Also see the Standards and Guidelines chapter for more on the *BABOK®* KAs.)
Business analyst (BA)	"Business analysis may be performed by people with job titles such as systems analyst, process analyst, project manager, product manager, developer, QA analyst, business architect, or consultant, among others."[30] (*BABOK®*) "Business Analyst is an individual within an organization who defines, manages, or monitors Business Processes. They are usually distinguished from the IT specialists or programmers who implement the Business Process within a BPMS [Business Process Management System]."[31] (BPMN)	A *business analyst (BA)* is a liaison between business stakeholders (those requiring a solution) and the solution provider. The solution may or may not involve IT. The BA is expected to discover, analyze, negotiate, represent, verify, and validate the requirements for a solution. Any practitioner of business analysis may be considered a business analyst, although the role may not match their formal job title. (See *business analysis*.)
Business architecture	"A formal blueprint of governance structures, business semantics, and value streams across the extended enterprise."[32]	The *business architecture* is a repository for knowledge about a business, including its processes and supporting organizational structure. Business architecture also contains a set of business goals and a roadmap for the evolution of the business.[33] The BA contribution to business architecture includes documentation and models describing external environments and the business units, business concepts and objects, business functions, and processes that comprise the business domain.

Term	What They Say (Standard or Guideline)	What It Means to the BA
Business case	"Justification for a significant item of expenditure. Includes information about costs, benefits, options, issues, risks, and possible problems."[34] (ITIL)	A *business case* is the business rationale for an initiative. For example, if the project were to upgrade a software system, the business case might describe the anticipated benefits to the business, such as increased market share. The BA may be asked to present a business case for proposed changes during the initiation of a project; this may be delivered verbally and/or as a formal document. The business case includes estimated project costs and business benefits, a preliminary analysis of options considered and/or rejected, and risks that might impact the success of the project.
Business Continuity Management (BCM)	"The Business Process responsible for managing Risks that could seriously affect the Business. BCM safeguards the interests of key stakeholders, reputation, brand, and value-creating activities. The BCM Process involves reducing Risks to an acceptable level and planning for the recovery of Business Processes should a disruption to the Business occur. BCM sets the Objectives, Scope and Requirements for IT Service Continuity Management."[35] (ITIL Service Design)	*Business Continuity Management* is the process within ITIL Service Design responsible for ensuring that the impact of a disruption on the business stays within acceptable limits. The BA is responsible for eliciting and documenting the business continuity requirements that are input to BCM. Business continuity requirements are a component of the Business Service Level Requirements.
Business Continuity Plan	"A Plan defining the steps required to Restore Business Processes following a disruption. The Plan will also identify the triggers for Invocation, people to be involved, communications, etc. IT Service Continuity Plans form a significant part of Business Continuity Plans."[36] (ITIL Service Design)	The *Business Continuity Plan* defines the circumstances and process for activating a contingency when a disruption occurs to business operations and the process for restoring the service. The BA is responsible for eliciting and documenting business continuity requirements that are input to the Business Continuity Plan. Business continuity requirements are a component of the Business Service Level Requirements.

Glossary of BA Terms (continued)

Term	What They Say (Standard or Guideline)	What It Means to the BA
Business Impact Analysis (BIA)	"BIA is the Activity in Business Continuity Management that identifies Vital Business Functions and their dependencies. These dependencies may include Suppliers, people, other Business Processes, IT Services, etc. BIA defines the recovery requirements for IT Services. These requirements include Recovery Time Objectives, Recovery Point Objectives, and minimum Service Level Targets for each IT Service."[37] (ITIL Service Strategy)	*BIA* is the analysis of Vital Business Functions (VBFs) and the impact on the business if they are not available. The BA contributes to BIA in a number of contexts, for example, when making a business case for the project and when determining the requirements for recovery of an essential service after a failure.
Business model		A *business model* is an abstract representation of a business area. The *business model* describes both the structure of the business as well as the ways its processes are carried out. The BA contribution to the business model includes static (structural) business models, such as data and object models, and business-process models. Business models created by the BA form part of the requirements package and may reside within the business architecture.
Business object	(Business modeling extension to UML)	A *business object* is something that the business area keeps track of, monitors, or controls. A business object is an occurrence (specific instance) of an entity class. The BA is responsible for documenting rules regarding types of business objects and including these in the static business model. (See *object*, *entity class*).
Business process	"A Process that is owned and carried out by the Business. A Business Process contributes to the delivery of a product or Service to a Business Customer. For example, a retailer may have a purchasing Process that helps to deliver Services to its Business Customers. Many Business Processes rely on IT Services."[38] (ITIL)	A *business process* is a set of business activities for delivering a service or part of a service to a customer. A business process may or may not be supported by IT services.

Term	What They Say (Standard or Guideline)	What It Means to the BA
Business Process Diagram (BPD)	"A Business Process Diagram (BPD) is the diagram that is specified by BPMN. A BPD uses the graphical elements and the semantics that support these elements as defined in this specification."[39] (BPMN)	A *Business Process Diagram* describes the sequencing of activities within a business process. The rules for the diagram are defined in the BPMN standard. The BA uses BPDs to analyze and document As-Is and To-Be business processes. (See *Business Process Modeling Notation*.)
Business Process Improvement		*Business Process Improvement* is an initiative taken to optimize a business process or processes. *Business Process Improvement* may or may not involve an IT solution.
Business Process Modeling Notation (BPMN)	"The primary goal of BPMN is to provide a notation that is readily understandable by all business users, from the business analysts that create the initial drafts of the processes to the technical developers responsible for implementing the technology that will perform those processes, and finally, to the business people who will manage and monitor those processes. Thus BPMN creates a standardized bridge for the gap between the business process design and process implementation."[40] (OMG)	*Business Process Modeling Notation* is a standard for modeling business processes, maintained by the OMG (Object Management Group). The BA uses BPMN to model As-Is and To-Be business processes. (See *Business Process Diagram*.)
Business Relationship Management	"The Process or Function responsible for maintaining a Relationship with the Business. Business Relationship Management usually includes Managing personal Relationships with Business managers, providing input to Service Portfolio Management, ensuring that the IT Service Provider is satisfying the Business needs of the Customers. This Process has strong links with Service Level Management."[41] (ITIL Service Strategy)	*Business Relationship Management* is the process within ITIL Service Strategy that manages the relationship between the IT service provider and the business. The BA contributes to Business Relationship Management by ensuring that business stakeholders' needs are represented over the course of an IT project. The BA also receives input from Business Relationship Management regarding the level to which existing IT services satisfy customer needs.

Glossary of BA Terms (continued)

Term	What They Say (Standard or Guideline)	What It Means to the BA
Business Relationship Manager (BRM)	"A Role responsible for maintaining the Relationship with one or more Customers. This Role is often combined with the Service Level Manager Role."[42] (ITIL Service Strategy)	*Business Relationship Managers* provide a consolidated view of costs and risks across customers and contracts and provide insight into how proposed changes will impact other services currently supplied to customers. They are often marketing and sales representatives. The BA seeks input from BRMs in analyzing the risks and proposed benefits of an IT project.
Business requirement		*Business requirement* is a term that is used in various ways. In some usages, it refers to a high-level business objective; in others, it refers to any requirement from the business area. Following is the definition used in this handbook: A *business requirement* is any requirement (capability that a solution must provide or a condition that it must meet) that stems from the business side. Business requirements include higher-level business objectives (such as increased market share) and lower-level requirements that the business requires of an IT solution (such as user requirements). Business requirements describe what is required by the business, while specifications describe how those requirements will be met by the solution. (See *Requirement, Specification.*)

Term	What They Say (Standard or Guideline)	What It Means to the BA
Business Requirements Document (BRD)	"The business requirements document describes the behavior required of a software application. The primary target audience for a BRD is the customer and users."[43] *(BABOK®)* "A business requirements document (BRD) details the business solution for a project including the documentation of customer needs and expectations. If an initiative intends to modify existing (or introduce new) hardware/software, a new BRD should be created. The BRD process can be incorporated within a Six Sigma DMAIC (define, measure, analyze, improve, control) culture."[44]	*Business Requirements Document* is a term that may be used in various ways; it may refer to business objectives or to more comprehensive requirements documentation. Following is the definition used in this handbook; the BRD, as defined here, is equivalent to the Requirements Package referred to by the *BABOK®*. The *Business Requirements Document* is the consolidated documentation of all of the requirements (capabilities that a solution must provide or conditions that it must meet) that stem from the business. Ideally, the BRD is an electronic assembly of smaller documents, each housed separately in a repository. The level of detail that is viewable in the BRD should be adjustable as appropriate for its intended readers. Separate housing of the subdocuments should allow them to be assembled into various other packages and views as appropriate. Business Requirements documentation forms a key part of the ITIL Service Design Package (SDP).[45]
Business rule		A *business rule* is a constraint, procedure, or directive that governs an aspect of the business. Business rules documented by the BA include methods and formulae used to derive business information, multiplicity rules (describing numerical limits on links between business objects), and condition-response rules. Business rules may be housed in a business rules folder, in an automated business rules engine and in the static model. (See *static model, decision table.*)

Glossary of BA Terms (continued)

Term	What They Say (Standard or Guideline)	What It Means to the BA
Business service	"An IT Service that directly supports a Business Process, as opposed to an infrastructure service, which is used internally by the IT Service Provider and is not usually visible to the business. The term *business service* is also used to mean a Service that is delivered to business customers by business units. For example, delivery of financial services to Customers of a bank, or goods to the Customers of a retail store. Successful delivery of business services often depends on one or more IT Services."[46] (ITIL)	A *business service* represents a capability or need that the business area provides to those who interact with it. A business service may be realized with or without IT. (Please note that the preceding is consistent with the second of the two ITIL definitions for a business service. The alternative ITIL definition excludes non-IT services; it applies the term to computer services that are used directly in business processes [as opposed to infrastructure services].) The BA is responsible for analyzing business services within the context of an initiative to document the business architecture, a business process improvement initiative, or a change to supporting IT Services. (See *Business Service Catalogue*.)
Business Service Catalogue	(See ITIL definition for Service Catalogue.)	A *Business Service Catalogue* contains policies, service level arrangements, and other items related to current business services and maps dependencies between business services and business processes and departments. The catalogue includes information about deliverables, prices, contact points, ordering, and request processes. The Business Service Catalogue is managed by the ITIL process, Service Catalogue Management.
Business Service Pipeline	(See ITIL definition for Service Pipeline.)	The *Business Service Pipeline* is a catalogue of business services in development. It forms part of the Business Service Portfolio. The BA provides input for changes to the Business Service Pipeline. (See *Service Pipeline, Business Service*.)

Glossary of BA Terms (continued)

Term	What They Say (Standard or Guideline)	What It Means to the BA
Business Service Portfolio	(See ITIL definition for Service Portfolio.)	The *Business Service Portfolio* consists of the Business Service Pipeline (business services in development), Business Service Catalogue (current business services) and Retired Business Services. (See *Business Service Pipeline, Business Service Catalogue*.)
Business unit	"A segment of the business that has its own Plans, Metrics, income, and costs. Each business unit owns Assets and uses these to create value for Customers in the form of goods and Services."[47] (ITIL Service Strategy)	A *business unit* is a component of the business that acts as an autonomous organization, with its own assets and business plans.
Business use case	"A business use case describes a business process, documented as a sequence of actions, that provides observable value to a business actor. . . . The flow of events, or workflow, is a key element of a business use case."[48] (Business modeling extension to UML)	A *business use case* is a business process representing a specific workflow in the business—an interaction that a stakeholder has with the business that achieves a business goal. It may involve both manual and automated processes and may take place over an extended period of time.

The BA is responsible for analyzing and documenting business use cases. Business use cases documented by the BA may form part of the requirements package and may reside within the business architecture. (See *business use-case diagram, business use-case realization*.) |
| Business use-case description (specification) | | A business use-case description (referred to in RUP as a business use-case specification) describes the interaction across the business boundary, typically using text supplemented with diagrams (such as activity diagrams) when the alternative flows connect in complex ways. |

Glossary of BA Terms (continued)

Term	What They Say (Standard or Guideline)	What It Means to the BA
Business use-case diagram	"A business use-case diagram can have business actors and business workers interacting with business use cases."[49] (Business modeling extension to UML)	A *business use-case diagram* describes which stakeholders (external business actors and internal workers) participate in which business use cases, the dependencies between business use cases, and the relationships amongst actors. Business use-case diagrams may form part of the requirements package and may reside within the business architecture.
Business use-case realization	Business modeling extension to UML (see *realization*)	A *business use-case realization* describes the internal process used to implement a business use case (business service). A business use-case realization differs from a business use case, which excludes internal steps. The BA analyzes and documents business use-case realizations graphically, using workflow diagrams, such as activity diagrams (indicating participants using partitions). (See *business use case, activity diagram*.)
Capability Maturity Model Integration (CMMI)	"Integration (CMMI) is a process improvement approach developed by the Software Engineering Institute (SEI) of Carnegie Mellon University. CMMI provides organizations with the essential elements of effective processes. It can be used to guide process improvement across a project, a division, or an entire organization. CMMI helps integrate traditionally separate organizational functions, set process improvement goals and priorities, provide guidance for quality processes, and provide a point of reference for appraising current processes."[50] (ITIL Continual Service Improvement)	*CMMI* is a set of best practices for improving processes in an organization or a project. Its predecessor, SW-CMM (also known as CMM) was upgraded to CMMI in 2000.

Term	What They Say (Standard or Guideline)	What It Means to the BA
Capacity	"[Capacity is] the maximum Throughput that a Configuration Item or IT Service can deliver whilst meeting agreed Service Level Targets. For some types of CI, Capacity may be the size or volume, for example a disk drive."[51] (ITIL Service Design)	*Capacity* refers to a maximum amount that a component or service must be able to handle without an unacceptable degradation in performance. Capacity requirements are a component of the non-functional requirements documented by the BA and packaged in documents such as the SRS, Statement of Requirement (SOR), SLR, and BRD. (See *Capacity Management*.)
Capacity Management	"The Process responsible for ensuring that the Capacity of IT Services and the IT Infrastructure is able to deliver agreed Service Level Targets in a Cost Effective and timely manner. Capacity Management considers all Resources required to deliver the IT Service, and plans for short-, medium-, and long-term Business Requirements."[52] (ITIL Service Design)	*Capacity Management* is a process within ITIL Service Design responsible for ensuring that capacity requirements are met. The BA supports Capacity Management through the documentation of capacity requirements and supervision of testing. (See *Capacity*.)
Cardinality	"The number of elements in a set."[53] (UML) (Data modeling)	*Cardinality* refers to the number of allowable elements in a set. Cardinality is often expressed as a number or a range of numbers. Within data modeling, cardinality refers to the number of occurrences that may participate in a relationship. Within the UML, it refers, more generally, to the number of items that may appear in any set; if the cardinality is expressed as a range, it is termed a *multiplicity*. Cardinalities documented by the BA include the cardinality of an attribute (for example, the number of Revision Dates stored in a Document object) and the cardinality of an association end (for example, the number of Accounts that a Customer may have).

Glossary of BA Terms (continued)

Term	What They Say (Standard or Guideline)	What It Means to the BA
Cause-and-Effect graph	(Root-cause analysis)	A *Cause-and-Effect* graph is a diagram that traces an effect back to its root causes. It is also known as an *Ishikawa diagram* or *fishbone diagram*. Cause-and-Effect graphs are used by the BA to identify high-priority areas that a process improvement effort should focus on in order to achieve a desired result or avoid an undesirable one. (See *root-cause analysis*.)
Certified Business Analysis Professional (CBAP)™	"The IIBA has created the Certified Business Analysis Professional (CBAP), a designation awarded to candidates who have successfully demonstrated their expertise in this field. This is done by detailing hands-on work experience in business analysis through the CBAP application process and passing the IIBA CBAP examination."[54]	*Certified Business Analysis Professional* is a professional designation in business analysis administered by the IIBA. (See *International Institute of Business Analysis*.)
Change	"The addition, modification or removal of anything that could have an effect on IT Services. The Scope should include all IT Services, Configuration Items, Processes, Documentation, etc."[55] (ITIL Service Transition)	A *change* refers to any alteration that could have an impact on the delivery of IT services. Changes for which the BA is responsible include changes to requirements documentation and business models. The BA is also responsible for analyzing the impact on the business of changes to underlying IT components and supporting IT services.
Change Advisory Board (CAB)	"A group of people that advises the Change Manager in the Assessment, prioritization, and scheduling of Changes. This board is usually made up of representatives from all areas within the IT Service Provider, representatives from the Business and Third Parties such as Suppliers."[56] (ITIL Service Transition)	The *Change Advisory Board* is a group that meets regularly to evaluate and prioritize changes. The composition of the CAB may change from meeting to meeting, based on the nature of the change. The BA should be included in the CAB or advise the CAB, in order to ensure that stakeholder needs are properly communicated to solution providers.

Glossary of BA Terms (continued)

Term	What They Say (Standard or Guideline)	What It Means to the BA
Change Management	"The Process responsible for controlling the life cycle of all Changes. The primary objective of Change Management is to enable beneficial Changes to be made, with minimum disruption to IT Services."[57] (ITIL Service Transition)	*Change Management* is the process within ITIL Service Transition responsible for controlling changes to services and related documentation. The BA contribution to Change Management includes participating and contributing to the CAB, as well as reviewing and creating business and user-level Requests for Change (RFCs). (See *Change Advisory Board, Request for Change*.)
Change Manager	"The main duties of the change manager, some of which may be delegated, are. . .receives, logs, and allocates a priority, in collaboration with the initiator, to all RFCs; decides. . .what is to be changed and people's areas of Expertise; chairs all CAB and ECAB meetings; liaises with all necessary parties to coordinate change building, testing, and implementation, in accordance with schedules; reviews all implemented changes to ensure that they have met their objectives"[58] (ITIL Service Transition)	The *Change Manager* is primarily concerned with protecting the production environment and ensuring that change-related incidents are minimized. The Change Manager is responsible for a final step in the approval process, ensuring that the Change Management process is followed by reviewing a checklist of items. The checklist provides verification that the sponsor has agreed to the change and that funding is available for allocated resources.
Change Schedule	"A Document that lists all approved Changes and their planned implementation dates. A Change Schedule is sometimes called a Forward Schedule of Change, even though it also contains information about Changes that have already been implemented."[59] (ITIL Service Transition)	The *Change Schedule* is a schedule of changes and the dates planned for their implementation. BA estimates of work effort provide input for the Change Schedule.

Term	What They Say (Standard or Guideline)	What It Means to the BA
Class	"A class describes a set of objects that share the same specifications of features, constraints, and semantics."[60] "Class is a kind of classifier whose features are attributes and operations."[61] (UML)	A *class* is a category that a group of objects may belong to. Objects in the same class share the same attributes (properties) and operations. The BA is responsible for modeling entity classes; these represent types of objects that are tracked by the business. Examples of classes that a BA might be responsible for modeling are Insurance Application, Supplier, and Invoice. Other non-BA classes, such as Control classes, are used in the design of object-oriented software. (See *entity class*, *object-oriented*.)
Class diagram	"A class diagram is a diagram where the primary symbols in the contents area are class symbols."[62] (UML)	*Class diagrams* may be drawn from a business or technical perspective. The BA is primarily concerned with business-perspective class diagrams that describe business nouns, concepts, categories of business objects, and their relationships to each other. Class diagrams created by the BA are included in the business model. The BA may also be asked to review technical-perspective class diagrams; these are used in the design of programs and databases. (See *business model*, *class*.)
Classifier	"A collection of instances that have something in common. A classifier can have features instances. Classifiers include interfaces, classes, datatypes, and components."[63] (UML)	A *classifier* is a category or type. The term classifier is more general than the term class. (All classes are classifiers; not all classifiers are classes.) Examples of classifiers that a BA may be responsible for defining include entity classes (such as Customer) and business datatypes (such as Address). (See *entity class*.)

Term	What They Say (Standard or Guideline)	What It Means to the BA
Commercial Off-The-Shelf (COTS)	"Application software or Middleware that can be purchased from a Third Party."[64] (ITIL Service Design)	A *Commercial Off-The-Shelf* solution is a ready-made, commercially available solution produced by a third-party software vendor. Requirements produced by the BA may serve as the basis for the selection of a COTS solution. The BA may also be responsible for verifying that a proposed or chosen COTS solution meets those requirements.
Communication Diagram	"Communication Diagrams focus on the interaction between Lifelines where the architecture of the internal structure and how this corresponds with the message passing is central. The sequencing of Messages is given through a sequence numbering scheme."[65] (UML)	A *communication diagram* depicts how objects send messages to each other, using a format that focuses on structure. The BA may use communication diagrams to describe how business areas, business systems, and IT systems communicate with each other. (See *interaction diagram*.)
Concurrency	"A measure of the number of Users engaged in the same Operation at the same time."[66] (ITIL)	*Concurrency* requirements describe how many users must be able to do the same thing simultaneously. Concurrency requirements are a component of the non-functional requirements documented by the BA and packaged in documents such as the SRS, Statement of Requirement (SOR), SLR, and BRD.
Condition-response table		A *condition-response table* shows a system's response to simple (non-compounded) input conditions. The BA uses condition-response tables to express business rules. Only simple (non-compounded) conditions are readily handled by a condition-response table. (See *decision table* for business rules related to complex conditions.)
Configuration	"A generic term, used to describe a group of Configuration Items that work together to deliver an IT Service, or a recognizable part of an IT Service."[67] (ITIL Service Transition)	A *configuration* is an assembly of parts that contributes to the delivery of an IT service. (See *Configuration Item.*)

Glossary of BA Terms (continued)

Term	What They Say (Standard or Guideline)	What It Means to the BA
Configuration Item (CI)	"Any Component that needs to be managed in order to deliver an IT Service. Information about each CI is recorded in a Configuration Record within the Configuration Management System and is maintained throughout its life cycle by Configuration Management. CIs are under the control of Change Management. CIs typically include IT Services, hardware, software, buildings, people, and formal documentation such as Process documentation and SLAs."[68] (ITIL Service Transition)	A *Configuration Item* is any item related to an IT Service, which needs to be managed so that changes to it occur in a controlled manner. According to ITIL guidelines, information about the CI and its relationships to other CIs is stored in a Configuration Management Data Base (CMDB)—a part of the Configuration Management System (CMS) and under the control of the Service Asset and Configuration Management process.

Any BA artifact linked to an IT service might be treated as a CI—if changes to it need to be controlled. Examples include business process models, business rules, Service Level Requirements, and functional requirements. (See *Service Asset and Configuration Management, Configuration Management Database, Configuration Management System*). |
| **Configuration Management** | "The Process responsible for maintaining information about Configuration Items required to deliver an IT Service, including their Relationships. This information is managed throughout the life cycle of the CI. Configuration Management is part of an overall Service Asset and Configuration Management Process."[69] (ITIL Service Transition) | In ITIL, *Configuration Management* is a sub-process within the Service Asset and Configuration Management process. Configuration Management is responsible for managing Configuration Items (CIs) and their relationship to other CIs. The process is listed under ITIL Service Transition, but, in fact, is activated any time a change is made to a CI.

Any BA artifacts whose changes must be controlled may be placed under the control of Configuration Management; these include business-perspective static models, as well as functional and non-functional requirements documentation. (See *Service Asset and Configuration Management, Configuration Management Database, Configuration Management System*). |

Term	What They Say (Standard or Guideline)	What It Means to the BA
Configuration Management Database (CMDB)	"A database used to store Configuration Records throughout their life cycle. The Configuration Management System maintains one or more CMDBs, and each CMDB stores Attributes of CIs, and Relationships with other CIs."[70] (ITIL Service Transition)	A *Configuration Management Database* is a table or set of tables used to record Configuration Items (CIs). The CMDB records data associated with each CI (for example, the author and creation date for a Service Level Requirement) and the relationship between a CI and other CIs (such as the links between an IT service and the IT components that support it). (See *Service Asset and Configuration Management*, *Configuration Management System*, *Configuration Item*.)
Configuration Management System (CMS)	"A set of tools and databases that are used to manage an IT Service Provider's Configuration data. The CMS also includes information about Incidents, Problems, Known Errors, Changes and Releases; and may contain data about employees, Suppliers, locations, Business Units, Customers and Users. The CMS includes tools for collecting, storing, managing, updating, and presenting data about all Configuration Items and their Relationships. The CMS is maintained by Configuration Management and is used by all IT Service Management Processes."[71] (ITIL Service Transition)	The *Configuration Management System* is the system that manages the Configuration Management Database. (See *Service Asset and Configuration Management*, *Configuration Management Database*.)
Constraint	"Constraints pose restrictions on the solution option. . . . Business constraints are things like budget limitations. . . . Technical constraints include any enterprise architecture standards that must be adhered to."[72]	A *constraint* is any restriction placed on the solution, such as the constraint that it use a specified technology. Constraints may arise from the business or technical side. Constraints are a component of the non-functional requirements documented by the BA and packaged in documents such as the SRS, Statement of Requirement (SOR), SLR, and BRD.

Term	What They Say (Standard or Guideline)	What It Means to the BA
Context diagram	(Structured Analysis)	In structured analysis, a *context diagram* (also known as *Level 0 DFD*) describes the flow of information between a system and entities outside it. The system that is the subject of a context diagram may be a real-life system, such as an organization, or an IT system. The BA uses context diagrams to provide an overview of the information that passes between a business (or business unit) and its environment, or to summarize the information that passes between an IT system and the users who access it, the external systems it services, and the systems whose services it uses. The BA may include the context diagram in the Vision and Scope document, the SRS,[73] or as part of the business or system architecture.
Continual Service Improvement (CSI)	"A stage in the life cycle of an IT Service. . .responsible for managing improvements to IT Service Management Processes and IT Services. The Performance of the IT Service Provider is continually measured and improvements are made to Processes, IT Services and IT Infrastructure in order to increase Efficiency, Effectiveness, and Cost Effectiveness."[74] (ITIL Continual Service Improvement)	*Continual Service Improvement* is an ITIL Service Life Cycle phase whose purpose is to continually (periodically) improve service management processes and services to ensure customer satisfaction. The senior BA is responsible for supporting the Continual Service Improvement of Business Analysis processes and templates, for example, by designing and improving requirements documentation templates and BA best practices.

Glossary of BA Terms (continued)

Term	What They Say (Standard or Guideline)	What It Means to the BA
Control Objectives for Information and Related Technology (COBIT)	"COBIT is an IT governance framework and supporting toolset that allows managers to bridge the gap between control requirements, technical issues, and business risks. COBIT enables clear policy development and good practice for IT control throughout organizations. COBIT emphasizes regulatory compliance, helps organizations to increase the value attained from IT, enables alignment, and simplifies implementation of the COBIT framework."[75]	*Control Objectives for Information and Related Technology* is a set of best practices, published by the IT Governance Institute, that provide guidance in managing IT processes. (See www.isaca.org.) The BA may be responsible for including within the business requirements control measures required for regulatory compliance, other audit requirements, or corporate policy.
Critical Success Factor (CSF)	"Something that must happen if a Process, Project, Plan, or IT Service is to succeed. KPIs (Key Performance Indicators) are used to measure the achievement of each CSF. For example, a CSF of 'protect IT Services when making Changes' could be measured by KPIs such as 'percentage reduction of unsuccessful Changes,' 'percentage reduction in Changes causing Incidents,' etc."[76] (ITIL)	A *Critical Success Factor* is a measurable outcome that must be attained in order for a project to be considered a success. Each CSF must be associated with one or more metric, referred to as a Key Performance Indicator (KPI); for example, the CSF "increase market share" is deemed successful if the KPI "percentage increase in market share" is 20% or over. The requirements gathered by the BA must support the attainment of CSFs. The BA is responsible for eliciting and documenting CSFs for the project.
Customer	"Someone who buys goods or Services. The Customer of an IT Service Provider is the person or group that defines and agrees to the Service Level Targets."[77] (ITIL)	The *customer* is the person or organization that will pay for the final product or service.
Database Management System (DBMS)		A *Database Management System* is a software system for managing a database. It includes facilities for defining, creating, and accessing data tables. The BA's business-perspective static models (ERDs, class diagrams, and so on) are used as input to the design of DBMS tables.

Glossary of BA Terms (continued)

Term	What They Say (Standard or Guideline)	What It Means to the BA
Data dictionary	"The data dictionary is an organized listing of all the data elements that are pertinent to the system, with precise, rigorous definitions so that both user and systems analyst will have a common understanding of all inputs, outputs, components of stores, and intermediate calculations."[78]	A *data dictionary* lists and describes every data element relevant to a system. The data dictionary promotes reuse. For example, the BA may document the length and valid range for a data item once in the data dictionary, then refer to this item as an attribute of a class, a data item in a use case, or a field in a screen or report mock-up.
Data Flow Diagram (DFD)	"The data flow diagram is a modeling tool that allows us to picture a system as a network of functional processes, connected to one another by 'pipelines' and 'holding tanks' of data."[79] (Structured Analysis)	A *Data Flow Diagram* depicts the flow of information through a system and between the system and its environment. The diagram indicates processes and subprocesses in the context of the flow of data from input to output. The BA uses DFDs to model the flow of information though a business system and to depict the decomposition of business processes into progressively smaller processes. Business-perspective DFDs produced by the BA contribute to the business architecture. Where an IT solution is contemplated, they are used as input to the design of an IT system that automates the business processes they describe.
Data model		A *data model* is an abstract representation of the data in a system, including data structures and relationships. The most common depiction of the data model used by the BA is the Entity Relationship Diagram (ERD). The BA uses the data model to define business concepts, to express business rules related to objects tracked by the business, and to define the business information that must be tracked by the IT solution. The business data model documented by the BA is a component of the business architecture and forms part of the requirements package for an IT project. (See *Entity Relationship Diagram*.)

Glossary of BA Terms (continued)

Term	What They Say (Standard or Guideline)	What It Means to the BA
Decision table		A *decision table* documents the ways that a system responds to complex conditions; a complex condition is a combination of more than one simple condition, such as "Account has been placed on hold" AND "Insufficient funds available." The BA uses decision tables to document condition-response business rules where many interrelated factors influence the outcome. The BA includes links and references to decision tables in business-process requirements documentation (such as business use-case descriptions [specifications]) as well as user requirements (such as system-use case descriptions [specifications]). (See *business rule*.)
Demand Management	"Activities that understand and influence Customer demand for Services and the provision of Capacity to meet these demands."[80] (ITIL Service Strategy)	*Demand Management* is a process within ITIL Service Strategy for predicting the demand for services and aligning supply accordingly. The BA supports Demand Management by analyzing the business area to determine patterns of activity and predict demand.
Description		A *description* is something that tells you what something is like. It may be in the form of text and/or diagrams. For example, a system use-case description usually consists of text describing the user-IT interaction; if the flows connect in complex ways, the description often also contains a workflow (activity) diagram.

Glossary of BA Terms (continued)

Term	What They Say (Standard or Guideline)	What It Means to the BA
Design	"[Design's]. . .primary purpose is to decide how the system will be implemented. During design, strategic and tactical decisions are made to meet the required functional and quality requirements of a system."[81] (UML) "An Activity or Process that identifies Requirements and then defines a solution that is able to meet these Requirements."[82] (ITIL Service Design)	*Design*, as the term is generally used (including in this handbook), refers to the activity or process of specifying *how* the solution is to be built. It differs from analysis, which focuses on *what* the business requires the solution to do or achieve. (Please note, however, that the ITIL definition of design includes both requirements identification and technical specification.) The BA's requirements are input to design. The BA is also involved in validating the design to ensure it conforms to the requirements. (See analysis.)
Domain model	"An object model of the domain that incorporates both behavior and data."[83]	A *domain model* is an abstract model of a system (or aspect of a system) that describes the entities that comprise it and their relationships. The BA may build a domain model of the business; it would include descriptions of business concepts as well as descriptions, data requirements, structural and operational rules regarding the types of organizations, people, transactions, products, and services tracked by the business.
Dynamic model	Also referred to as the behavioral model: ". . .the dynamic, behavioral constructs (e.g., activities, interactions, state machines) used in various behavioral diagrams, such as activity diagrams, sequence diagrams, and state machine diagrams."[84] (UML)	The *dynamic model*, also known as the *behavioural model*, describes how a system acts. It differs from the static (or structural) model, which focuses on what a system and its components *are*. Dynamic-modeling diagrams that the BA is responsible for include use-case diagrams, activity diagrams, and state-machine (statechart) diagrams. (See *static model*.)
Elicitation	"Elicitation describes how we work with stakeholders to find out what their needs are and ensure that we have correctly and completely understood their needs."[85] *(BABOK®)*	*Elicitation* is a *BABOK®* Knowledge Area (KA) that refers to the engagement with stakeholders for the purpose of discovering and validating requirements.

Glossary of BA Terms (continued)

Term	What They Say (Standard or Guideline)	What It Means to the BA
Emergency Change Advisory Board (ECAB)	"A sub-set of the Change Advisory Board that makes decisions about high-impact Emergency Changes. Membership of the ECAB may be decided at the time a meeting is called and depends on the nature of the Emergency Change."[86] (ITIL Service Transition)	The *Emergency Change Advisory Board* is a body that meets to deal with emergency changes. The ECAB is composed of select members from the Change Advisory Board (CAB), but its exact composition may vary for each meeting. The BA advises the ECAB and may be a member of it. (See *Change Advisory Board*.)
Encapsulation		*Encapsulation* is an object-oriented (OO) principle that states that the description of a class encompasses both its operations (actions) and attributes (data) and that no object may refer directly to another's attributes or rely on a knowledge of the methods used to implement its operations. Encapsulation requires that objects only interact by passing messages.
Enterprise Analysis (EA)	"Enterprise Analysis describes how we take a business need, refine and clarify the definition of that need, and define a solution scope that can feasibly be implemented by the business. It covers problem definition and analysis, business case development, feasibility studies, and the definition of a solution scope."[87] (*BABOK®*)	*Enterprise Analysis* is a *BABOK®* Knowledge Area (KA) that refers to the analysis of the business environment and the business rationale for a change. The BA performs Enterprise Analysis activities at the initiation of a project, for example, in preparing a business case or a stakeholder impact analysis. The BA also performs Enterprise Analysis activities in order to define and document the business architecture. The BA contribution to Enterprise Analysis includes static (structural) modeling and process modeling in order to describe the business, its structure, and its operations.
Enterprise Architecture (EA)	"A coherent whole of principles, methods, and models that are used in the design and realization of an enterprise's organizational structure, business processes, information systems, and infrastructure."[88] (Also, see *architecture*.)	*Enterprise Architecture* is a blueprint describing the current and future state of an enterprise, its structure, processes, assets, and infrastructure. The BA contribution to the Enterprise Architecture includes static models and process models that describe the business, its structure, and its operations.

Term	What They Say (Standard or Guideline)	What It Means to the BA
Entity, entity class	"An entity represents an object of interest in the application which may be concrete (e.g., a person) or abstract (e.g., a conference). A more precise term is entity instance. An entity class represents a particular set of entities in the application."[89] A standard stereotype for "a persistent information component representing a business concept."[90] (UML)	The term *entity* is sometimes used informally to refer to what are more specifically referred to as either *entity instances* or *entity classes* (also known as *entity types*). From the BA perspective, an entity instance is an object tracked by the business (such as Flight 905); an entity class (or entity type) is a category that a group of objects belongs to (such as Flight). Objects that belong to the same entity class are treated similarly by the business. For example, the business tracks the same properties (attributes) for all objects in the same entity class.[91] (See *Entity Relationship Diagram, data modeling, Unified Modeling Language.*)
Entity Relationship Diagram (ERD)	"An entity relationship diagram (also known as an ERD, or E-R diagram) is a network model that describes the stored data layout of a system at a high level of abstraction."[92]	An *Entity Relationship Diagram* describes how information about one subject is cross-referenced against another, for example, the link between Invoice and Product information. The ERD is a data-modeling tool; its UML counterpart is the *class diagram*. The BA uses business-perspective ERDs to express business rules and to define informational items and requirements. The BA may also be asked to review technical ERDs, used to design relational databases.
Escalation	"An Activity that obtains additional Resources when these are needed to meet Service Level Targets or Customer expectations. Escalation may be needed within any IT Service Management Process, but is most commonly associated with Incident Management, Problem Management, and the management of Customer complaints."[93] (ITIL Service Operation)	To *escalate* an incident means to bring in additional resources to deal with it. The BA is responsible for ensuring that escalation procedures for new or revised incidents resulting from a change are documented before the change is put into place.

Term	What They Say (Standard or Guideline)	What It Means to the BA
Event	"A change of state that has significance for the management of a Configuration Item or IT Service. The term Event is also used to mean an Alert or notification created by any IT Service, Configuration Item, or Monitoring tool. Events typically require IT Operations personnel to take actions, and often lead to Incidents being logged."[94] (ITIL Service Operation) "An event is the specification of some occurrence that may potentially trigger effects by an object."[95] (UML)	In ITIL, an *event* is a happening that must be logged and/or managed. If the event causes or may cause a disruption of services, the event is treated as an incident. The BA is responsible for ensuring that requirements for the monitoring of and response to events are included in the requirements documentation. (See incident, *Event Management*.) Within the UML and elsewhere, an event represents a happening or condition that triggers a response. The BA models events on state-machine (statechart) diagrams, on workflow diagrams, and, in the user requirements, as triggers for user-IT interactions (system use cases) and alternate flows.
Event Management	"The Process responsible for managing Events throughout their life cycle. Event Management is one of the main Activities of IT Operations."[96] (ITIL Service Operation)	*Event Management* is the process within ITIL Service Operation for detecting random and planned events that have an impact on the delivery of IT services and for taking appropriate management action. BA deliverables such as activity diagrams, state-machine (statechart) diagrams, and system use-case documentation (triggers) serve as input to Event Management. (See *event*.)
Extension point	"An extension point is a reference to a location within a use case at which parts of the behavior of other use cases may be inserted. Each extension point has a unique name within a use case."[97] (UML)	An *extension point* is a labeled location, or set of locations, within a use case. The extension points mark spots in a base use case where extending use cases may alter its behaviour. The BA indicates extension points on use-case diagrams and/or in the documentation for the base use case. (See *extend*.)

Glossary of BA Terms (continued)

Term	What They Say (Standard or Guideline)	What It Means to the BA
Extend/extending use case	An extend relationship is a "relationship from an extending use case to an extended use case that specifies how and when the behavior defined in the extending use case can be inserted into the behavior defined in the extended use case. . . . The extension takes place at one or more specific extension points defined in the extended use case."[98] "The base use case does not depend on performing the behavior of the extension use case."[99] (UML)	One use case can be described as *extending* a base use case if it adds to or alters the behaviour of the base at specified extension points (locations) and under a specified condition. The BA uses extending use cases to alter the requirements for a user task without modifying the original user requirements—for example, in order to define requirements for an optional software upgrade or to isolate a group of changes to a workflow that only apply under a specific set of circumstances. An example of an extending use case is "Apply for preferred mortgage," which extends the base use case "Apply for mortgage" when the condition "Customer has requested preferred rate" is true. (See *base use case, use case*.)
Fault tolerance	"The ability of an IT Service or Configuration Item to continue to Operate correctly after Failure of a Component part."[100] (ITIL Service Design)	*Fault tolerance* refers to an item's ability to continue to function after a breakdown of one of its components. Fault tolerance can be achieved through redundancy. Fault-tolerance requirements are a component of the non-functional requirements documented by the BA and packaged in documents such as the Software Requirements Specifications (SRS), Statement of Requirement (SOR), Service Level Requirements (SLR), and Business Requirements Document (BRD).
Feature	"A feature is a set of logically related functional requirements that provides a capability to the user and enables the satisfaction of a business requirement."[101]	A *feature* is a capability that a solution is required to deliver. It typically refers to a critical item that a customer or user requires in the solution and may be fulfilled by one or more functional or non-functional requirements. Features are documented by the BA and are a component of the Vision Document and requirements documentation.

Glossary of BA Terms (continued)

Term	What They Say (Standard or Guideline)	What It Means to the BA
Fit for purpose	"An informal term used to describe a Process, Configuration Item, IT Service, etc., that is capable of meeting its objectives or Service Levels. Being Fit for Purpose requires suitable design, implementation, control, and maintenance."[102] (ITIL)	An item or service that is *fit for purpose* works as intended, delivering the required functionality. The BA role includes ensuring that a solution is fit for purpose, for example by supporting black-box testing. (See *fit for use*.)
Fit for use	"Meets certain specifications under the specified terms and conditions of use."[103] (ITIL)	An item or service that is *fit for use* has sufficient capacity, continuity, and security to support warranties and allow for the promised value of the service to be realized. (See *fit for purpose*.)
Five Whys	(Root-cause analysis)	The *Five Whys* is a problem-solving technique in which the question "why?" is asked successively until the root cause of a problem or effect is uncovered. Adherents contend that, typically, asking "why?" about a topic five times will get to the root of the topic. Asking fewer times will not dig deep enough, and asking more will lead to redundancy. (See *root-cause analysis*.)
Focus group		A *focus group* is a small group of representative customers or users. The BA convenes focus groups of users in order to analyze a business process or to elicit user requirements for an IT system or enhancement.
Fork	On activity diagrams, "a fork node is a control node that splits a flow into multiple concurrent flows."[104] (UML) On state machine diagrams, "fork vertices serve to split an incoming transition into two or more transitions terminating on orthogonal target vertices (i.e., vertices in different regions of a composite state)."[105]	A *fork* is a UML modeling element that indicates a point after which outgoing flows or transitions may occur in any order. The BA uses forks on activity diagrams to indicate concurrent processing and on state-machine diagrams to indicate concurrent states (states that an object may be in at the same time). A fork is often combined with a join that marks the point where all incoming flows or transitions must occur before the process (or object life cycle) proceeds.

Glossary of BA Terms (continued)

Term	What They Say (Standard or Guideline)	What It Means to the BA
Forward Schedule of Changes	See *Change Schedule*. (ITIL)	
Function	"A team or group of people and the tools they use to carry out one or more Processes or Activities. For example the Service Desk. The term Function also has two other meanings: • An intended purpose of a Configuration Item, Person, Team, Process, or IT Service. For example, one Function of an Email Service may be to store and forward outgoing mails; one Function of a Business Process may be to dispatch goods to Customers. • To perform the intended purpose correctly, 'The computer is Functioning.'"[106] (ITIL)	In ITIL, a *function* usually refers to a business unit with specified responsibilities and resources. An example of an ITIL function is the Service Desk. Such functions are named using noun phrases, in contrast to processes, which are verbs. A function may participate in many processes, and a process may require the involvement of a number of functions. The term function is also used to refer to a unit of behaviour, for example the business function, "Place an order," or the system function, writeOrderRecord.
Functional decomposition chart		A *functional decomposition chart* describes how complex functions and processes are broken down into simpler processes. Business-perspective functional decomposition charts produced by the BA contribute to the business architecture. Where an IT solution is contemplated, functional decomposition charts are used as input to the design of an IT solution.
Functional escalation	"Transferring an Incident, Problem or Change to a technical team with a higher level of expertise to assist in an Escalation."[107] (ITIL Service Operation)	To escalate an incident is to bring in added resources to deal with it; in *functional escalation*, the added resources provide greater expertise. (See *escalation*.)

Glossary of BA Terms (continued)

Term	What They Say (Standard or Guideline)	What It Means to the BA
Functional requirement	"Functional requirements define the software functionality the developers must build into the product to enable users to accomplish their tasks."[108] "Typically, requirements are broadly categorized as functional or non-functional. Functional requirements describe capabilities the system will be able to perform in terms of behaviors or operations—a specific system action or response. Functional requirements are best expressed as a verb phrase."[109]	Please note that the use of the term functional requirement is not uniform; in some usages it refers only to system-perspective requirements. Following is the definition used in this handbook: A *functional requirement* describes what the system must be able to do; it is an externally visible behaviour that a system must be able to perform. Functional requirements include features and behaviours written from the customer, user, and system perspective. Use cases are a recommended means for representing user-perspective functional requirements. An example of a system-perspective functional requirement is "The system must be able to assign a unique tracking number to each order." The BA is responsible for eliciting, documenting, validating, and verifying functional requirements. Functional requirements are a component of the requirements documented by the BA and packaged in documents such as the SRS, Statement of Requirement (SOR), S(L)R, and BRD.
Gap Analysis	"Gap analysis is done to map the gap which exists between implied and specified customer requirements and an existing process."[110]	A *Gap Analysis* is an analysis of the difference between customer needs and an existing system. The BA performs a Gap Analysis to determine how much of a customer's needs are not met by the current IT system or an off-the-shelf solution.
Gate Review	"Gating is the limitation of opportunities for deviation from the proven steps in the manufacturing process. The primary objective is to minimize human error."[111]	A *Gate Review* is a meeting held at specified points in a project to assess progress and determine whether the project may proceed to the next step. The BA may be asked to participate in or provide input for Gate Reviews at various points during the project life cycle.

Glossary of BA Terms (continued)

Term	What They Say (Standard or Guideline)	What It Means to the BA
Generalization	"A generalization is a taxonomic relationship between a more general classifier and a more specific classifier. Each instance of the specific classifier is also an indirect instance of the general classifier. Thus the specific classifier inherits the features of the more general classifier."[112] (UML)	The BA uses *generalization* to model business categories that have sub-types. For example, the category (entity class) Loan Product may be modeled as a generalization of Mortgage Product and Line Of Credit. Generalization is a strategy for reuse and reducing redundancies, as features common to all subtypes are documented only once (in the generalized class). The use of generalization also allows the BA to proceed from the known to the unknown— by modeling general categories first and adding in subtypes as they become known. (See *specialized class, generalized class.*)
Generalized class	(See *class and generalization.*) (UML)	A *generalized class* describes features common to a group of classes, referred to as its *specialized* classes. Specialized classes inherit the attributes, operations, and relationships of the generalized class. Generalized classes are also known as *generalization classes, superclasses, parent classes,* and *base classes.* (See *generalization* for more on the BA perspective.)
Harel statechart diagram		A *Harel statechart diagram* describes the life cycle of an object and the rules that govern its changes of state (status). Statecharts have been incorporated into the UML where they are referred to as state-machine diagrams. (See *state-machine diagram.*)
Incident	"An unplanned interruption to an IT Service or reduction in the Quality of an IT Service. Failure of a Configuration Item that has not yet affected Service is also an Incident."[113] (ITIL Service Operation)	An *incident* is an event that causes or may cause a disruption or degradation of an IT service. The BA is responsible for documenting expected events resulting from implementation of the solution and the procedures for dealing with them.

Term	What They Say (Standard or Guideline)	What It Means to the BA
Incident Management	"The Process responsible for managing the life cycle of all Incidents. The primary Objective of Incident Management is to return the IT Service to Customers as quickly as possible."[114] (ITIL Service Operation)	*Incident Management* is the process within ITIL Service Operation responsible for managing events that disrupt or might disrupt a service in order to ensure that the regular state of affairs is resumed as quickly as possible.
Include/included use case	"A relationship from a base use case to an inclusion use case, specifying how the behavior for the base use case contains the behavior of the inclusion use case. The behavior is included at the location which is defined in the base use case. The base use case depends on performing the behavior of the inclusion use case, but not on its structure (i.e., attributes or operations)."[115] "The include relationship is intended to be used when there are common parts of the behavior of two or more use cases. This common part is then extracted to a separate use case, to be included by all the base use cases having this part in common."[116] (UML)	When a number of use cases share common steps, those steps may be factored out into an *included use case*. Each of the base use cases that refer to it is said to *include* this new use case. For example, each of the two use cases Withdraw Cash and Pay Bills includes the use case Check Available Funds. The BA uses included use cases to reduce redundancies in the requirements documentation. (See *base use case*, *use case*.)
Information Technology (IT)	"The use of technology for the storage, communication, or processing of information. The technology typically includes computers, telecommunications, applications, and other software. The information may include business data, voice, images, video, etc. Information Technology is often used to support business processes through IT Services."[117] (ITIL)	*Information Technology* refers to the software and hardware used to support business services and processes. Projects involving the BA may or may not involve an IT solution.

Glossary of BA Terms (continued)

Term	What They Say (Standard or Guideline)	What It Means to the BA
Information Security Management (ISM)	"The Process that ensures the Confidentiality, Integrity, and Availability of an Organisation's Assets, information, data, and IT Services. Information Security Management usually forms part of an Organisational approach to Security Management which has a wider scope than the IT Service Provider, and includes handling of paper, building access, phone calls, etc., for the entire Organisation."[118] (ITIL Service Design)	*Information Security Management* is the process within ITIL Service Design responsible for aligning IT and business security and for ensuring that information security is managed in all service management activities. Business and user security requirements are a component of the non-functional requirements documented by the BA and packaged in documents such as the SRS, Statement of Requirement (SOR), SLR, and BRD.
Inheritance	"The mechanism by which more specific elements incorporate structure and behavior of more general elements."[119] (UML)	In object-orientation, an object may *inherit* the features or properties of another element. The BA uses inheritance when a number of types (entity classes) share some but not all features. The shared features are described once in a generalized class. Each variation is modeled as a subtype—referred to, in the UML, as a specialized class. Each subtype inherits all the operations, attributes, and relationships of the generalized class. For example, the subtype Chequing Account inherits the attributes, etc., defined for its generalized class, Account.
Instance	"An entity that has unique identity, a set of operations that can be applied to it, and state that stores the effects of the operations."[120] (UML)	An object is an *instance* of (specific case of) a class. For example, Acme Inc. is an instance of the Customer class.
Integrated Computer Aided Manufacturing Definition Languages (IDEF)		*Integrated Computer Aided Manufacturing Definition Languages* is a standard for modeling systems used in military and other sectors. IDEF includes data, object, and process modeling standards. The BA may be required to create, update, and interpret IDEF diagrams.

Glossary of BA Terms (continued)

Term	What They Say (Standard or Guideline)	What It Means to the BA
Interaction diagram	"A generic term that applies to several types of diagrams that emphasize object interactions. These include communication diagrams, sequence diagrams, and the interaction overview diagram."[121] "In the Annexes one may also find optional diagram notations such as Timing Diagrams and Interaction Tables."[122] (UML)	In the UML, an *interaction diagram* describes how objects communicate through the passing of messages over the course of a scenario (or a group of scenarios). The term is a general one that includes the communication diagram and sequence diagram. Interaction diagrams are used primarily in design.[123] The BA may be expected to review design interaction diagrams to ensure they support the requirements. (See *communication diagram, sequence diagram*.)
Interface	"A named set of operations that characterize the behavior of an element."[124] (UML)	An *interface* is a UML modeling element; it is equivalent to a generalized class that only has operations, but no methods for carrying them out. Any class that conforms to an interface must support the operations defined in that interface. Interfaces are often used by technical designers but may also be used by BAs. For example, the BA may declare an interface that defines the set of messages that redundant, interchangeable IT system must be able to receive and process in order to support service continuity requirements. (See *generalized actor, generalized class*.)
International Institute of Business Analysis (IIBA)	"The IIBA is the independent non-profit professional association serving the growing field of Business Analysis."[125]	*The International Institute of Business Analysis* is a professional body dedicated to the practice of business analysis. It publishes the *Business Analysis Body of Knowledge (BABOK)®* and grants professional certification in business analysis (CBAP).

Glossary of BA Terms (continued)

Term	What They Say (Standard or Guideline)	What It Means to the BA
International Organization for Standardization (ISO)	"ISO is the world largest standards developing organization. Between 1947 and the present day, ISO has published more than 17,000 International Standards, ranging from standards for activities, such as agriculture and construction, through mechanical engineering to medical devices to the newest information technology developments."[126]	*The International Organization for Standardization* is an organization that sets standards in a wide range of industries, including IT.
Iteration	"The purpose of an iteration is to produce a working version. . .of the solution. . . .This does not mean that all the requirements that will ultimately be satisfied need to be known before the development iterations start. Instead, we strive to have just enough understanding of the requirements to set a meaningful objective for the current iteration."[127]	An *iteration* is a cycle within a project that is managed using iterative incremental development, an approach whereby the product is developed and released in stages. Each iteration may involve some analysis, design, and coding and must result in useful added functionality. (See *iterative incremental development*.)
Iterative incremental development	"A style of development that involves the iterative application of a set of activities to evaluate a set of assertions, resolve a set of risks, accomplish a set of development objectives, and incrementally produce and refine an effective solution. It is iterative in that it involves the successive refinement of the understanding of the problem, the solution's definition, and the solution's implementation by the repetitive application of the core development activities. It is incremental in that each pass through the iterative cycle grows the understanding of the problem and the capability offered by the solution. Several or more applications of the iterative cycle are sequentially arranged to compose a project."[128]	*Iterative incremental development* is an approach to software development where the software is developed in iterations (cycles), with each iteration adding an increment of value to the user. In each cycle, some analysis, design, testing, and coding may occur. Also referred to as *iterative development*. Iterative, incremental development is fundamental to agile approaches.

Glossary of BA Terms (continued)

Term	What They Say (Standard or Guideline)	What It Means to the BA
IT Infrastructure Library (ITIL)	"A set of Best Practice guidance for IT Service Management. ITIL is owned by the OGC and consists of a series of publications giving guidance on the provision of Quality IT Services, and on the Processes and facilities needed to support them."[129] (ITIL; see www.itil.co.uk for more information.)	*IT Infrastructure Library* is a library of best practices that provide guidance in the management of IT services. The BA is a key role player in implementing ITIL best practices and achieving its objective of IT services that match customer expectations. The BA is involved in many ITIL processes, such as Service Level Management and Change Management, and plays a key role during ITIL Service Strategy and Service Design.
IT service	"A Service provided to one or more Customers by an IT Service Provider. An IT Service is based on the use of Information Technology and supports the Customer's Business Processes. An IT Service is made up from a combination of people, processes, and technology and should be defined in a Service Level Agreement."[130] (ITIL)	An *IT service* is one that the IT organization must provide to its customers. In ITIL, the service includes all of the resources and processes required for implementation. The BA defines requirements for IT services in the requirements package, such as the SRS, SOR, and S(L)R. (See *business service*.)
IT Service Management (ITSM)	"The implementation and management of Quality IT Services that meet the needs of the Business. IT Service Management is performed by IT Service Providers through an appropriate mix of people, Process and Information Technology."[131] (ITIL)	*IT Service Management* is the discipline of managing IT services, with the goal of matching the IT solution to the customer need. As the person responsible for communicating between the business stakeholder and the solution provider, the BA plays a key role in successful implementation of ITSM best practices. An approach to ITSM that has wide popularity is ITIL. (See *IT Infrastructure Library*.)

Glossary of BA Terms (continued)

Term	What They Say (Standard or Guideline)	What It Means to the BA
IT Service Continuity Management (ITSCM)	"The Process responsible for managing Risks that could seriously affect IT Services. ITSCM ensures that the IT Service Provider can always provide minimum agreed Service Levels, by reducing the Risk to an acceptable level and Planning for the Recovery of IT Services. ITSCM should be designed to support Business Continuity Management."[132] (ITIL Service Design)	*IT Service Continuity Management* is the process within ITIL Service Design that supports business continuity by ensuring IT facilities can be resumed after a failure within the agreed timeframe. The BA is responsible for providing the business continuity requirements that provide input to ITSCM; these requirements are part of the non-functional requirements, which may be included in documentation, such as the Service Level Requirements (SLR), Statement of Requirement (SOR), or Software Requirements Specification (SRS). (See *Business Continuity Management*.)
IT Service Management Forum (itSMF®)	"The itSMF® is the only truly independent and internationally recognized forum for IT Service Management professionals worldwide. This not-for-profit organisation is a prominent player in the on-going development and promotion of IT Service Management 'best practice' standards and qualifications and has been since 1991."[133]	*IT Service Management Forum®* is an organization that promotes best practices in IT Service Management (ITSM), including the promotion of ITIL and the publication of ITIL and non-ITIL books related to IT service management.
Joint Application Development/ Design (JAD)		*Joint Application Design* is an approach to software advancement, developed by Toby Crawford and Chuck Morris at IBM in 1977. The JAD approach brings together business stakeholders and the technical team for marathon analysis and design sessions that result in various types of deliverables, including requirements and design artifacts, prototypes, and working code. A BA may be asked to participate in or facilitate JAD sessions.[134]

Term	What They Say (Standard or Guideline)	What It Means to the BA
Key Performance Indicator (KPI)	"A Metric that is used to help manage a Process, IT Service, or Activity. Many Metrics may be measured, but only the most important of these are defined as KPIs and used to actively manage and report on the Process, IT Service, or Activity. KPIs should be selected to ensure that Efficiency, Effectiveness, and Cost Effectiveness are all managed."[135] (ITIL Service Design and Continual Service Improvement)	A *Key Performance Indicator* is something that can be measured, such as a percentage increase or decrease in response time, down time, and so on. The BA documents KPIs for Critical Success Factors (CSF), Service Level Targets, and other objectives.
Knowledge Area (KA)	"A knowledge area groups a related set of tasks and techniques."[136] (*BABOK®*)	A Knowledge Area is a cluster of BA techniques and best practices defined in the *BABOK®*. The *BABOK®* defines six KAs: • BAP & M: Business Analysis Planning and Monitoring • EA: Enterprise Analysis • E: Elicitation • RA: Requirements Analysis • SA & V: Solution Assessment and Validation • RM & C: Requirements Management and Communication (See *Business Analysis Book of Knowledge®*. Also see "IIBA and *BABOK®*" in the Standards and Guidelines chapter of this handbook for more on KAs.)
Legacy system		A *legacy system* is a system in the twilight of its life cycle that is developed and hosted on aging technology.[137]
Line of Service (LOS)	"A Core Service or Supporting Service that has multiple Service Level Packages. A Line of Service is managed by a Product Manager and each Service Level Package is designed to support a particular market segment."[138] (ITIL Service Strategy)	A *Line of Service* is a grouping of IT services. LOSes are managed like a product at the highest level in the provider's catalogue. They are composed of core, supporting, and enabling services to address specific market segments.[139]

Term	What They Say (Standard or Guideline)	What It Means to the BA
Maintainability	"A measure of how quickly and Effectively a Configuration Item or IT Service can be restored to normal working after a Failure. Maintainability is often measured and reported as MTRS. Maintainability is also used in the context of Software or IT Service Development to mean ability to be Changed or Repaired easily."[140] (ITIL Service Design)	A *maintainability* requirement describes the ease with which an item (service, component, artifact, etc.) can be changed or repaired. *Maintainability* requirements are a component of the non-functional requirements documented by the BA and packaged in documents such as the SRS, Statement of Requirement (SOR), SLR, and BRD.
Mean Time Between Failures (MTBF)	"A Metric for measuring and reporting Reliability. MTBF is the average time that a Configuration Item or IT Service can perform its agreed Function without interruption. This is measured from when the CI or IT Service starts working, until it next fails."[141] (ITIL Service Design)	The *Mean Time Between Failures* (MTBF) is the average time an item or service is operational ("up") before it fails. Target MTBFs are a component of the non-functional requirements documented by the BA and packaged in documents such as the SRS, Statement of Requirement (SOR), and SLR.
Mean Time Between System/Service Incidents (MTBSI)	"A Metric used for measuring and reporting Reliability. MTBSI is the mean time from when a System or IT Service fails, until it next fails. MTBSI is equal to MTBF + MTRS."[142] (ITIL Service Design)	*Mean Time Between System/Service Incidents* is the average time between failures of the same system or service. As opposed to MTBF (which is measured from the time the item goes up till it goes down), MTBSI is measured from the time the item last failed until it fails again. Target MTBSes are a component of the non-functional requirements documented by the BA and packaged in documents such as the SRS, Statement of Requirement (SOR), and SLR.
Mean Time To Repair (MTTR)	"The average time taken to repair a Configuration Item or IT Service after a Failure. MTTR is measured from when the CI or IT Service fails until it is repaired. MTTR does not include the time required to Recover or Restore. MTTR is sometimes incorrectly used to signify Mean Time to Restore Service."[143] (ITIL)	*Mean Time To Repair (MTTR)* is the average time it takes to fix an item or service, from the time it is reported until the repair is complete – but not including time to recover or restore. Target MTTRs are a component of the non-functional requirements documented by the BA and packaged in documents such as the SRS, Statement of Requirement (SOR) and SLR.

Term	What They Say (Standard or Guideline)	What It Means to the BA
Mean Time to Restore Service (MTRS)	"The average time taken to restore a Configuration Item or IT Service after a Failure. MTRS is measured from when the CI or IT Service fails until it is fully restored and delivering its normal functionality."[144] (ITIL)	*Mean Time to Restore Service* is the average time for an item or service to become operational following a failure. It differs from MTTR in that MTRS includes time to recover or restore. Target MTRSes are a component of the non-functional requirements documented by the BA and packaged in documents such as the SRS, Statement of Requirement (SOR), and SLR.
Message	"A specification of the conveyance of information from one instance to another, with the expectation that activity will ensue. A message may specify the raising of a signal or the call of an operation."[145] (UML)	In OO (object orientation), a *message* is a request that one object sends to another. When a message is passed between objects, the message represents a class operation of the receiving object. When the objects are IT systems, the messages represent electronic requests or transactions. The BA may be asked to review messages appearing on technical communication diagrams and sequence diagrams to ensure they comply with and implement the requirements. In addition, business-perspective sequence diagrams, including messages, are sometimes prepared by BAs (though this practice is not recommended in this handbook[146])—for example, to describe business use-case realizations (cross-functional workflow).
Method	"The implementation of an operation. It specifies the algorithm or procedure associated with an operation."[147] (UML)	In the UML, a *method* is the procedure used to carry out an operation: While an *operation* represents the facade, or interface, shown to the world outside the object, the method is the internal mechanism for implementing the operation. The BA documents the methods used to implement the operations of business entity classes.[148]

Term	What They Say (Standard or Guideline)	What It Means to the BA
Mitigate		To *mitigate* a risk is to take action to reduce the exposure to the risk or to reduce its consequences. Proactive mitigation aims to reduce the chance of the risk occurring; reactive mitigation is a contingency plan (Plan B) to deal with the risk if it occurs. The BA contributes to risk analysis and planning, including planning for risk mitigation.
Model		A *model* is an abstract representation of something. It is often expressed in diagrams, such as flowcharts, block diagrams, and ERDs.
Multiplicity	"A multiplicity is a definition of an inclusive interval of non-negative integers beginning with a lower bound and ending with a (possibly infinite) upper bound. A multiplicity element embeds this information to specify the allowable cardinalities for an instantiation of this element."[149] "Multiplicity specifications may be given for association ends, parts within composites, repetitions, and other purposes. Essentially a multiplicity is a (possibly infinite) subset of the non-negative integers."[150] (UML)	*Multiplicity* is a range that represents the number of times an element can occur. The term is similar to cardinality, but is more specific: Cardinality refers to any specification of the number of elements in a set, whereas multiplicity must be expressed as a range. Applied to an end of an association, multiplicity represents the number of objects that may be linked to another object (whose type appears at the other end of the association). The BA depicts the multiplicities of association ends on class diagrams. Applied to an attribute, multiplicity represents the allowable number of the attribute's values that are tracked for each object.

Glossary of BA Terms (continued)

Term	What They Say (Standard or Guideline)	What It Means to the BA
Net Present Value (NPV)		*Net Present Value* is the value of an item, expressed in today's currency. NPV is used to correct for the effect of time on the value of money (time value of money). The BA uses NPV in analyzing future costs or benefits in order to correct for inflation and/or compound interest. NPV is calculated according to the formula $NPV = NFV / (1 + i)^n$, where i is the factor being corrected for (interest or inflation rate) and n is the number of terms (e.g., years) between the present and the time for which the future value is expressed.
Non-functional requirement	"Quality of service requirements are most often used to describe the system or system environment. They are also known as non-functional requirements."[151] *(BABOK®)* "In addition to the functional requirements, which describe the behavior the system must exhibit and the operations it performs, the SRS contains nonfunctional requirements. These might include standards, regulations, . . . contracts to which the product must conform, . . . performance requirements, . . . and constraints."[152]	*Non-functional requirements* are any requirements that don't result in observable behaviour, such as security requirements, performance requirements, reliability, and compliance requirements. Non-functional requirements are documented by the BA and packaged in documents such as the SRS, Statement of Requirement (SOR), SLR, and BRD. Also referred to as quality requirements and Service Level Requirements. (See *Service Level Requirement*.)
Object	"An instance of a class."[153] (UML)	An *object* is a thing; it is an *instance* of (specific case of) a class (category). For example, the customer "Jane Dell Ray" is an object—an instance of the class Customer. A BA analyzes rules related to business objects.[154] A *business object* is something responsible for carrying out business activities and/or something that business needs to track. A business object is an instance of an entity class. Invoice #220 is an example of a business object. (See *entity class*.)

Glossary of BA Terms (continued)

Term	What They Say (Standard or Guideline)	What It Means to the BA
Object Management Group (OMG)	"Founded in 1989, the Object Management Group, Inc. (OMG) is an open membership, not-for-profit computer industry standards consortium that produces and maintains computer industry specifications for interoperable, portable, and reusable enterprise applications in distributed, heterogeneous environments. Membership includes Information Technology vendors, end users, government agencies, and academia."[155]	The *Object Management Group* is a non-profit organization that maintains the UML and BPMN modeling standards among many other standards. (See *www.omg.org*.)
Object-oriented (OO)		*Object-oriented* is an approach to analysis, design, and coding based upon a view of a system as a set of basic units, called *objects*, each of which represents the information and operations related to one aspect of the system. A system described as *object-oriented* must also support other concepts, such as classes and inheritance.

OO supplies the BA with a set of tools and concepts for modeling a business area, including its business processes, concepts, and types of business objects. The most popular standard for OO modeling is the Unified Modeling Language (UML). OO is also the basis for the languages most used for new development, such as Java and C++ in the .NET framework. |
| Office of Government Commerce (OGC) | "OGC owns the ITIL brand (copyright and trademark). OGC is a UK Government department that supports the delivery of the government's procurement agenda through its work in collaborative procurement and in raising levels of procurement skills and capability within departments. It also provides support for complex public sector projects."[156] | The *Office of Government Commerce* is the UK government department that owns ITIL, a set of best practices and guidelines for delivering IT services. |

Term	What They Say (Standard or Guideline)	What It Means to the BA
Operation	[Operation is the] "day-to-day management of an IT Service, System, or other Configuration Item. *Operation* is also used to mean any pre-defined Activity or Transaction. For example, loading a magnetic tape, accepting money at a point of sale, or reading data from a disk drive."[157] (ITIL Service Operation) "A feature which declares a service that can be performed by instances of the classifier of which they are instances."[158] (UML) "Operations of a class can be invoked on an object. . . . An operation invocation may cause changes to the values of the attributes of that object."[159] (UML)	In ITIL, the term *operation* refers to an activity involved in the running of an IT service or system. In the UML, an operation is a function that an object may carry out or that is carried out on the object. Operations are defined at the class level. For example, "Apply price increase" might be modeled as an operation of the Product class. Though class operations are not widely included in BA models at present, they are useful in that context for reducing redundancies in the documentation. For example, if a Withdraw Funds operation must always be implemented on an account using a standard set of verifications, the BA may model it as an operation of the Account class, along with a method (procedure) for carrying it out. The method for the operation can then be applied whenever withdrawals occur, for example, during bill payments or fund transfers. (See *method*.)
Package	"A package is used to group elements, and provides a namespace for the grouped elements."[160] (UML)	A *package* is a container used to organize a model's elements into groups. Packages may be nested within other packages. The names of modeling elements within a package must be unique, but identical element names may appear across packages. The BA uses packages in the dynamic model to organize and bundle use cases and use-case diagrams and in the static (structural) model to bundle entity classes and class diagrams. (See *package diagram*.)
Package diagram	A diagram that depicts how model elements are organized into packages and the dependencies among them, including package imports and package extensions.[161] (UML)	A *package diagram* is a UML diagram that depicts how a model's elements are bundled into packages and the dependencies between elements. It is a type of structural (static) diagram. (See *package*.)

Glossary of BA Terms (continued)

Term	What They Say (Standard or Guideline)	What It Means to the BA
Pareto chart	Also called Pareto diagram. "Focuses on efforts or the problems that have the greatest potential for improvement by showing relative frequency and/or size in a descending bar graph. Based on the proven Pareto principle: 20% of the sources cause 80% of any problems."[162]	A *Pareto chart* plots events against their frequency of occurrence. It is often used with the "80/20" rule to find the roughly 20% of events that are thought to be the source of 80% of the problems. The BA uses Pareto charts to help determine the critical root causes to address in an IT project.
Payback period		The *payback period* is the time it takes to pay off the initial investment. The payback period is calculated according to the following formula: (Payback period in years) = (Initial investment) / (Net benefit per year). The BA includes the payback period in the business case for a proposed solution.
Performance test		A *performance test* is a system test that checks the speed of the system, such as how fast it responds (response time) or how many transactions it can process per unit time (throughput). The BA must ensure that performance tests are planned and executed to ensure that performance requirements documented with the non-functional requirements are satisfied by the solution.
Phase		A *phase* is a span of time within a process, marked at each end by well-defined milestones with specific exit criteria; each phase has its own theme of behaviour. The BA is most active during the early phases of a project.

Term	What They Say (Standard or Guideline)	What It Means to the BA
Plan-Do-Check-Act	"A four-stage cycle for Process management, attributed to Edward Deming. Plan-Do-Check-Act is also called the Deming Cycle. PLAN: Design or revise Processes that support the IT Services. DO: Implement the Plan and manage the Processes. CHECK: Measure the Processes and IT Services, compare with Objectives and produce reports. ACT: Plan and implement Changes to improve the Process."[163] (ITIL Continual Service Improvement)	*Plan-Do-Check-Act* is a guideline for managing a process. On an IT project, it involves planning for the change, executing it, verifying whether the change met its objectives, and planning and implementing corrective action based on the results. On an iterative incremental project, a Plan-Do-Check-Act cycle is executed for each iteration. Within ITIL, the approach is also applied to the continual (periodic) improvement of IT Service Management processes.
Process map	"Illustrated description of how things get done, which enables participants to visualize an entire process and identify areas of strength and weaknesses. It helps reduce cycle time and defects while recognizing the value of individual contributions."[164]	A *process map* is an abstract representation of the procedures used to implement tasks (such as services, processes, and operations). The process map is expressed using diagrams. Process maps are used by the BA to analyze As-Is and To-Be business processes. Process mapping tools used by the BA include the activity diagram and Business Process Diagram (BPD). (See *activity diagram*, *Business Process Diagram*.)
Project	"A temporary endeavor undertaken to create a unique product, service, or result."[165]	A *project* is an activity with specified objectives, resources, and time frames. The BA is a key player involved in projects whose goal is to provide a solution to a business problem, acting as an intermediary between the business and the solution provider; the solution may or may not involve IT.
Project Management Body of Knowledge (PMBOK)	"The Project Management Body of Knowledge (PMBOK) document. . .is a codification of knowledge specifically related to the management of projects."[166]	The *Project Management Body of Knowledge* is a set of guidelines for managing projects. The PMBOK is maintained and published by the Project Management Institute. (See *www.pmi.org* for more information.)

Glossary of BA Terms (continued)

Term	What They Say (Standard or Guideline)	What It Means to the BA
POLDAT Framework		*POLDAT* is a corporate analysis approach for depicting an enterprise's processes, organization, location, data, application, and technology within the Enterprise Architecture.
Polymorphism	"Operations are specified in the model and can be dynamically selected only through polymorphism."[167] (UML)	*Polymorphism* is an object-oriented concept that denotes the ability to take on many forms. With respect to operations, it means that the same operation may be associated with a variety of methods for carrying it out.

The BA uses polymorphic operations, in conjunction with generalized classes, to declare generic operations that are carried out in different ways depending on the subtype that an object belongs to. For example, the BA may define a generic operation Determine Service Charge for a generalized class, Account, without ascribing a method to it. For each of the subtypes (specializations) of Account, such as Chequing Account and Savings Account, the BA documents the polymorphic operation Determine Service Charge and ascribes a type-specific method to it for determining the charge. |
| **Post-condition** | "A constraint expresses a condition that must be true at the completion of an operation."[168] | A *post-condition* is one that is guaranteed to be true when a task completes. Post-conditions may be attached to any sized task, such as a business process, user task (system use case), or class operation.

Post-conditions commonly documented by the BA include post-conditions of business and system use cases. (See *pre-condition*, *operation*, *use case*.) |

Term	What They Say (Standard or Guideline)	What It Means to the BA
Post-Implementation Review (PIR)	"A Review that takes place after a Change or a Project has been implemented. A PIR determines if the Change or Project was successful, and identifies opportunities for improvement."[169]	A *Post-Implementation Review* is a meeting held after an initiative to determine whether or not it was successful. The BA may be asked to participate in a PIR after a project to determine if it met its objectives, to identify opportunities for improvement, and to identify lessons learned that can be applied to other projects.
Pre-condition	"A constraint expresses a condition that must be true when an operation is invoked."[170]	A *pre-condition* is something that must be true before a task may begin. The task may be of any size, such as a business process, user task, or class operation. The BA documents pre-conditions for various tasks, including business and system use cases and class operations. (See *post-condition, operation, use case*.)
Primary actor	(Use-case modeling)	A *primary actor* is a user role or external system that initiates a use case. The BA indicates that an actor is the primary actor for a use case by depicting an arrow from the actor to the use case on a use-case diagram. Primary actors may also be indicated in the textual documentation of a use case.
Primary key	(Data and object modeling)	A *primary key* is a unique identifier. Primary keys are included in the data model (ERD and accompanying documentation) and/or static OO model (class diagrams and accompanying documentation) While the assignment of primary keys is largely a technical responsibility, the BA indicates primary keys if they are constrained by the business.

Glossary of BA Terms (continued)

Term	What They Say (Standard or Guideline)	What It Means to the BA
Problem Management	"Problem Management is the process responsible for managing the life cycle of all problems. The primary Service Operation processes objectives of Problem Management are to prevent problems and resulting incidents from happening, to eliminate recurring incidents, and to minimize the impact of incidents that cannot be prevented."[171] (ITIL Service Operation)	*Problem Management* is the process within ITIL Service Operation responsible for managing knowledge about known problems. Problem Management services Incident Management by assisting in the diagnosis of the underlying problems behind an incident and by providing known workarounds; Incident Management supports Problem Management by supplying statistics and records of incidents. Problem Management provides information to and receives information from the BA. For example, Problem Management provides information used by the BA to make the business case for a project; the BA supplies input to Problem Management in the form of analyses of known problems and workarounds based on interviews with business stakeholders and users of a system.
Process	"A structured set of Activities designed to accomplish a specific Objective. A Process takes one or more defined inputs and turns them into defined outputs."[172] (ITIL) "A Process is any activity performed within a company or organization."[173] (BPMN)	A *process* is a repeatable series of steps used to achieve a result. It may be of any size and may or may not involve IT. A process can be thought of as a factory that consumes input data and produces output data. For example, the Calculate Income Tax process uses earnings and other financial input data to produce Tax Payments. (See *process model*.)
Process model	"The types of activities that are a part of a Process Model are Process, Sub-Process, and Task."[174] (BPMN)	A *process model* is an abstract representation of a process, including the sequencing of its activities and its decomposition into subprocesses. The BA creates process models to describe business processes and user tasks. Process-modeling diagrams used by the BA include activity diagrams and BPDs. (See *process, activity diagram, Business Process Diagram*.)

Glossary of BA Terms (continued)

Term	What They Say (Standard or Guideline)	What It Means to the BA
Process owner	"A Role responsible for ensuring that a Process is Fit for Purpose. The Process Owner's responsibilities include sponsorship, Design, Change Management, and continual improvement of the Process and its Metrics. This Role is often assigned to the same person who carries out the Process Manager Role, but the two Roles may be separate in larger Organizations."[175] (ITIL)	A *process owner* is an executive role responsible for ensuring the quality of a process. The BA seeks the input of business process owners in order to gain an understanding of problems and issues with current business processes and to ensure that IT changes are consistent with the business processes they support.
Product manager	'Product Manager is. . .responsible for managing services as a product over their entire life cycle from concept to retirement through design, transition, and operation. They are instrumental in the development of Service Strategy and its execution through the Service life cycle. . . . Product Managers are recognized as the subject matter experts on Lines of Service (LOS) and the Service Catalogue. They understand Service Models and their internal structure and dynamics to be able to drive changes and improvements effectively. They have a consolidated view of costs and risks across LOS, just as BRMs [Business Relationship Managers] maintain a similar view across customers and contracts."[176] (ITIL)	*Product manager* is a tactical role responsible for planning and managing the development of products and services that are packaged and marketed together as a group.\n\nProduct managers are amongst the stakeholders whose needs are analyzed by the BA. They provide insight regarding the impact on the business if the proposed changes are made or are not made and define the overall risk profile and costs across Lines of Service.
Production Verification Testing (PVT)		*Production Verification Testing* is testing done in the production environment to verify the satisfactory operation of the implemented solution.[177] Also known as *Production Validation Testing*.
Projected Service Outages (PSO)	"A Document that identifies the effect of planned Changes, maintenance Activities and Test Plans on agreed Service Levels."[178] (ITIL Service Transition)	*Projected Service Outages* is a document outlining planned activities that might lead to a disruption of services and their projected effect on those services.\n\nThe change schedule and test plans that the BA contributes to provide input to the PSO.

Glossary of BA Terms (continued)

Term	What They Say (Standard or Guideline)	What It Means to the BA
Prototype		A *prototype* is a simulation of the system, used to derive and test requirements. The prototype may be low-tech (sketch, system use-case description) or automated (active screen). Automated prototypes may be discarded after their use in analysis and design, or they may be developed further and incorporated into the final system. Prototypes are developed by the designer, not the BA. However, they are often developed incrementally alongside the user tasks (system use cases) for which they serve as interfaces.
Quality requirements	"Quality requirements describe the designability, reliability, usability, maintainability, efficiency, human engineering, testability, understandability, maintainability, scalability, and portability expectations for the system."[179]	See *alternate term, non-functional requirements*.
RACI chart		A *RACI chart* is a table used to identify the involvement of stakeholders in a process or artifact. Stakeholders indicated as Responsible are those who perform the task (or create the artifact). One person is designated as Accountable; this person is ultimately answerable for the performance of the task (or the correctness of the artifact). Those designated as Consulted provide input. Informed stakeholders are notified but do not contribute to the task or artifact. A RACI chart may be used or reviewed by a BA to specify the involvement of various roles and stakeholders in a project, to indicate the involvement of stakeholders in a business process, and to indicate the persons involved in the creation, sign-off, and distribution of a BA artifact.

Term	What They Say (Standard or Guideline)	What It Means to the BA
Rational Unified Process (RUP)	"The Rational Unified Process (RUP) is an iterative software development process framework created by the Rational Software Corporation, now a division of IBM, in 1995. RUP is not a single concrete prescriptive process, but rather an adaptable process framework, intended to be tailored by the development organizations and software project teams that will select the elements of the process that are appropriate for their needs. The Rational Unified Process is also a software process product, originally developed by Rational Software, and now available from IBM. The product includes a hyperlinked knowledge base with sample artifacts and detailed descriptions for many different types of activities. It is iterative, architecture-centric, and use-case-driven and supported by a palette of software development tools."[180] "Develop iteratively, manage requirements, use a component architecture, model visually, continuously verify quality, manage change—these strategies are often referred to as the best practices of the Rational Unified Process."[181]	IBM *Rational Unified Process* is a use-case driven, iterative, and architecture-centric software development framework originally developed by Rational Software. RUP encapsulates the following key concepts[182]: • Early resolution of risk driving the iterative planning activity • Whole team focus on use-case modeling as key to building the right system • Early architecture definition as foundation for development • Measurement of progress based on executable software rather than documentation • Verification of quality throughout the development life cycle • Institutionalization of industry-proven best practices driving predictability and repeatability
Realization	"A classifier that specifies a domain of objects and that also defines the physical implementation of those objects."[183] "A specialized abstraction relationship between two sets of model elements, one representing a specification (the supplier) and the other representing an implementation of the latter (the client). Realization can be used to model stepwise refinement, optimizations, transformations, templates, model synthesis, framework composition, etc."[184] (UML)	A realization is an *implementation.* In the business use-case model, the BA models the façade of a business service as a business use case; the internal process for implementing the service is modeled by the BA as a business use-case realization. In the system use-case model, the BA models a user-IT interaction as a system use case; the design that implements the system use case is modeled as a system use-case realization by the technical system analyst.

Term	What They Say (Standard or Guideline)	What It Means to the BA
Redundancy requirement	"Synonym for Fault Tolerance."[185] (ITIL)	A *redundancy requirement* expresses a need for duplicated assets in order to support reliability and sustainability requirements. Redundancy, reliability, and sustainability requirements are a component of the non-functional requirements documented by the BA and packaged in documents such as the SRS, Statement of Requirement (SOR), SLR, and BRD.
Redundant requirement		A *redundant requirement* is one that appears more than once in the documentation or that may be derived in more than one way. The aim of the BA should be to reduce redundancies in the requirements as much as is practically possible in order to reduce the risk of internal inconsistencies and to increase the maintainability of the documentation. BA tools for decreasing redundancies include extending and included use cases. (See *extending use case, included use case.*)
Regression testing	"Regression testing is that testing that is performed after making a functional improvement or repair to the program. Its purpose is to determine if the change has regressed other aspects of the programs. It is usually performed by rerunning some subset of the program's test case."[186]	*Regression testing* is retesting to ensure that items that were not supposed to have changed remain unaffected by the solution. The CAB or ECAB ensures that the appropriate degree of regression testing is performed based on the nature of the change. (See *Change Advisory Board.*)

Term	What They Say (Standard or Guideline)	What It Means to the BA
Relationship	"An abstract concept that specifies some kind of connection between elements. Examples of relationships include associations and generalizations."[187] (UML)	In data modeling, a *relationship* is a connection between entities, indicating that occurrences of one entity are linked to occurrences of the entity at the other end of the relationship. A verb is used to name a relationship. For example, a Customer *owns* an Account. In the UML, the term refers to any type of connection between classes. One type of relationship, the UML association, is equivalent to the data-modeling relationship. Other types of UML relationships include generalization and aggregation. The BA indicates relationships related to business objects on Entity Relationship Diagrams (ERDs) and class diagrams. (See *association, generalization, aggregation*.)
Request for Change (RFC)	"A formal proposal for a Change to be made. An RFC includes details of the proposed Change, and may be recorded on paper or electronically. The term RFC is often misused to mean a Change Record, or the Change itself."[188] (ITIL Service Transition)	A *Request for Change* is a formal request for a change to be made to a system or component. The BA may encounter RFCs at various levels. For example, a high-level RFC to change a business process might trigger a business process improvement project. This project may trigger mid-level RFCs to change business and IT services and these, in turn, may generate RFCs to change IT components.
Request for Information (RFI)		A *Request for Information* is a formal request for information, made by a client to potential suppliers, in order to assist in the initial investigation of a solution.
Request for Proposal	"An RFP or RFQ is a document that is distributed to parties outside the organization to serve as the basis for the contracting of solution development services."[189] (BABOK®)	A *Request for Proposal* is a formal invitation to solution providers to submit a proposal for a solution. RFPs are issued for COTS (Commercial-Off-The-Shelf) solutions as well as customized software systems.

Glossary of BA Terms (continued)

Term	What They Say (Standard or Guideline)	What It Means to the BA
Requirement	"A formal statement of what is needed, for example, a Service Level Requirement, a Project Requirement, or the required Deliverables for a Process."[190] (ITIL Service Design) "A requirement is (1) A condition or capability needed by a stakeholder to solve a problem or achieve an objective; (2) A condition or capability that must be met or possessed by a solution or solution component to satisfy a contract, standard, specification, or other formally imposed documents; a documented representation of a condition or capability as in (1) or (2). . . . The elicitation, analysis, and communication of requirements, with the objective of ensuring that they are visible to and understood by all stakeholders, is central to the discipline of business analysis."[191] *(BABOK®)* "A desired feature, property, or behavior of a system"[192] (UML)	A *requirement* is a capability that a solution must provide or a condition that it must meet. Examples of requirements include the capability to conduct online transactions and the condition that the solution comply with a set of regulations. Within a business analysis context, a requirement is differentiated from a specification, in that a requirement describes *what* is required, whereas a specification defines how it will be satisfied. There are many types of requirements for which the BA is responsible; these may be broadly categorized as high-level business objectives, as well as functional and non-functional requirements. (See *functional requirement, non-functional requirement.*)
Requirements Analysis (RA)	"Requirements Analysis describes how we progressively elaborate the solution definition in order to enable the project team to design and build a solution that will meet the needs of the business and stakeholders. In order to do that, we have to analyze the stated requirements of our stakeholders to ensure that they are correct, assess the current state of the business to identify and recommend improvements, and ultimately verify and validate the results."[193] *(BABOK®)*	*Requirements Analysis* is the *BABOK®* Knowledge Area (KA) responsible for analyzing and modeling stakeholder requirements. RA tools used by the BA include data modeling and process modeling tools, such as ERDs and flowcharts. (See *static analysis, dynamic analysis, data model, process model.*)
Requirements attributes table		A *requirements attributes table* is used to document the properties of requirements, such as their authorship, priority, and so on. The senior BA is responsible for working with the project manager to determine which requirements attributes to track and for managing the requirements attributes table.

Glossary of BA Terms (continued)

Term	What They Say (Standard or Guideline)	What It Means to the BA
Requirements-based testing		*Requirements-based testing* is testing to determine the degree to which a system complies with the require-ments. It is also known as *black-box testing*. (See *black-box test*.)
Requirements traceability matrix		A *requirements traceability matrix* is a table used to trace requirements backwards to the business processes and objectives they support and for-wards to the subsequent artifacts, events, and changed configuration items that result from them. The senior BA, working in consultation with the project manager, is responsible for designing and managing the requirements traceability matrix.
Relational Database Management System (RDBMS)		A *Relational Database Management System* is software for defining, cre-ating, updating, and accessing a relational database. Relational data-bases are non-hierarchical sets of tables, whose design is based on an approach developed by Edgar Codd, founded on set theory. Popular implementations of RDBMS include SQL/DS and DB2 and Oracle. Alternative approaches to Database Management Systems (DBMSes) include hierarchical and network databases. The business data models created by the BA describe business rules, con-cepts, and data requirements that stem from the business. The BA's data models are mapped by technical analysts (systems analysts and data analysts) to technical-perspective data models, which are in turn, implemented as Database Management Systems.

Glossary of BA Terms (continued)

Term	What They Say (Standard or Guideline)	What It Means to the BA
Return On Investment (ROI)		*Return On Investment* is percentage net benefit relative to initial investment. ROI is calculated according the following formula: ROI = (annual net benefit) / (initial investment) The BA uses ROI in preparing the cost-benefit analysis for a proposed change.
Reverse engineering		To *reverse-engineer* is to work backwards from the final product in order to derive its underlying analysis and design models. For example, an existing, undocumented RDBMS may be reverse-engineered to produce a data model; once the data model has been generated, it can be modified in response to changing business rules and forward-engineered into a revised RDBMS.
Risk	"A possible Event that could cause harm or loss or affect the ability to achieve Objectives. A Risk is measured by the probability of a Threat, the Vulnerability of the Asset to that Threat, and the Impact it would have if it occurred."[194] (ITIL)	According to a common definition, a *risk* is something that is unknown or uncertain that may impact the success or failure of a project; in practice, the term usually denotes a negative impact. The BA contributes to risk analysis and planning.
Risk Management	"The Process responsible for identifying, assessing and controlling Risks."[195] (ITIL)	*Risk Management* is a process for identifying, planning for, and mitigating risks. The BA contributes to Risk Management. (See *risk, Risk Management strategy.*)

Term	What They Say (Standard or Guideline)	What It Means to the BA
Risk Management strategy		A *Risk Management strategy* is a strategy for responding to identified risks. Strategies for managing risks generally fall into one of the following categories: Avoid (eliminate the risk), Transfer (make the risk someone else's responsibility), Accept (live with the consequences), and Mitigate (take action to reduce exposure or impact). The BA contributes to strategies related to risks in the Risk Management Plan. (See *mitigate*. Also see the sections "Risk Analysis Table Template" and "Risk Management Plan" [within the Requirements Work Plan Template] in the Templates chapter of this handbook.)
Root-cause analysis (RCA)	"Study of original reason for non-conformance with a process. When the root cause is removed or corrected, the nonconformance will be eliminated."[196]	*Root-cause analysis* is an approach to solving problems that focuses on identifying their underlying root causes. (See *Five Whys, Cause-and-Effect graph.*)
Role Map	"For complex problems, the relationships among user roles can be represented diagrammatically in a separate user role map."[197] (UML extension)	A *Role Map* is a special form of the use-case diagram that only shows actors (users and external systems) and the relationships between them, such as user types with overlapping roles. The BA creates Role Maps to centralize the definition of actors so that their treatment may be standardized in models and the requirements documentation. Role Maps are also used as input for the definition of user groups and associated access privileges by the network administrator. (See *use-case diagram, actor.*)

Term	What They Say (Standard or Guideline)	What It Means to the BA
Scenario	"A specific sequence of actions that illustrates behaviors. A scenario may be used to illustrate an interaction or the execution of a use case instance."[198] (UML)	A *scenario* is one specific interaction—one pass through a use case. A number of flows of a use case may be executed in a single scenario. For example, a single scenario may begin with steps within the Basic Flow, branch to an Alternate Flow, return to the Basic Flow, branch to another Alternate Flow, and then end.
Schedule of Changes	See *Change Schedule* (ITIL)	
Scope	"Solution scope is the set of capabilities a solution must support to meet the business need. Project scope is the work necessary to construct and implement a particular solution."[199] *(BABOK®)*	*Scope* is a delineation of what is included in and what is excluded from a solution or a project. The BA manages the scope of the solution, while the project manager manages the scope of a project.
Secondary actor	(Use case)	A *secondary actor* is an actor (user role or external system) that participates in a use case after it has been initiated. A secondary actor may receive messages and reports while the use case is executing and may provide input to the use case after it has begun. The BA indicates a secondary actor on a use-case diagram by drawing an arrow from the use case to the actor. (See *actor, primary actor, use case*.)

Glossary of BA Terms (continued)

Term	What They Say (Standard or Guideline)	What It Means to the BA
Security requirements	"The overall aim of IT security is 'balanced security in depth,' with justifiable controls implemented to ensure that the Information Security Policy is enforced and that continued IT services within secure parameters . . .continue to operate. . . . For many organizations, the approach taken to IT security is covered by an Information Security Policy owned and maintained by Information Security Management."[200] (ITIL Service Design) "Security requirements protect the data that the system uses or creates. They describe the potential risk that individuals will attempt to gain illegitimate access to information stored within the solution or that individuals with legitimate access will use the information in illegitimate ways. They include strategies to prevent access and mitigate the risks involved."[201] (BABOK®)	*Security requirements* are requirements to ensure the confidentiality, integrity, and availability of an organization's assets, information, data, and IT services. Security requirements are a component of the non-functional requirements documented by the BA and packaged in documents such as the SRS, Statement of Requirement (SOR), SLR, and BRD.
Sequence diagram	"A diagram that depicts an interaction by focusing on the sequence of messages that are exchanged, along with their corresponding event occurrences on the lifelines. Unlike a communication diagram, a sequence diagram includes time sequences but does not include object relationships. A sequence diagram can exist in a generic form (describes all possible scenarios) and in an instance form (describes one actual scenario)."[202] (UML)	A *sequence diagram* is a UML diagram that indicates the sequence in which objects pass messages to each other over the course of one or more scenarios. The diagram is typically used by systems analysts to assist in the mapping of system use cases (created by the BA) to design specifications. It is often included as part of a system use-case realization.
Service	"A means of delivering value to Customers by facilitating Outcomes Customers want to achieve without the ownership of specific Costs and Risks."[203] (ITIL)	A *service* is something of value offered to customers. In ITIL, the term refers to the capability offered to customers, as well as the infrastructure for delivering it.

Term	What They Say (Standard or Guideline)	What It Means to the BA
Service Acceptance Criteria (SAC)	"A set of criteria used to ensure that an IT Service meets its functionality and Quality Requirements and that the IT Service Provider is ready to operate the new IT Service when it has been deployed."[204] (ITIL Service Transition)	*Service Acceptance Criteria* are the criteria used to determine whether a service or solution meets its functional and non-functional requirements and that the solution provider is ready for deployment. The BA is responsible for ensuring that SACs are documented as part of the requirements package.
Service Asset and Configuration Management (SACM)	"The Process responsible for both Configuration Management and Asset Management."[205] (ITIL Service Transition)	*Service Asset and Configuration Management* is the process within ITIL Service Transition responsible for defining service assets, artifacts, infrastructure components, and financial assets. SACM is a large process that incorporates Asset Management and Configuration Management. BA artifacts whose changes must be managed may be registered as Configuration Items (CIs) and placed under the control of SACM. SACM also provides input to the BA regarding the impact of proposed changes on other CIs, such as services, customers, and suppliers. (See *Configuration Item*.)
Service Catalogue	"A database or structured Document with information about all Live IT Services, including those available for Deployment. The Service Catalogue is the only part of the Service Portfolio published to Customers, and is used to support the sale and delivery of IT Services. The Service Catalogue includes information about deliverables, prices, contact points, ordering, and request."[206] (ITIL Service Design)	A *Service Catalogue* is a catalogue of all active services. The Service Catalogue is one part of the Service Portfolio, which also includes retired services and those under development. (See *Service Pipeline*, *Service Portfolio*).

Term	What They Say (Standard or Guideline)	What It Means to the BA
Service Design	"A stage in the life cycle of an IT Service. Service Design includes a number of Processes and Functions and is the title of one of the Core ITIL publications."[207] (ITIL Service Design; see *Design*.)	*Service Design* is the ITIL Service Life Cycle phase whose purpose is to analyze and design services and processes. (Please note that in contrast to other common usages, the ITIL definition of *design* includes analysis activities.) Service Design aims to ensure a holistic approach to all aspects of the design of new or changed services including functional, management, and operational aspects. The BA is a key player in Service Design, responsible for the gathering, analysis, documentation, and management of requirements.
Service Design Package	"Document(s) defining all aspects of an IT Service and its Requirements through each stage of its Life cycle. A Service Design Package is produced for each new IT Service, major Change, or IT Service Retirement."[208] (ITIL)	A *Service Design Package* is the comprehensive package of a service's requirements and specifications. The BA is responsible for contributing to the Service Design Package requirements that stem from the business side, including functional and non-functional requirements. (See *business requirement*.)
Service Desk	"The Single Point of Contact between the Service Provider and the Users. A typical Service Desk manages Incidents and Service Requests, and also handles communication with the Users."[209] (ITIL Service Operation)	*Service Desk* is the term for the function within ITIL Service Design that is the single point of contact for the user in dealing with problems related to IT services. The Service Desk handles help calls and other incidents according to defined escalation procedures. The Service Desk also handles standard service requests, such as requests to upgrade a service. The BA seeks the input of the Service Desk in order to gain an understanding of existing problems and in order to elicit the needs of the Service Desk resulting from a proposed change. Changes to IT services often require increased Service Desk resources, training programs for the Service Desk, and procedures for dealing with new incidents and service requests.

Glossary of BA Terms (continued)

Term	What They Say (Standard or Guideline)	What It Means to the BA
Service Level Agreement (SLA)	"An Agreement between an IT Service Provider and a Customer. The SLA describes the IT Service, documents Service Level Targets, and specifies the responsibilities of the IT Service Provider and the Customer. A single SLA may cover multiple IT Services or multiple Customers."[210] (ITIL Service Design, Continual Service Improvement)	A *Service Level Agreement* is a formal agreement between a service provider and a customer that describes what will be delivered and specifies the required quality levels.
Service Level Management (SLM)	"The Process responsible for negotiating Service Level Agreements, and ensuring that these are met. SLM is responsible for ensuring that all IT Service Management Processes, Operational Level Agreements, and Underpinning Contracts, are appropriate for the agreed Service Level Targets. SLM monitors and reports on Service Levels, and holds regular Customer reviews."[211] (ITIL Service Design, Continual Service Improvement)	*Service Level Management* is a formal ITIL process within the Service Design Life Cycle phase whose purpose is to ensure that the agreed level of IT service provision is attained for present and future services. The BA supports Service Level Management by analyzing and documenting Service Level Requirements.
Service Level Manager		The *Service Level Manager* works with customers and suppliers of services to ensure Service Level Agreements (SLAs) are defined, agreed on, and met. The BA supports the Service Level Manager by analyzing and documenting Service Level Requirements.[212]
Service Level Requirement (SLR)	"A Customer Requirement for an aspect of an IT Service. SLRs are based on Business Objectives and are used to negotiate agreed Service Level Targets."[213] (ITIL Service Design, Continual Service Improvement)	A *Service Level Requirement* is a customer requirement that must be satisfied in the solution. Despite the general phraseology of the ITIL definition, the term is sometimes used to mean non-functional requirements (such as performance requirements) and sometimes to include both functional and non-functional requirements. In this handbook, the acronym S(L)R is used to refer to any type of customer requirement, while SLR refers specifically to non-functional requirements and across-the-board system capabilities.

Glossary of BA Terms (continued)

Term	What They Say (Standard or Guideline)	What It Means to the BA
Service Level Target	"A commitment that is documented in a Service Level Agreement. Service Level Targets are based on Service Level Requirements, and are needed to ensure that the IT Service design is Fit for Purpose. Service Level Targets should be SMART, and are usually based on KPIs."[214] (ITIL Service Design, Continual Service Improvement)	A *Service Level Target* is a specified level of service that is guaranteed in a Service Level Agreement, such as a performance target. The BA documents the Service Level Requirements that form the basis of the targets.
Service Manager		A *Service Manager* is responsible for continual service improvement, for evaluating the emerging needs of customers, and for ensuring that tactical, operational needs for the service are met. The Service Manager is amongst the stakeholders whose needs are analyzed by the BA prior to a change.[215]
Service Operation	"A stage in the life cycle of an IT Service. Service Operation includes a number of Processes and Functions and is the title of one of the Core ITIL publications."[216] (ITIL)	*Service Operation* is the ITIL Service Life Cycle phase whose purpose is to provide and manage services for business stakeholders within a specified level. The BA supports Service Operation by ensuring that non-functional requirements are taken into consideration up front before deployment.
Service Owner	"A Role which is accountable for the delivery of a specific IT Service."[217] (ITIL Continual Service Improvement)	*Service Owner* is an executive business function, with hiring and firing authority, responsible at a high level for a service. The BA seeks the input of Service Owners to ensure that business objectives (financial, etc.) for the service are addressed and realized.
Service Pipeline	"A database or structured Document listing all IT Services that are under consideration or Development, but are not yet available to Customers. The Service Pipeline provides a Business view of possible future IT Services and is part of the Service Portfolio which is not normally published to Customers."[218] (ITIL Service Strategy)	The *Service Pipeline* is the catalogue of services that are being considered for new development or are under development.

The BA documents requirements for IT services listed in the Service Pipeline. |

Glossary of BA Terms (continued)

Term	What They Say (Standard or Guideline)	What It Means to the BA
Service Portfolio	"The complete set of Services that are managed by a Service Provider. The Service Portfolio is used to manage the entire life cycle of all Services, and includes three Categories: Service Pipeline (proposed or in Development), Service Catalogue (Live or available for Deployment), and Retired Services."[219] (ITIL Service Strategy)	The *Service Portfolio* is the comprehensive catalogue of services that includes current services, those under development, and retired services.
Service Strategy	"The title of one of the Core ITIL publications. Service Strategy establishes an overall Strategy for IT Services and for IT Service Management."[220] (ITIL Service Strategy)	*Service Strategy* is an ITIL Service Life Cycle phase whose purpose is to achieve superior performance versus competing alternatives and guide the development of service management as a strategic organizational capability and asset. The BA supports Service Strategy by contributing to the strategic audit of currently available services and by determining requirements for services required by customers.
Service Transition	"A stage in the life cycle of an IT Service. Service Transition includes a number of Processes and Functions and is the title of one of the Core ITIL publications."[221] (ITIL Service Transition)	*Service Transition* is the ITIL Service Life Cycle phase whose purpose is to manage processes, systems, and functions required for implementing and releasing a change into production. The BA supports Service Transition by ensuring that the IT transition process supports the change process of the business and that the service meets the requirements of business stakeholders.
Service Utility	"The Functionality of an IT Service from the Customer's perspective. The Business value of an IT Service is created by the combination of Service Utility (what the Service does) and Service Warranty (how well it does it)."[222] (ITIL Service Strategy)	*Service Utility* refers to what a service does (rather than how well it does it). The BA documents the Service Utility required from the solution in the functional requirements. (See *service warranty*.)

Term	What They Say (Standard or Guideline)	What It Means to the BA
Service validation and testing	"The Process responsible for Validation and Testing of a new or Changed IT Service. Service Validation and Testing ensures that the IT Service matches its Design Specification and will meet the needs of the Business."[223] (ITIL Service Transition)	*Service validation and testing* is a process within ITIL Service Transition whose purpose is to ensure that a service meets or exceeds business and operational requirements and adds value to the business. The BA creates requirements that are the basis for service validation and testing and is responsible for supervising testing. (See *validation, verification*.)
Service Warranty	"Assurance that an IT Service will meet agreed Requirements. This may be a formal Agreement such as a Service Level Agreement or Contract, or may be a marketing message or brand image. The Business value of an IT Service is created by the combination of Service Utility (what the Service does) and Service Warranty (how well it does it)."[224] (ITIL Service Strategy)	*Service Warranty* refers to how well a service performs. Service Warrantees that must be guaranteed by a solution are defined by the BA in the Service Level (non-functional) Requirements. (See *service utility*.)
Six Sigma	"A vision of quality which equates with only 3.4 defects per million opportunities for each product or service transaction. Strives for perfection."[225]	*Six Sigma* is a set of best practices for improving processes by eliminating defects. (Six Sigma refers to six standard deviations from the mean of a metric.)
SMART requirements		Requirements documented by the BA must be *SMART*: Specific, Measurable, Achievable/Appropriate, Realistic/Relevant, and Timely/Time-bound/Testable.
Software Development Life Cycle		A *Software Development Life Cycle* (also known as *System Development Life Cycle*) is a defined process for developing software that describes the phases (stages) of an IT project and defines activities and responsibilities. SDLCs for IT projects can be broadly categorized as *waterfall* (development occurring in a single pass) and *iterative incremental* (multiple passes). (See *phase, waterfall, iterative incremental development, agile*.)

Glossary of BA Terms (continued)

Term	What They Say (Standard or Guideline)	What It Means to the BA
Software Requirements Specification (SRS)	"A Software Requirements Specification (also known as a System Requirements Specification) describes the behavior and implementation of a software application. The primary target audience for an SRS is the development team that will be required to implement the solution. An SRS includes a description of the problem domain, a decomposition of the problem domain, a description of the functional requirements that govern the solution, the relevant quality of service [non-functional] requirements, assumptions, and constraints affecting the solution and may include requirements attributes and traceability information if the solution is complex enough to warrant it."[226]	Requirements are often packaged into a number of documents, each with a different focus. Business objective and high-level requirements are often captured in a Customer Wants and Needs (or similar) document, while requirements that relate specifically to the IT solution are packaged in a *Software Requirements Specification*. SRS contents include non-functional IT Service Level Requirements, user profiles (such as Role Maps), and functional requirements (such as user requirements). (See *Statement of Requirement*.)
Solution	"A solution meets a business need by solving problems or allowing the organization to take advantage of an opportunity. A solution can be subdivided into components, including the information systems that support it, the processes that manage it, and the people who operate it."[227] *(BABOK®)*	A *solution* is a change intended to meet the needs of the business area. The change may or may not involve an IT solution. The BA is responsible for documenting and managing the requirements that form the basis for selecting and measuring the quality of a solution.
Specialized class	"One classifier may specialize another by adding or redefining features."[228] *(UML)*	The BA uses *specialized classes* to model subtypes, modeling the general type as a generalized class, and each subtype as a specialization of it. Specialization provides an effective mechanism for reuse in the requirements documentation: features common to all subtypes are documented once in a generalized class, while the peculiarities of each subtype are described in the relevant specialized classes. Also known as a *specialization*, *subclass*, *child class*, and *derived class*. (See *generalization*, *inheritance*, *polymorphism*.)

Term	What They Say (Standard or Guideline)	What It Means to the BA
Specification	[Specifications are] "a set of requirements for a system or other classifier."[229] (UML) "A requirement is. . .a condition or capability that must be met. . .to satisfy a contract, standard, specification, or other formally imposed documents."[230] (BABOK®)	The use of the term specification varies between standards. For example, the UML definition of specification includes requirements that originate from the business area. This handbook differentiates between requirements and specifications as follows (and as suggested by the BABOK®). A requirement describes a need; a specification describes *how* the solution will meet those needs. The technical team (such as the systems analyst) is responsible for creating the specifications using the BA's requirements as input.
State-machine diagram	"A diagram that depicts discrete behavior modeled through finite state-transition systems. In particular, it specifies the sequences of states that an object or an interaction goes through during its life in response to events, together with its responses and actions."[231] (UML)	A *state-machine diagram* (also known as a Harel statechart) is a diagram that depicts the different states (statuses) of an object, the rules that govern how it passes from state to state, and the behavior of the object in each state. The BA uses state-machine diagrams to describe the life cycle of business objects. For example, a state-machine diagram for an insurance claim might describe the events that causes a claim to pass from an Initiated state to Adjusted and Paid states. (See *Harel statechart diagram*.)
Statement of Requirement (SOR)	"A Document containing all Requirements for a product purchase, or a new or changed IT Service."[232] (ITIL Service Design)	A *Statement of Requirement* is the ITIL equivalent to an SRS. (See *Software Requirements Specification*.)

Term	What They Say (Standard or Guideline)	What It Means to the BA
Static model	Also known as *structural model.* An aspect of a model is considered structural if it "emphasizes the structure of the objects in a system, including their types, classes, relationships, attributes, and operations."[233] (UML)	The *static model* is the portion of the model that focuses on structural aspects of a system, in particular, the types of objects that it consists of and their relationships to each other. The BA uses the static model to define business concepts and business rules related to objects, for example, the rule that a business account may be owned by more than one customer. These rules may be documented as part of the business architecture and/or in order to define business rules that must be met by an IT solution. The main static modeling diagrams used by the BA are the Entity Relationship Diagram (data modeling) and the class diagram (UML). (See *data modeling, class diagram, Entity Relationship Diagram.*)
Stereotype	"A class that defines how an existing metaclass (or stereotype) may be extended, and enables the use of platform or domain specific terminology or notation in addition to the ones used for the extended metaclass. Certain stereotypes are predefined in the UML, others may be user defined. Stereotypes are one of the extensibility mechanisms in UML."[234] (UML)	A *stereotype* is a feature that may be tied to a UML modeling element to modify its meaning. The UML includes a number of stereotypes as well as the capability for practitioners to add their own stereotypes. Stereotypes used by the BA include Business Worker, applied to an actor to indicate that a participant works within the business area, and business use case, applied to a use case to indicate that the interaction is with a business area.

Glossary of BA Terms (continued)

Term	What They Say (Standard or Guideline)	What It Means to the BA
Structured Analysis		*Structured Analysis* is a set of techniques for analyzing any system, such as a business area or an IT system. Structured Analysis is based on the view that processes are best viewed as procedures that convert input data to output data. In Structured Analysis, the system is analyzed using functional decomposition—with each process decomposed into smaller and smaller processes, each of which, ideally, performs a single (though possibly high-level) function. The BA uses Structured Analysis within the context of Enterprise Analysis to analyze the functions and processes of a business area and/or to analyze those aspects of the business that must be supported by an IT solution. An alternative to Structured Analysis is Object-Oriented (OO) Analysis. (See *Data Flow Diagram, object-oriented.*)
Structured walkthrough		A *structured walkthrough* is a meeting held to review a project deliverable in order to verify its quality. The BA may be asked to conduct and be the subject of a structured walkthrough of any of the requirements documentation that he or she has authored. The BA may also be invited to participate in structured walkthroughs of design artifacts to ensure they meet the requirements.
Subclass		*Subclass* is an alternative term for specialized class. (See *specialized class.*)

Term	What They Say (Standard or Guideline)	What It Means to the BA
Supplier Management	"The Process responsible for ensuring that all Contracts with Suppliers support the needs of the Business, and that all Suppliers meet their contractual commitments."[235]	*Supplier Management* is the process for managing the relationships with suppliers. The BA seeks the input of the supplier manager in order to gain an understanding of the capabilities of suppliers and their contractual commitments.
SWOT Analysis		*SWOT Analysis* is an approach to analyzing a project or change based on strengths, weaknesses, opportunities, and threats.

The BA uses SWOT Analysis in preparing the business case and risk analysis for an IT project or proposed business change. |
| **System Development Life Cycle (SDLC)** | | See *Software Development Life Cycle*. |
| **System test** | "System testing is the process of attempting to demonstrate how [a product or] program does not meet its objectives. . . . System testing. . .is impossible if the project has not produced a written set of measurable objectives."[236] | *System tests* are those designed to check whether the solution has met its measurable objectives. The term is generally applied to the testing of the solution for compliance with non-functional requirements and service level targets. Examples of system tests include stress tests, volume tests, and performance testing. |
| **System use case** | (Extended UML) (See *use case*.) | A system use case is a user task; the task must be complete from the user's point of view[237] and yield a result of value to the user.[238] It represents a way that the software is used by an actor (user or external system). A system use case may be of any size, but it typically denotes an interaction that is triggered by one actor and that takes place over a single session with the IT system.

System use cases provide the BA with a framework for modeling user tasks and documenting user requirements. |

Term	What They Say (Standard or Guideline)	What It Means to the BA
System use-case diagram	(Extended UML) (See *use-case diagram*.)	A *system use-case diagram* depicts who does what with an IT system; it depicts the actors (user roles and external systems) that interact with the system and connects them to the user tasks (system use cases) they have access to. A system use-case diagram may also show dependencies between system use cases and relationships between user roles.
Systems analyst		Usage of the term *systems analyst* is non-uniform. As used in this book, the term refers to the software designer, a role distinct from the business analyst. In other usages, it may refer to a role responsible for the analysis and modeling not only of software, but also of business structure and processes (and a role that, consequently, overlaps that of the BA.)
Task		A task is "a piece of work often to be finished within a certain time."[239]
Technical service	A synonym for an infrastructure service: "An IT Service that is not directly used by the Business, but is required by the IT Service Provider so they can provide other IT Services. For example, Directory Services, naming services, or communication services."[240] (ITIL)	A *technical service* is an underlying IT service that supports other IT services but is not used directly by the business.
Template		A *template* is a standardized form used for textual documentation.
Tool		Within the context of this book, the term *tool* is used for any job aid or technique that facilitates the practice of business analysis. Examples of BA tools are Pareto Analysis and class diagrams. (Tools are described in the BA Toolkit chapter of this book.) The term tool is also used to denote software used in the development process; an example of such a tool is IBM Rational Rose.

Glossary of BA Terms (continued)

Term	What They Say (Standard or Guideline)	What It Means to the BA
Total Cost of Ownership (TCO)	"A methodology used to help make investment decisions. TCO assesses the full life cycle Cost of owning a Configuration Item, not just the initial Cost or purchase price."[241] (ITIL Service Strategy)	*Total Cost of Ownership* is the full cost of an item over its entire lifespan. TCO includes the initial investment, maintenance, and overhead costs.

The BA includes TCO as part of a cost-benefit analysis for a proposed change. |
| **Total Cost of Utilization (TCU)** | "A methodology used to help make investment and Service Sourcing decisions. TCU assesses the full life cycle Cost to the Customer of using an IT Service."[242] (ITIL Service Strategy) | *Total Cost of Utilization* is the total cost to the customer of using a service during the entire period it is used.

The BA may include TCU in the cost-benefit analysis of a proposed new or changed service. |
| **Traceability** | "Requirements traceability supports the ability to trace a requirement through the development life cycle. The ability to track the requirements is an important technique used to detect missing functionality or identity if implemented functionality is not supported by a specific requirement."[243] | *Traceability* is the ability to track an item to other items. *Forward traceability* refers to the ability to trace forward to a subsequent item, for example, from a requirement to the design specifications and test cases that result from it. *Backward traceability* refers to the ability to trace back to prior items, for example, from a user requirement to the business objectives it supports. *Horizontal traceability* refers to the ability to track dependencies between items of the same type, for example, how a change in one IT service impacts other IT services.

The BA is responsible for managing requirements traceability: the tracking of requirements and requirements artifacts to other items related to the project, product, or service. |

Term	What They Say (Standard or Guideline)	What It Means to the BA
Trigger	"The trigger specifies the event that gets the use case started."[244]	A *trigger* is an event or condition that forces a response. The trigger may kick-start a task (such as a system use case) or force a control flow or state transition. Examples of triggers include "Supplies fall below a set point," "User cancels," and "System error." The BA documents triggers in models (for example, on activity diagrams and state-machine diagrams) and in the requirements documentation.
Underpinning Contract (UC)	"A Contract between an IT Service Provider and a Third Party. The Third Party provides goods or Services that support delivery of an IT Service to a Customer. The Underpinning Contract defines targets and responsibilities that are required to meet agreed Service Level Targets in an SLA."[245] (ITIL Service Design)	An *Underpinning Contract* is a contract made between the service provider and a third party that provides supporting services.
Unified Modeling Language (UML)	"The Unified Modeling Language—UML—is OMG's most-used specification, and the way the world models not only application structure, behavior, and architecture, but also business process and data structure."[246]	The *Unified Modeling Language* is a standard notation owned by the Object Management Group (OMG), a not-for-profit computer industry specifications consortium. The UML is used for the specification, visualization, and modeling of the structure and behaviour of business and software systems The BA uses UML tools and techniques to model the business area, often as part of an IT initiative. UML tools used by the BA include class diagrams, activity diagrams, and use cases.
Unified Process		The *Unified Process* is the open-source framework for iterative development that forms the basis for IBM RUP. (See *Rational Unified Process*.)

Glossary of BA Terms (continued)

Term	What They Say (Standard or Guideline)	What It Means to the BA
Usability	"The ease with which an Application, product, or IT Service can be used. Usability Requirements are often included in a Statement of Requirements."[247] (ITIL Service Design)	*Usability* requirements relate to the ease with which a user must be able to use the system. They are also referred to as *human-factor* requirements. Usability may include requirements to comply with guidelines that cover how the interface deals with errors, exhibits consistency, acknowledges transactions, and so on. Usability requirements are a component of the non-functional requirements documented by the BA and packaged in documents such as the SRS, Statement of Requirement (SOR), SLR, and BRD.
Use case	"The specification of a sequence of actions, including variants, that a system can perform, interacting with actors of the system."[248] (UML) "A technique used to define required functionality and Objectives and to Design Tests. Use Cases define realistic scenarios that describe interactions between Users and an IT Service or other System."[249] (ITIL Service Design)	A *use case* represents a use of the system under discussion—a type of interaction between an actor and the system that yields a result of value to the initiating actor. The system may be of any type (business or IT), though an IT system is often implied when the term is unqualified. (See *system use case*). The description of a use case should include all of the different ways that it could play out. (See *system use case*, *business use case*.)
Use-case brief		A *use-case brief* is a short paragraph (two to six sentences) describing the use case, mentioning only the most significant activities and failures.[250]
Use-case description/specification		A *use-case description* (referred to in RUP as *use-case specification*) describes the various ways that an interaction may play out. It may take the form of text and/or diagrams. (Text is usually used, with the addition of workflow diagrams when the flows connect in complex ways.)

Glossary of BA Terms (continued)

Term	What They Say (Standard or Guideline)	What It Means to the BA
Use-case diagram	"A diagram that shows the relationships among actors and the subject (system), and use cases."[251] (UML)	A *use-case diagram* depicts the types of interactions that each actor has with the system. The diagram connects actors to the use cases they initiate or participate in. It may also indicate relationships between actors (such as those whose roles overlap) and dependencies between use cases. The BA uses different types of use-case diagrams for different types of systems. A business use-case diagram depicts interactions with the business area; a system use-case diagram depicts interactions with the IT system.
User Acceptance Testing (UAT)	"As the solution is built and available for testing, the Business Analyst role involves supporting the Quality Assurance activities. They may help business stakeholders with user acceptance testing, defect reporting, and resolution."[252]	*User Acceptance Testing* is testing done by the user or on the user's behalf prior to sign-off. Prior to the test, the user agrees that if the system passes the UAT, the solution will be accepted. UAT is performed after extensive testing has already occurred. The UAT may follow a formal or informal process. In a formal process, precise test scripts and expected results are designed beforehand. In an informal process, the goals of the tests are defined, but the detailed steps are not. The BA supports quality assurance activities including User Acceptance Testing.
User requirement	"User requirements describe the needs of a particular set of stakeholders in regard to a proposed solution. They may be used to describe how a particular set of users of a solution will interact with it or how a product will meet the needs of different customer groups."[253]	A user requirement is one that must be satisfied by an IT solution, written from the perspective of the end user. A recommended practice is to document user requirements as system use cases. User requirements are a component of the functional requirements documented by the BA and packaged in documents such as the SRS, Statement of Requirement (SOR), S(L)R, and BRD. (See *functional requirement*.)

Glossary of BA Terms (continued)

Term	What They Say (Standard or Guideline)	What It Means to the BA
User task		A *user task* is a piece of meaningful work that a user accomplishes with the assistance of an IT system; it is typically completed in a single interaction and yields a result of value to the user. (As used in this handbook, the term user task is equivalent to system use case, but [unlike system use case] is not specific to the use-case modeling approach. (See *system use case*.)
Validate	"To ensure that the stated requirements correctly and fully implement the business requirements as defined during Enterprise Analysis."[254] *(BABOK®)*	To *validate* a deliverable of an activity means to check whether the output of the activity properly reflects the input to the activity. To validate the requirements means to check whether they reflect and conform to the inputs to requirements elicitation and analysis; these inputs include high-level business requirements (business objectives, etc.), architectural documents, and the input provided by business stakeholders during requirements elicitation events. Validation of the requirements is a responsibility of the BA. To validate a specification means to check whether it conforms to the inputs to the design activity, such as the requirements and design architecture. Validation of the design specifications is carried out by technical team members, such as system analysts, with BAs playing a supporting role. To validate a solution means to check whether it satisfies the inputs to the coding and construction of the solution, for example, that it has been built to the design specifications and that it meets the requirements. The BA plays a supporting role in validating a solution.

Glossary of BA Terms (continued)

Term	What They Say (Standard or Guideline)	What It Means to the BA
Verify	"Requirements verification ensures that requirements are defined clearly enough to allow solution design and implementation to begin. Customer, user, and project team collaboration is required to complete this activity."[255] (*BABOK*® 1.6)	To *verify* an output of an activity is to check whether it can be effectively used by its intended users as input to subsequent activities. To verify the requirements is to ensure they can be used as input to subsequence steps in the development process. The BA should ensure that the technical team verifies that the requirements are of sufficient quality to be used as input to the creation of design specifications. To verify the specifications is to ensure that they are of sufficient quality to be used effectively to construct a solution. Coders and other implementers should verify that the specifications can be used to construct the code, tables, and so on. To verify a solution means to check that it produces output of sufficient quality that it can be effectively used by the intended users of the output. This includes checking the correctness and usefulness of data and reports and ensuring that the data is properly stored in tables. The BA plays a supporting role in solution verification.
Vital Business Function (VBF)	"The business critical functions of the business, supported by an IT service."[256] (ITIL)	A *Vital Business Function* is a function that is critical for the business. The BA documents VBFs as part of Business Impact Analysis (BIA). (See *Business Impact Analysis*.)
Waterfall	"The traditional waterfall method advocates gathering all requirements in the beginning of the project; while in the Iterative/Agile approaches requirements may be defined throughout the life cycle."[257] (*BABOK*®)	A *waterfall* approach is an approach to developing software where each step must be completed before the next begins. (See *System Development Life Cycle, iterative incremental development*.)

Glossary of BA Terms (continued)

Term	What They Say (Standard or Guideline)	What It Means to the BA
Worker	"A worker is a class that represents an abstraction of a human that acts within the system. A worker interacts with other workers and manipulates entities while participating in use case realizations."[258] (Extended UML)	A *worker* is a human role within the business area that participates in implementing a business process (business use case). The BA depicts workers on business use-case diagrams.
Zachman Framework	"A 'language' to facilitate communication, research, and implementation of Enterprise Architecture concepts."[259]	*The Zachman Framework*, developed by John Zachman, is a classification scheme for describing aspects of an enterprise.

[1] *OMG Unified Modeling Language (OMG UML), Superstructure, V2.1.2,* Nov. 2007 (OMG), p. 217.

[2] *OMG Unified Modeling Language (OMG UML), Superstructure, V2.1.2,* Nov. 2007 (OMG), p. 311.

[3] *OMG Unified Modeling Language (OMG UML), Superstructure, V2.1.2,* Nov. 2007 (OMG), p. 311.

[4] *UML 2.0: Infrastructure - Final Adopted Specification* (OMG, 2003), p. 4.

[5] *OMG Unified Modeling Language (OMG UML), Superstructure, V2.1.2,* Nov. 2007 (OMG), p. 586.

[6] *UML 2.0: Infrastructure - Final Adopted Specification* (OMG, 2003), p. 4.

[7] Note that in the UML, aggregation is a type of association.

[8] Kent Beck, Mike Beedle, et al. *Manifesto for Agile Software Development.* http://agilemanifesto.org/.

[9] Kent Beck, Mike Beedle, et al. *Manifesto.* http://agilemanifesto.org/principles.html.

[10] *UML 2.0: Infrastructure - Final Adopted Specification* (OMG, 2003), p. 4.

[11] ITIL® V3 Glossary v01 (30 May 2007), p. 3.

[12] *UML 2.0: Infrastructure - Final Adopted Specification* (OMG, 2003), p. 5.

[13] In the UML, an *association* is only one type of relationship possible between classes. (Other examples are aggregation and generalization.) The relationships specified in data modeling correspond to UML associations.

[14] *UML 2.0: Infrastructure - Final Adopted Specification* (OMG, 2003), p. 5.

[15] *ITIL® V3 Glossary v01,* 30 May 2007 (OGC), p 4.

[16] *ITIL V3 Core Book: Service Design,* Glossary (OGC, 2007), p. 290.

[17] *ITIL V3 Core Book: Service Design,* Glossary (OGC, 2007), p. 290.

[18]*OMG Unified Modeling Language (OMG UML), Superstructure*, V2.1.2, Nov. 2007 (OMG), p. 591.

[19]*OMG Unified Modeling Language (OMG UML), Superstructure*, V2.1.2, Nov. 2007 (OMG), p. 593.

[20]*ITIL V3 Core Book: CSI*, Glossary (OGC, 2007), p. 193.

[21]*ITIL Core Book: Service Transition* (OGC, 2007), p. 92. See Figure 4.21 (in the BA Toolkit chapter), indicating Baseline Points.

[22]*ITIL V3 Core Book: CSI*, Glossary , (OGC, 2007), p. 193.

[23]Glenford Myers, *The Art of Software Testing* (Wiley and Sons, 1979), p. 8.

[24]*American Marketing Association Dictionary*, http://www.marketingpower.com/_layouts/Dictionary.aspx?dLetter=B.

[25]*ITIL V3 Core Book: Service Strategy*, Glossary, (OGC, 2007), p. 235.

[26]Adam Frankl, "Validated Requirements from Business Use Cases and the Rational Unified Process," 15 Aug 2007, http://www.ibm.com/developerworks/rational/library/aug07/frankl/index.html.

[27]*The Guide to the Business Analysis Body of Knowledge®*, Version 2.0 Framework, p. 2, www.theiiba.org.

[28]*The Guide to the Business Analysis Body of Knowledge®*, Version 2.0 Framework, p. 2, www.theiiba.org.

[29]*The Guide to the Business Analysis Body of Knowledge®*, Version 2.0 Framework, p. 2, www.theiiba.org.

[30]*The Guide to the Business Analysis Body of Knowledge®*, Version 2.0 Framework, p. 2, www.theiiba.org.

[31]*Business Process Modeling Notation*, V1.2 (Beta 3), Feb. 2008, p. 280.

[32]BPM Institute, Business Architecture Home Page, http://www.bpminstitute.org/topics/business-architecture.html.

[33]From a note from Chris Reynolds.

[34]*ITIL V3 Core Book: Service Strategy*, Glossary (OGC, 2007), p. 235.

[35]*ITIL V3 Core Book: Service Design*, Glossary (OGC, 2007), p. 292.

[36]*ITIL V3 Core Book: Service Design*, Glossary, (OGC, 2007), p. 292.

[37]*ITIL V3 Core Book: Service Strategy*, Glossary (OGC, 2007), p. 235.

[38]*ITIL V3 Core Book: Service Strategy*, Glossary (OGC, 2007), p. 235.

[39]*Business Process Modeling Notation* v1.2 (beta 3) (OMG), p. 280.

[40]*Business Process Modeling Notation*, v1.2 (beta 3) (OMG), p. 1.

[41]*ITIL V3 Core Book: Service Design*, Glossary (OGC, 2007), p. 292. (The definition is missing from the ITIL Service Strategy Core Book.)

[42]*ITIL V3 Core Book: Service Strategy*, Glossary (OGC, 2007), p. 235.

[43] *A Guide to the Business Analysis Body of Knowledge®*, Release 1.6 ©2006, International Institute of Business Analysis. p. 207. (At the time of writing, there is no reference to the BRD in the current draft for *BABOK®* Release 2.)

[44] J. DeLayne Stroud, "Business Requirements Document: A High-Level Review," http://finance.isixsigma.com/library/content/c080123b.asp.

[45] *ITIL Core Book: Service Design*, Glossary (OMG, 2007), p. 227.

[46] *ITIL® V3 Glossary*, v01, 30 May 2007, www.itsmf.co.uk (OGC), p. 8.

[47] *ITIL V3 Core Book: Service Strategy*, Glossary (OGC, 2007), p. 235.

[48] Adam Frankl, "Validated Requirements from Business Use Cases," http://www.ibm.com/developerworks/rational/library/aug07/frankl/index.html.

[49] Arthur V. English, *Business Modeling with UML: Understanding the Similarities and Differences Between Business Use Cases and System Use Cases*, IBM Developer Works/Rational, 2007, http://www.ibm.com/developerworks/rational/library/apr07/english.

[50] *ITIL® V3 Glossary*, v01, 30 May 2007, www.itsmf.co.uk (OGC), p. 8. See http://www.sei.cmu.edu/cmmi/ for more information on this topic.

[51] *ITIL V3 Core Book: Service Design*, Glossary (OGC, 2007), p. 293.

[52] *ITIL V3 Core Book: Service Design*, Glossary (OGC, 2007), p. 293.

[53] *UML 2.0: Infrastructure - Final Adopted Specification*, (OMG, 2003), p. 5.

[54] International Institute of Business Analysis, Certification, http://www.theiiba.org/AM/Template.cfm?Section=Certification.

[55] *ITIL V3 Core Book: Service Transition*, Glossary (OGC, 2007), p. 228.

[56] *ITIL V3 Core Book: Service Transition*, Glossary (OGC, 2007), p. 228.

[57] *ITIL V3 Core Book: Service Transition*, Glossary (OGC, 2007), p. 228.

[58] *ITIL V3 Core Book: Service Transition*, Glossary (OGC, 2007), p. 186.

[59] *ITIL V3 Core Book: Service Transition*, Glossary (OGC, 2007), p. 229.

[60] *OMG Unified Modeling Language (OMG UML), Superstructure*, V2.1.2, Nov. 2007 (OMG), p. 49.

[61] *OMG Unified Modeling Language (OMG UML), Superstructure*, V2.1.2, Nov. 2007 (OMG), p. 49.

[62] *OMG Unified Modeling Language (OMG UML), Superstructure*, V2.1.2, Nov. 2007 (OMG), p. 681.

[63] *UML 2.0: Infrastructure - Final Adopted Specification*, 2003 (OMG), p. 6.

[64] *ITIL V3 Core Book: Service Design*, Glossary (OGC, 2007), p. 294.

[65] *OMG Unified Modeling Language (OMG UML), Superstructure*, V2.1.2, Nov. 2007 (OMG), p. 513.

[66] *ITIL V3 Core Book: Service Design*, Glossary (OGC, 2007), p. 294.

[67] *ITIL V3 Core Book: Service Transition*, Glossary (OGC, 2007), p. 230.

[68] *ITIL V3 Core Book: Service Transition*, Glossary (OGC, 2007), p. 230.

[69] *ITIL V3 Core Book: Service Transition*, Glossary (OGC, 2007), p. 230.

[70] *ITIL® V3 Glossary*, v01, 30 May 2007, www.itsmf.co.uk (OGC), p. 13.

[71] *ITIL V3 Core Book: Service Transition*, Glossary (OGC, 2007), p. 230.

[72] *A Guide to the BABOK®*, 4/7/2005 (IIBA), p. 4.

[73] Karl E Wiegers, *Software Requirements, Second Edition*, Microsoft Press, 2003, p. 105.

[74] *ITIL V3 Core Book: CSI*, Glossary (OGC, 2007), p. 196.

[75] See COBIT at the ISACA web site at
www.isaca.org/Template.cfm?Section=COBIT6&Template=/TaggedPage/TaggedPageDisplay.cfm
&TPLID=55&ContentID=7981. Source COBIT 4.1 ©1996-2007 ITGI. All rights reserved. Used by
permission.

[76] *ITIL V3 Core Book: Service Strategy*, Glossary (OGC, 2007), p. 239.

[77] *ITIL V3 Core Book: Service Design*, Glossary (OGC, 2007), p. 296.

[78] Edward Yourdon, Structured Analysis Wiki,
http://yourdon.com/strucanalysis/wiki/index.php?title=Chapter_10.

[79] Yourdon, Structured Analysis Wiki,
http://yourdon.com/strucanalysis/wiki/index.php?title=Chapter_9.

[80] *ITIL V3 Core Book: Service Design*, Glossary (OGC, 207), p. 296.

[81] *UML 2.0: Infrastructure - Final Adopted Specification*, 2003 (OMG), p. 8.

[82] *ITIL V3 Core Book: Service Design*, Glossary (OGC, 2007), p. 296.

[83] Martin Fowler, *Patterns of Enterprise Application Architecture* (Addison-Wesley Professional,
2002), as described in "Domain Model," http://martinfowler.com/eaaCatalog/domainModel.html.

[84] *OMG Unified Modeling Language (OMG UML), Superstructure*, V2.1.2, Nov. 2007 (OMG),
p. 215.

[85] *The Guide to the Business Analysis Body of Knowledge®*, Version 2.0 Framework, IIBA, p. 8.

[86] *ITIL V3 Core Book: Service Transition*, Glossary (OGC, 2007), p. 233.

[87] *The Guide to the Business Analysis Body of Knowledge®*, Version 2.0 Framework, IIBA, p. 7.

[88] Marc Lankhorst, *Enterprise Architecture at Work: Modelling, Communication, and Analysis*
(Springer, 2005), p.3.

[89] *Entity-Relationship Approach*, ER '93: 12th International Conference on the Entity-Relationship
Approach, Arlington, Texas, USA, December 15-17, 1993. Proceedings by Ramez Elmasri, Vram
Kouramajian, Bernhard Thalheim (Springer, 1994), p. 243.

[90] *OMG Unified Modeling Language (OMG UML), Superstructure*, V2.1.2, Nov. 2007 (OMG),
p. 694.

[91] Other ways that the business treats objects in the class the same way include the types of relationships an object in the class may have with other objects and operations that may be performed on or by objects in the class (and the rules regarding those operations).

[92] Yourdan, Structured Analysis Wiki,
http://yourdon.com/strucanalysis/wiki/index.php?title=Chapter_12.

[93] *ITIL V3 Core Book: Service Operation*, Glossary (OGC, 2007), p. 232.

[94] *ITIL V3 Core Book: Service Operation*, Glossary (OGC, 2007), p. 232.

[95] *UML Superstructure Version 2.0 Revised Final Adopted Specification* (ptc/04-10-02) October 8, 2004 (OMG), p. 478.

[96] *ITIL V3 Core Book: Service Operation*, Glossary (OGC, 2007), p. 232.

[97] *Unified Modeling Language: Superstructure version 2.1.1 formal/2007-02-03* (OMG), p. 590.

[98] *Unified Modeling Language: Superstructure version 2.1.1 formal/2007-02-03* (OMG), p. 587.

[99] *UML 2.0: Infrastructure - Final Adopted Specification*, 2003 (OMG), p. 9.

[100] *ITIL® V3 Glossary*, v01, 30 May 2007 (OGC), www.itsmf.co.uk, p. 21.

[101] Wiegers, *Software Requirements*, p. 8.

[102] *ITIL V3 Core Book: Service Operation*, Glossary (OGC, 2007), p. 233.

[103] *ITIL V3 Core Book: Service Transition*, Glossary (OGC, 2007), p. 115.

[104] *Unified Modeling Language: Superstructure version 2.1.1 formal/2007-02-03* (OMG), p. 374.

[105] *Unified Modeling Language: Superstructure version 2.1.1 formal/2007-02-03* (OMG), p. 540.

[106] *ITIL® V3 Glossary*, v01, 30 May 2007 (OGC), www.itsmf.co.uk, p. 22.

[107] *ITIL® V3 Glossary*, v01, 30 May 2007 (OGC), www.itsmf.co.uk, p. 22.

[108] Wiegers, *Software Requirements*, p. 8.

[109] *A Guide to the BABOK®*, 4/7/2005 (IIBA), p. 4.

[110] iSixSigma Dictionary, http://software.isixsigma.com/dictionary/Gap_Analysis-629.htm.

[111] iSixSigma Dictionary, http://software.isixsigma.com/dictionary/Gating-131.htm.

[112] *Unified Modeling Language: Superstructure version 2.1.1 formal/2007-02-03* (OMG), p. 71.

[113] *ITIL V3 Core Book: Service Operation*, Glossary (OGC, 2007), p. 234.

[114] *ITIL® V3 Glossary*, v01, 30 May 2007 (OGC), www.itsmf.co.uk, p. 23.

[115] *UML 2.0: Infrastructure - Final Adopted Specification*, 2003 (OMG). p.10.

[116] *Unified Modeling Language: Superstructure version 2.1.1 formal/2007-02-03* (OMG), p. 591.

[117] *ITIL V3 Core Book: Service Strategy*, Glossary (OGC, 2007), p. 242.

[118] *ITIL V3 Core Book: Service Design*, Glossary (OGC, 2007), p. 300.

[119] *UML 2.0: Infrastructure - Final Adopted Specification*, 2003 (OMG), p. 10.

[120] *UML 2.0: Infrastructure - Final Adopted Specification*, 2003 (OMG), p. 10.

[121] *UML 2.0: Infrastructure - Final Adopted Specification*, 2003 (OMG), p. 10.

[122] *Unified Modeling Language: Superstructure, version 2.1.1 formal/2007-02-03* (OMG), p. 504.

[123] The sequence diagram—a type of interaction diagram—is sometimes used in a BA context to describe cross-functional workflow in business use-case realizations. However, sequence diagrams are not readily understood by business stakeholders. For BA purposes, and especially when communicating with business stakeholders, the activity diagram with partitions (swimlanes) is the recommended UML alternative.

[124] *UML 2.0: Infrastructure - Final Adopted Specification*, 2003 (OMG), p.10.

[125] International Institute of Business Analysis, http://www.theiiba.org//AM/Template.cfm?Section=Home.

[126]"*The ISO Story*," International Organization for Standardization, http://www.iso.org/iso/about/the_iso_story.htm. The updated number of standards (17,000) was provided in an e-mail from Rosemary Maginniss of ANSI to the author.

[127]Ian Spence and Kurt Bittner, "What Is Iterative Development? Part 2: The Customer Perspective," 15 April 2005, http://www.ibm.com/developerworks/rational/library/content/RationalEdge/apr05/bittner-spence.

[128]Spence and Bittner, "What Is Iterative Development? Part 1: The Developer Perspective," 15 March 2005, http://www.ibm.com/developerworks/rational/library/mar05/bittner.

[129]*ITIL V3 Core Book: Service Design*, Glossary (OGC, 2007), p. 301.

[130]*ITIL V3 Core Book: Service Design*, Glossary (OGC, 2007), p. 301.

[131]*ITIL V3 Core Book: Service Design*, Glossary (OGC, 2007), p. 301.

[132]*ITIL V3 Core Book: Service Design*, Glossary (OGC, 2007), p. 301.

[133]itSMF Chapter, IT Service Management Forum (bottom of home page), http://itsmfi.net.

[134]For more on JAD, please see Robert T. Futrell, Donald F. Shafer, and Linda I. Safer, *Quality Software Project Management* (Prentice Hall PTR, 2002).

[135]*ITIL V3 Core Book: Service Design*, Glossary (OGC, 2007), p. 301.

[136]*The Guide to the Business Analysis Body of Knowledge®, Version 2.0 Framework*, IIBA, p. 4.

[137]This description was provided in an e-mail from Ken Clyne to the author.

[138]*ITIL V3 Core Book: Service Strategy*, Glossary (OGC, 2007), p. 244.

[139]Definition provided by Rick Guyatt.

[140]*ITIL® V3 Glossary, v01*, 30 May 2007 (OGC), www.itsmf.co.uk , p. 29.

[141]*ITIL V3 Core Book: Service Design*, Glossary (OGC, 2007), p. 301.

[142]*ITIL V3 Core Book: Service Design*, Glossary (OGC, 2007), p. 301.

[143]*ITIL V3 Core Book: Service Operation*, Glossary (OGC, 2007), p. 237.

[144]*ITIL V3 Core Book: Service Operation*, Glossary (OGC, 2007), p. 237.

[145]*UML 2.0: Infrastructure - Final Adopted Specification*, 2003 (OMG), p.11.

[146]As noted elsewhere, the recommended UML diagram for business use-case realizations is the activity diagram, with partitions representing the participants.

[147]*UML 2.0: Infrastructure - Final Adopted Specification*, 2003 (OMG), p.11.

[148]However, it should be noted that at present, the modeling of operations and methods is not a common BA activity.

[149]*OMG Unified Modeling Language (OMG UML), Superstructure*, V2.1.2, Nov. 2007 (OMG), p. 94.

[150]*UML 2.0: Infrastructure - Final Adopted Specification*, 2003 (OMG), p. 12.

[151]*A Guide to the Business Analysis Body of Knowledge®*, Release 1.6, 2006, International Institute of Business Analysis, p. 198.

[152]Wiegers, *Software Requirements*, p. 8.

[153] *UML 2.0: Infrastructure - Final Adopted Specification*, 2003 (OMG), p. 12.

[154] More specifically, business analysis focuses on *types* of business objects, referred to as *entity classes.*

[155] *Business Process Modeling Notation*, v1.3 (beta 3), 2008, p. 23.

[156] *ITIL V3 Core Book: Service Design*, Glossary (OGC, 2007), p. 303.

[157] *ITIL® V3 Glossary*, v01, 30 May 2007 (OGC), www.itsmf.co.uk, p. 32.

[158] *UML 2.0: Infrastructure - Final Adopted Specification*, 2003 (OMG), p. 12.

[159] *OMG Unified Modeling Language (OMG UML), Superstructure*, V2.1.2, Nov. 2007 (OMG), p. 50.

[160] *OMG Unified Modeling Language (OMG UML), Superstructure*, V2.1.2, Nov. 2007 (OMG), p. 107.

[161] *UML 2.0: Infrastructure - Final Adopted Specification*, 2003 (OMG), p. 13.

[162] SixSigma *Glossary of Terms and Definitions*, General Electric Company, http://www.ge.com/sixsigma/glossary.html.

[163] *ITIL V3 Core Book: Continual Service Improvement*, Glossary (OGC, 2007), p. 204.

[164] SixSigma *Glossary of Terms and Definitions*, General Electric Company, http://www.ge.com/sixsigma/glossary.html.

[165] Douglas C. Bower and Derek H. T. Walker, abstract for *Planning Knowledge for Phased Rollout Projects* (Project Management Institute), posted on Project Management Institute, Marketplace, http://www.pmi.org/Marketplace/Pages/ProductDetail.aspx?GMProduct=00101038200&iss=1.

[166] Joan Knutson, abstract for *The PMBOK and PMP Exam* (Project Management Institute), posted on Project Management Institute, Marketplace, http://www.pmi.org/Marketplace/Pages/ProductDetail.aspx?GMProduct=00100615500&iss=1.

[167] *OMG Unified Modeling Language (OMG UML), Superstructure*, V2.1.2, Nov. 2007 (OMG), p. 217.

[168] *UML 2.0: Infrastructure - Final Adopted Specification*, 2003 (OMG), p. 13.

[169] *ITIL V3 Core Book: Service Transition*, Glossary (OGC, 2007), p. 240.

[170] *UML 2.0: Infrastructure - Final Adopted Specification*, 2003 (OMG), p. 14.

[171] *ITIL® V3 Glossary*, v01, 30 May 2007 (OGC), www.itsmf.co.uk, p. 36.

[172] *ITIL V3 Core Book: Service Strategy*, Glossary (OGC, 2007), p. 247.

[173] *Business Process Modeling Notation*, v1.2 (beta 3), p. 287.

[174] *Business Process Modeling Notation*, v1.2 (beta 3), p. 18.

[175] *ITIL V3 Core Book: Service Operation*, Glossary (OGC, 2007), p. 241.

[176] *ITIL V3 Core Book: Service Strategy*, Glossary (OGC, 2007), p. 221.

[177] Definition provided by Chris Reynolds.

[178] *ITIL® V3 Glossary*, v01, 30 May 2007 (OGC), www.itsmf.co.uk, p. 37.

[179] *A Guide to the Business Analysis Body of Knowledge®*, Release 1.6 ©2006, International Institute of Business Analysis, p. 100.

[180]From an e-mail from Philippe Krutchen to Ken Clyne.

[181]Mats Wessberg, "Introducing the IBM Rational Unified Process Essentials by Analogy," 2005, http://www.ibm.com/developerworks/rational/library/05/wessberg.

[182]This RUP description was provided by Ken Clyne in an e-mail to the author.

[183]*Unified Modeling Language: Superstructure version 2.1.1 formal/2007-02-03* (OMG), p. 696.

[184]*UML 2.0: Infrastructure - Final Adopted Specification*, 2003 (OMG), p. 14.

[185]*ITIL® V3 Glossary*, v01, 30 May 2007 (OGC), www.itsmf.co.uk, p. 38.

[186]Myers, *The Art of Software Testing*, p. 122.

[187]*UML 2.0: Infrastructure - Final Adopted Specification*, 2003 (OMG), p. 14.

[188]*ITIL® V3 Glossary*, v01, 30 May 2007 (OGC), www.itsmf.co.uk, p. 40.

[189]*A Guide to the Business Analysis Body of Knowledge®*, Release 1.6, ©2006, International Institute of Business Analysis, p. 207.

[190]*ITIL® V3 Glossary*, v01, 30 May 2007 (OGC), www.itsmf.co.uk, p. 40.

[191]*The Guide to the Business Analysis Body of Knowledge®*, Version 2.0 Framework (IIBA), p. 2, www.theiiba.org.

[192]*UML 2.0: Infrastructure - Final Adopted Specification*, 2003 (OMG), p. 15.

[193]*The Guide to the Business Analysis Body of Knowledge®*, Version 2.0 Framework, p. 9, www.theiiba.org.

[194]*ITIL® V3 Glossary*, v01, 30 May 2007 (OGC), www.itsmf.co.uk, p. 41.

[195]*ITIL® V3 Glossary*, v01, 30 May 2007 (OGC), www.itsmf.co.uk, p. 41.

[196]SixSigma *Glossary of Terms and Definitions*, http://www.ge.com/sixsigma/glossary.html.

[197]Larry Constantine, preprint, *User Roles and Personas*, p. 9, posted on http://www.foruse.com/articles/rolespersonas.pdf.

[198]*UML 2.0: Infrastructure - Final Adopted Specification*, 2003 (OMG), p. 15.

[199]*The Guide to the Business Analysis Body of Knowledge®* Version 2.0 Framework, International Institute of Business Analysis, p. 2.

[200]*ITIL Core Book: Service Design*, Glossary (OGC, 2007), p. 114.

[201]*A Guide to the Business Analysis Body of Knowledge®*, Release 1.6, ©2006, International Institute of Business Analysis, p. 201.

[202]*UML 2.0: Infrastructure - Final Adopted Specification*, 2003 (OMG), p. 15.

[203]*ITIL® V3 Glossary*, v01, 30 May 2007 (OGC), www.itsmf.co.uk, p. 42.

[204]*ITIL® V3 Glossary*, v01, 30 May 2007 (OGC), www.itsmf.co.uk, p. 42.

[205]*ITIL® V3 Glossary*, v01, 30 May 2007 (OGC), www.itsmf.co.uk, p. 43.

[206]*ITIL® V3 Glossary*, v01, 30 May 2007 (OGC), www.itsmf.co.uk, p. 43.

[207]*ITIL Core Book: Service Design*, Glossary (OGC, 2007), p. 309.

[208]*ITIL Core Book: Service Design*, Glossary (OGC, 2007), p. 309.

[209]*ITIL® V3 Glossary*, v01, 30 May 2007 (OGC), www.itsmf.co.uk, p. 44.

[210] *ITIL® V3 Glossary*, v01, 30 May 2007 (OGC), www.itsmf.co.uk, p. 44.

[211] *ITIL® V3 Glossary*, v01, 30 May 2007 (OGC), www.itsmf.co.uk, p. 44.

[212] For more on the Service Level Manager, see *ITIL V3 Core Book: Service Operation* (OGC, 2007), p. 87.

[213] *ITIL® V3 Glossary*, v01, 30 May 2007 (OGC), www.itsmf.co.uk, p. 45.

[214] *ITIL® V3 Glossary*, v01, 30 May 2007 (OGC), www.itsmf.co.uk, p. 45.

[215] For more on the Service Manager, see *ITIL V3 Core Book: CSI* (OGC, 2007), p. 133.

[216] *ITIL® V3 Glossary*, v01, 30 May 2007 (OGC), www.itsmf.co.uk, p. 45.

[217] *ITIL® V3 Glossary*, v01, 30 May 2007 (OGC), www.itsmf.co.uk, p. 45.

[218] *ITIL® V3 Glossary*, v01, 30 May 2007 (OGC), www.itsmf.co.uk, p. 45.

[219] *ITIL® V3 Glossary*, v01, 30 May 2007 (OGC), www.itsmf.co.uk, p. 46.

[220] *ITIL® V3 Glossary*, v01, 30 May 2007 (OGC), www.itsmf.co.uk, p. 47.

[221] *ITIL® V3 Glossary*, v01, 30 May 2007 (OGC), www.itsmf.co.uk, p. 47.

[222] *ITIL® V3 Glossary*, v01, 30 May 2007 (OGC), www.itsmf.co.uk, p. 47.

[223] *ITIL® V3 Glossary*, v01, 30 May 2007 (OGC), www.itsmf.co.uk, p. 47.

[224] *ITIL® V3 Glossary*, v01, 30 May 2007 (OGC), www.itsmf.co.uk, p. 47.

[225] SixSigma *Glossary of Terms and Definitions*, General Electric Company, http://www.ge.com/sixsigma/glossary.html.

[226] *A Guide to the Business Analysis Body of Knowledge®*, Release 1.6 ©2006, International Institute of Business Analysis, p. 207.

[227] *The Guide to the Business Analysis Body of Knowledge®*, Version 2.0 Framework, IIBA, p. 2.

[228] *UML 2.0 Superstructure Specification*, OMG, p. 38.

[229] *UML 2.0: Infrastructure - Final Adopted Specification*, OMG, p. 18.

[230] *The Guide to the Business Analysis Body of Knowledge®*, Version 2.0 Framework, p. 2.

[231] *UML 2.0 Infrastructure Specification*, OMG, p. 16.

[232] *ITIL® V3 Glossary*, v01, 30 May 2007 (OGC), www.itsmf.co.uk, p. 49.

[233] *UML 2.0 Infrastructure Specification*, OMG p. 17.

[234] *UML 2.0 Infrastructure Specification*, OMG p. 16.

[235] *ITIL V3 Core Book: Service Strategy*, Glossary (OGC, 2007), p. 312.

[236] Myers, *The Art of Software Testing*, p. 110.

[237] "A use case should be a complete task from a user's point of view." From *Applying Use Cases: A Practical Guide, 2nd Edition*, by Geri Schneider and Jason Winters (Addison-Wesley Professional, 2001), p. 14.

[238] In the UML, the term *use case* is used for an interaction with a system; a system use case is a use case for which the system is an IT system.

[239] *Merriam-Webster Online Dictionary*, http://www.merriam-webster.com/dictionary/task.

[240] *ITIL® V3 Glossary*, v01, 30 May 2007 (OGC), www.itsmf.co.uk, p. 24.

[241] *ITIL® V3 Glossary*, v01, 30 May 2007 (OGC), www.itsmf.co.uk, p. 52.

[242] *ITIL® V3 Glossary*, v01, 30 May 2007 (OGC), www.itsmf.co.uk, p. 52.

[243] *A Guide to the Business Analysis Body of Knowledge®*, Release 1.6 ©2006, International Institute of Business Analysis, p. 131.

[244] Alistair Cockburn, *Writing Effective Use Cases* (Addison-Wesley, 2000), p. 84.

[245] *ITIL® V3 Glossary*, v01, 30 May 2007 (OGC), www.itsmf.co.uk, p. 53.

[246] UML Resource Page, Object Management Group, Inc., http://www.uml.org.

[247] *ITIL® V3 Glossary*, v01, 30 May 2007 (OGC), www.itsmf.co.uk, p. 53.

[248] *UML 2.0 Infrastructure Specification, OMG Adopted Specification ptc/03-09-15*, 2003, Object Management Group, p.19.

[249] *ITIL Core Book: Service Design*, Glossary (OGC, 2007), p.314.

[250] For more on use-case briefs, see Cockburn, *Writing Effective Use Cases*, pp. 37–38.

[251] *UML 2.0 Infrastructure Specification*, OMG, p. 19.

[252] *A Guide to the Business Analysis Body of Knowledge®*, Release 1.6 ©2006, International Institute of Business Analysis, p. 14.

[253] *A Guide to the Business Analysis Body of Knowledge®*, Release 1.6 ©2006, International Institute of Business Analysis, p. 192.

[254] *A Guide to the Business Analysis Body of Knowledge®*, Release 1.6 ©2006, International Institute of Business Analysis, p. 207.

[255] *A Guide to the Business Analysis Body of Knowledge®*, Release 1.6 ©2006, International Institute of Business Analysis, p. 208.

[256] *A Dictionary of IT Service Management*, Evans and MacFarlane, itSMF®, 2001, p. 91.

[257] *A Guide to the Business Analysis Body of Knowledge®*, Release 1.6 ©2006, International Institute of Business Analysis, p. 104.

[258] Pan-Wei Ng, *Effective Business Modeling with UML: Describing Business Use Cases and Realizations*, The Rational Edge, November, 2002, Rational Software, p.23. (Originally posted on http://www.therationaledge.com/content/nov_02/t_businessModelingUML_pn.jsp.)

[259] Zachman Institute for Framework Advancement, http://www.zifa.com.

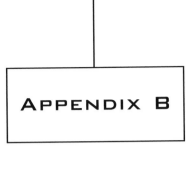

APPENDIX B

ACRONYMS

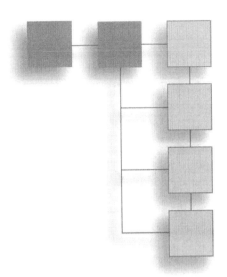

Following is a list of acronyms of interest to the business analyst.

BA: Business Analyst

BABOK®: *Business Analysis Body of Knowledge®*

BAP & M: Business Analysis Planning and Monitoring

BCM: Business Continuity Management

BCP: Business Continuity Plan

BIA: Business Impact Analysis

BPD: Business Process Diagram

BPI: Business Process Improvement

BPMN: Business Process Modeling Notation

BRD: Business Requirements Document

CAB: Change Advisory Board

CBAP™: Certified Business Analysis Professional™

CI: Configuration Item

CMDB: Configuration Management Database

CMMI: Capability Maturity Model Integration

CMS: Configuration Management System

COBIT: Control Objectives for Information and Related Technology

COTS: Commercial Off-The-Shelf

CSF: Critical Success Factor

CSI: Continual Service Improvement

DBMS: Data Base Management System

DFD: Data Flow Diagram

EA: Enterprise Analysis (also Enterprise Architecture)

ECAB: Emergency Change Advisory Board

ERD: Entity Relationship Diagram

FURPS+: Functionality, Usability, Reliability, Performance, and Supportability plus other constraints

IDEF: Integrated Computer-Aided Manufacturing (ICAM) Definition Languages

IIBA™: International Institute for Business Analysis™

ISM: Information Security Management

ISO: International Organization for Standardization

IT: Information Technology

ITIL: IT Infrastructure Library

ITSCM: IT Service Continuity Management

ITSM: IT Service Management

itSMF®: IT Service Management Forum®

JAD: Joint Application Development/Design

KA: Knowledge Area

KPI: Key Performance Indicator

LOS: Line of Service

MTBF: Mean Time Between Failures

MTBSI: Mean Time Between System/Service Incidents

MTRS: Mean Time to Restore Service

MTTR: Mean Time To Repair

NPV: Net Present Value

OMG: Object Management Group

OO: Object-Oriented

PIR: Post-Implementation Review

PMBOK: Project Management Body of Knowledge

POLDAT: Process, Organization, Location, Data, Application, and Technology

PSO: Projected Service Outages

PVT: Production Verification Testing (also Production Validation Testing)

RDBMS: Relational Data Base Management System

RA: Requirements Analysis

RACI: Responsible, Accountable, Consulted, Informed

RCA: Root Cause Analysis

RFC: Request For Change

RFI: Request For Information

RFP: Request For Proposal

ROI: Return On Investment

RUP: Rational Unified Process

SAC: Service Acceptance Criteria

SACM: Service Asset and Configuration Management

SDLC: System Development Life Cycle

SLA: Service Level Agreement

SLM: Service Level Management

SLR: Service Level Requirement

SOR: Statement of Requirement

SMART: Specific, Measurable, Achievable/Appropriate, Realistic/Relevant, and Timely/Time-Bound/Testable

SME: Subject Matter Expert

SRS: Software Requirements Specification (also known as System Requirements Specification)

SWOT: Strengths, Weaknesses, Opportunities, and Threats

TCO: Total Cost of Ownership

TCU: Total Cost of Utilization

UAT: User Acceptance Testing

UC: Underpinning Contract

UML: Unified Modeling Language

UP: Unified Process

VBF: Vital Business Function

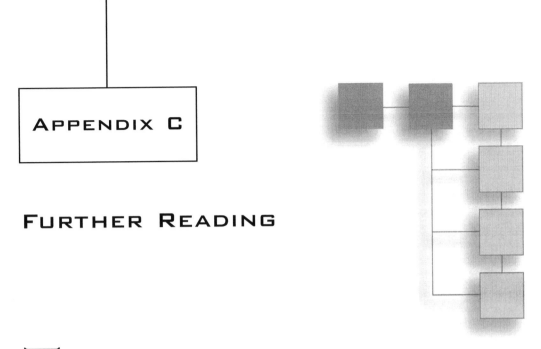

Appendix C

Further Reading

This appendix contains references to books and other resources related to business analysis, ITIL, and the UML and includes sources used in this handbook.

Books and Articles

Booch, Grady, James Rumbaugh, and Ivar Jacobson. *The Unified Modeling Language User Guide, Second Edition.* Addison-Wesley Professional, 2005.

Booch, Grady, Robert A. Maksimchuk, Michael W. Engel, Bobbi J. Young, Jim Conallen, and Kelli A. Houston. *Object-Oriented Analysis and Design with Applications, Third Edition.* Addison Wesley, 2007.

Benyon, Robert and Robert Johnston. *Service Agreements – A Management Guide.* itSMF®-NL. Van Haren, 2006.

Bittner, Kurt and Ian Spence. *Use Case Modeling.* Addison-Wesley Professional, 2002.

Clyne, Ken. Agile Risk Management. Advanced Technology Systems (ATS). Presentation to "Rational Comes To You" conference, Chicago, IL, Feb. 20, 2008.

Cockburn, Alistair. *Writing Effective Use Cases.* Addison-Wesley Professional, 2000.

Constantine, Larry. *Users, Roles, and Personas.* Constantine & Lockwood, 2005. Pre-print. http://www.foruse.com/articles/rolespersonas.pdf.

Eriksson, Hans-Erik and Magnus Penker. *Business Modeling with UML: Business Patterns and Business Objects.* Wiley, 2000.

Eriksson, Hans-Erik, Magnus Penker, Brian Lyons, and David Fado. *UML 2 Toolkit*. Wiley, 2003.

Evans, Ivor and Ivor MacFarlane. *A Dictionary of IT Service Management: Terms, Acronyms, and Abbreviations, Version 1 (North America)*. itSMF®, 2001.

Fowler, Martin. *UML Distilled: A Brief Guide to the Standard Object Modeling Language, Third Edition*. Addison-Wesley Professional, 2003.

Gamma, Erich, Richard Helm, Ralph Johnson, and John M. Vlissides. *Design Patterns: Elements of Reusable Object-Oriented Software*. Addison-Wesley Professional, 1994.

Grady, Robert. *Practical Software Metrics for Project Management and Process Improvement*. Prentice Hall PTR, 1992.

Hoffer, Jeffrey A, Joey F. George, and Joseph S. Valacich. *Modern Systems Analysis and Design, Fourth Edition*. Prentice Hall, 2004.

International Institute of Business Analysis. *Guide to the Business Analysis Body of Knowledge®*. Version 1.6, 2006. http://www.theiiba.org/AM/Template.cfm?Section= Body_of_Knowledge.

International Institute of Business Analysis. *Guide to the Business Analysis Body of Knowledge®*. Version 2.0 Framework. http://www.theiiba.org.

Johnson, Brian and John Higgins. *ITIL® and the Software Lifecycle: Practical Strategy and Design Principles*. Van Haren, 2007.

Kroll, Per and Philippe Krutchen. *The Rational Unified Process Made Easy: A Practitioner's Guide to the RUP*. Addison-Wesley Professional, 2003.

Krutchen, Philippe. *The Rational Unified Process: An Introduction (3rd Edition)*. Addison-Wesley Professional, 2003.

Larman, Craig. *Applying UML and Patterns: An Introduction to Object-Oriented Analysis and Design and Iterative Development, Third Edition*. Prentice Hall PTR, 2004.

Lyons, Brian G. *Three Key Features*. Number Six Software. PowerPoint presentation on iterative, use-case driven, architecture-centric processes. Provided to the author in an e-mail from Ken Clyne of Number Six Software.

Myers, Glenford. *The Art of Software Testing*. John Wiley, 1979.

Ng, Pan-Wei. "Effective Business Modeling with UML: Describing Business Use Cases and Realizations." *The Rational Edge*. 2002. Originally available at http://www.therationaledge.com/content/nov_02/t_businessModelingUML_pn.jsp.

Object Management Group (OMG). Business Process Maturity Model (BPMM), v1.0 - Beta 2. OMG Document Number: dtc/2007-11-01. November, 2007.

Object Management Group (OMG). Business Process Modeling Notation, v1.2 (beta 3). OMG Document Number: BMI/2008-02-07. February, 2008.

Object Management Group (OMG). OMG Unified Modeling Language (OMG UML), Infrastructure, V2.1.2. OMG Document Number: formal/2007-11-04. November, 2007.

Object Management Group (OMG). OMG Unified Modeling Language (OMG UML), Superstructure, V2.1.2. OMG Document Number: formal/2007-11-02. November, 2007.

Object Management Group (OMG). UML 2.0 Infrastructure Specification.[1] Document: ptc/03-09-15. December, 2003.

Office of Government Commerce. ITIL® V3 Acronyms v1.0. 30 May 2007. Download: www.get-best-practice.co.uk.

Office of Government Commerce. ITIL® V3 Glossary v01. Glossary of Terms and Definitions. 30 May 2007. http://www.get-best-practice.co.uk.

Office of Government Commerce. (ITIL® Core Book.) Continual Service Improvement. The Stationery Office. 2007.

Office of Government Commerce. (ITIL® Core Book.) Service Design. 2007.

Office of Government Commerce. (ITIL® Core Book.) Service Operation. 2007.

Office of Government Commerce. (ITIL® Core Book.) Service Strategy. 2007.

Office of Government Commerce. (ITIL® Core Book.) Service Transition. 2007.

Podeswa, Howard. *UML for the IT Business Analyst: A Practical Guide to Object-Oriented Requirements Gathering, Second Edition.* Cengage Learning, 2009. (ISBN: 1598638688)

Podeswa, Howard. *UML for the IT Business Analyst: A Practical Guide to Object-Oriented Requirements Gathering.* Thomson Course Technology, 2005. (ISBN: 1592009123)

Rational Software, Microsoft, Hewlett-Packard, Oracle, et al. *UML Extension for Business Modeling.* Rational Software Corporation, 1997. ftp://ftp.omg.org/pub/docs/ad/97-08-07.pdf.

---

[1]The UML 2 Infrastructure Specification, though superseded by more recent versions, has content omitted from later editions—a detailed "Terms and Definitions" section with definitions of UML terms.

Schneider, Geri and Jason P. Winters. *Applying Use Cases: A Practical Guide, Second Edition.* Addison-Wesley Professional, 2001.

Van Bon, Jan, ed. *Foundations of IT Service Management: Based on ITIL® V3.* Van Haren, 2007.

Wiegers, Karl E. *Software Requirements, Second Edition.* Microsoft Press, 2003.

Web Sites

(Please be advised that URLs are always subject to change.)

Agile Alliance: http://www.agilealliance.com/ (to join the agile community).

IIBA™ (International Institute of Business Analysis) home page: http://www.theiiba.org (to join, for latest versions of the *BABOK®*, links to certified education providers, and information regarding the Certified Business Analysis Professional™).

iSix Sigma: http://www.isixsigma.com (for Six Sigma resources and events).

Noble Inc. home page: http://nobleinc.ca; e-mail: info@nobleinc.ca (for courses and templates and based on this book).

OGC Best Management Practice: http://www.get-best-practice.co.uk/glossaries.aspx (for free ITIL® V3 downloads).

OMG (Object Management Group) home page: www.omg.org (for UML and BPMN specifications).

The Rational Edge **(e-zine)**: http://www-128.ibm.com/developerworks/rational/rationaledge/.

TSO (The Stationery Office) online bookshop: www.tsoshop.co.uk; e-mail: customer.services@tso.co.uk (to purchase ITIL V3 Core Books).

INDEX

Nobleinc

Wherever there has been innovation in the BA field, Noble has been there. Since 1998, Noble Inc.—an IBM Advanced Business Partner and IIBA-endorsed Education Provider (EEP)—has designed BA programs for major training centres in the U.S. and Canada, acted as SME to the Comptia/U.S. Government NITAS BA initiative and served as reviewer to the BABOK. Noble's chief course designer, Howard Podeswa, is a recognized leader in the field and author of the highly successful book, *UML for the IT Business Analyst*, and *The Business Analyst's Handbook*. Our services include IIBA-approved in-house training anywhere in the world and public courses offered through our affiliate network.

For more information on Noble services please contact info@nobleinc

Made in the USA
Middletown, DE
16 September 2015